# DRUG
# MISUSE

## AND THE

# ENVIRONMENT

A REPORT BY THE ADVISORY COUNCIL
ON THE MISUSE OF DRUGS

London: The Stationery Office

Applications for reproduction should be made in writing to
The Copyright Unit, Her Majesty's Stationery Office,
St Clement's House, 2–16 Colegate, Norwich, NR3 1BQ

ISBN 0 11 341183 9

Printed in the United Kingdom for The Stationery Office
J40919 C30 4/98 009091

ADVISORY COUNCIL ON THE MISUSE OF DRUGS

**Members**

Professor David Grahame-Smith

Mrs Joy Barlow

Mr Ronald Bartle

Mr David Bernstein

Mr Raj Boyjoonauth

Ms Anna Bradley

Mr Alexander Cameron

Dr William Clee

Dr Michael Donmall

Dr Anthony Duxbury

Professor Griffith Edwards

Dr Laurence Gruer

Ms Kim Hager

Ms Lorraine Hewitt

Mr Mike Hindson

Mr Roger Howard

Professor Ronald Jones

Ms Ruth Joyce

Mr James Kay

Professor Malcolm Lader

Mr David Massam

Professor Otto Meth-Cohn

Mr Michael Narayn Singh

Ms Sally O'Sullivan

Dr Diana Patterson

Mr Alistair Ramsay

Dr Sue Ruben

Dr James Robertson

Mr Ian Sherwood

Professor Gerry Stimson

Professor John Strang

Dr David Temple

Mr Peter Walker

# CONTENTS

# PREFACE

The Advisory Council has produced this report as the result of a perception that the world in which the individual lives has been a rather neglected area when considering how to tackle drug misuse. Efforts have tended to concentrate on enforcement of the law and treatment and education for the individual.

This report explores the environmental aspect of drug prevention and falls into two parts. The first part, comprising chapters 1-4, describes in detail the aims of the report, looks at the nature and extent of drug misuse, explores the environmental factors which influence drug misuse, and reviews current community-based drug prevention strategies. Thereafter in the second part, which takes account of the findings of the first part, we identify a number of subject areas which seem to us ripe for attention in one form or another in the cause of drug prevention.

Both parts are preceded by a brief summary of the report and the recommendations which emerge from it. We hope that readers will venture beyond the summary into the body of the report itself.

During our enquiry a number of themes have emerged which we believe warrant mention in this preface and which the reader will come across as he or she goes through the report.

In general, in taking environmentally-based drug prevention measures, involvement of the population is important; it is much better for people to be engaged in the process rather than having things done for them, or to them, from on high. We have found ourselves distrusting what we regard as negative solutions - for example, evicting tenants and excluding children from schools; we doubt that these quick fix solutions will in the long run be found to be successful. The problems of drug misuse and the solutions do not sit neatly in a single cubbyhole; they are inter-sectoral by which we mean that there are health, education, social service, employment, housing and criminal justice dimensions and it is important to remain mindful of the links and overlaps between them. Finally, we have often found ourselves without as solid a basis as we would have wished for knowing what works in terms of environmental prevention; this is a situation which needs remedying and makes plain the need for the results of those actions which are taken to be evaluated.

A report like this cannot, and should not expect to, have an immediate and massive impact. The fundamental nature of the issues involved makes it obvious that changes cannot be instantly brought about. However we believe that implementation of the recommendations and sustained effort would over time significantly help to ameliorate some of the problems for the benefit of society as a whole.

# SUMMARY AND RECOMMENDATIONS

## CHAPTER 1: THE AIMS OF THE REPORT

1.  The purpose of the report is to look at drug prevention from an environmental perspective and within that context make recommendations for action. It is the individual who is the ultimate agent who does or does not make the personal decision to misuse drugs and their personal capacity to make sensible and healthy choices will be weakened or supported by the world which surrounds them. **We recommend that environmental responses should feature more often and more strongly in the total mix of prevention activities both at national and local level. In our view prevention strategies which are blind to the environment have no future place** (paras 1.3 - 1.4).

2.  We believe that Drug Action Teams (and in Wales, Drug and Alcohol Action Teams) established by the Government's recent strategies should continue in being (para 1.7).

3.  Drug problems have an innate complexity. Different drugs are used in different ways and with different patterns and intensities and with different routes by different people and with different levels of risk (para 1.12).

4.  **When setting up drug prevention policies consideration will often need at the same time to be given to the place of alcohol, tobacco and volatile substances in the scheme of things. Drug prevention policies which ignore licit drugs lack credibility** (para 1.12).

5.  The environment is the totality of our surround. For the purpose of the report we have regarded the environment as an interactive whole where people are not only influenced by it but influence it themselves. Family, school, work and leisure environments, and peer group influences are part of the environment. So too are cultural beliefs, expectations and attitudes. The quality of the built environment can be relevant, as can be the degree of access to education, employment, welfare support, medical care, childcare, leisure activities and justice. The economic and commercial climate will bear also in many ways on the quality of the complex mix of social, cultural, interpersonal and physical factors which make up the environment. **The environment affects the choices which individuals can and do make, and this fact is crucial to the design of prevention policies** (paras 1.16 - 1.17).

6.      Drug prevention, we believe, must very much be the concern of generalists as well as specialists (para 1.23).

## CHAPTER 2: THE NATURE AND EXTENT OF ILLICIT DRUG USE IN THE UNITED KINGDOM

7.      **Drug prevention policies in the United Kingdom should be designed with an awareness that drug misuse is today a diverse, widespread and in some areas an enormously common problem** (para 2.1).

8.      The British Crime Survey for England and Wales and the equivalent survey for Scotland show that cannabis is the drug which has been most used ever with (in 1996) up to 27% of men and 18% of women between 16 and 59 having done so ever, with amphetamines, LSD and psilocybin following behind at around 7 - 11% for men and 3 - 7% for women. The total number to have ever taken cannabis is about 7 million and amphetamines about 2.5 million. Less commonly used drugs and those carrying greater social stigma are probably less well covered by surveys (paras 2.18 - 2.26).

9.      Surveys have shown that the use of tobacco, alcohol and solvents are predictors of the later use of illicit drugs (para 2.27). In some areas the majority of young people will have tried illicit drugs by their mid-teens (although looking at it the other way a significant proportion will not have). The much smaller numbers who use regularly, reminds us that because a young person has tried an illicit drug does not mean that they will necessarily develop a pattern of long term misuse (paras 2.28 - 2.33).

10.     It is quite likely that in the late 1980s something approaching a doubling in several types of drug misuse may have occurred. Whether those upward trends are still continuing or continuing at the same rate, only time will tell. Between the British Crime Surveys of 1994 and 1996 in the 16-29 age group the picture is more or less one of stability of use within the last year (paras 2.35 and 2.41).

11.     By combining the results of a 1992 OPCS Psychiatric Morbidity Survey with data from the 1991 census it is possible to arrive at an estimate for 1992 of about 725,000 persons having been dependent but the figure should be treated with caution because the definition of dependence used in the 1992 survey may lead to inflation in the prevalence estimate on illicit drugs in the preceding 12 months (paras 2.6 - 2.10).

12.     The Regional Drug Misuse Databases which record individuals starting treatment with an agency show men outnumbering women by 3:1 in the returns and illustrate

regional variations in the nature and prevalence of drug misuse and differences within the geographical areas covered by the Databases (paras 2.11 - 2.14).

13. Official data on drug-related deaths probably under-report the true extent of mortality associated with a drug using lifestyle but research has shown that the death rate amongst opiate misusers is nearly twelve times that of the general population. There are also gaps in the information available on morbidity but among intravenous drug users recorded prevalence rates of HIV infection in the United Kingdom are generally low, with a few places showing higher rates. Information for hepatitis C prevalence are not as complete as for hepatitis B but the available information gives cause for concern (paras 2.42 - 2.52).

14. Gender is a factor in drugs misuse. Female drug misusers tend to utilise drug services less frequently than their male counterparts. Female injectors may be at greater risk of HIV and other infections than male injectors as a result of being more likely to have sexual partners who are also injecting. In some cities there has been shown to be a strong association between female prostitution and drug misuse (paras 2.53 - 2.54).

15. The influence of ethnicity on illicit drug use is an under-researched topic. Information from the British Crime Survey 1996, however, shows that drug misuse is not confined to any particular ethnic group (para 2.55 - 2.56).

16. The relationship between unemployment and drug use is important if complicated. The British Crime Survey shows that among those in the 16-29 year age group who were unemployed as many as 45% reported drug use in the previous year, more than double the rate (22%) for those with full-time jobs. The OPCS Psychiatric Morbidity Survey also found that those who were unemployed were very considerably more likely to be drug dependent (paras 2.57 - 2.60).

17. Overall the chapter shows that the nature and extent of drug misuse differs by region, by age, by sex, by ethnicity and by employment status. There is a need to develop approaches to drug prevention which are sensitive to the diverse experiences of different social groups. **Policy makers should not become dulled to the extent and nature of the problem or ignore its complexity** (para 2.65).

18. **In support of prevention policies there is a need for strengthened research on the nature and extent of drug misuse in several respects. First, sharper understanding is needed of whether drug misuse is in some sense a seamless whole or whether it is a jigsaw of rather distinct, unrelated behaviour with different origins and outcomes. Second, we need better understanding of the contribution made to the cause of different types of drug misuse by environmental factors, personal factors, and the availability of drugs - such estimates need to be quantified** (para 2.67).

## CHAPTER 3: ENVIRONMENTAL FACTORS AND DRUG MISUSE

19.     Access to drugs is a necessary requirement of a misuser's external environment. At the initial stage access is likely to be provided by friends. Physical access is, however, only one aspect of access, the other being symbolic and cultural - essentially fashion. **Prevention strategies must deal with the fact of access as broadly defined** (paras 3.6 - 3.10).

20.     Whether there will be a transition from experimentation to regular use will depend on lifestyle - eg friendships, neighbourhood, family and compatibility with daily routines (paras 3.18 - 3.20).

21.     Both family influences and peer influences are key aspects of the environment which will have a significant impact on an individual's drug use (para 3.27).

22.     In looking at the influence of the family it is probably family process (eg a conflict ridden marriage, or absence of affection and control in a two-parent household) rather than family structure (eg the lone parent household) which provides the most reliable indicator of drug use by young people (para 3.30).

23.     Friendship networks are invariably the means by which people are introduced to drugs and will be a continuing feature of an individual's drug using career, including any future likelihood of cessation (para 3.32).

24.     The term "peer pressure" has unhelpful implications in that there is an absence of any notion of volition on the part of the individual - it suggests he or she is being coerced by deviant companions. Another way of looking at the situation is in terms of "peer clusters" where the individual is not an innocent victim, but is part of the cluster, helping to shape its attitudes and behaviour, equally a recipient and a source of drug encouragement (paras 3.34 - 3.35).

25.     Research suggests that high levels of parental monitoring could discourage both boys and girls from beginning to use drugs, help reduce levels of consumption among heavy using boys and encourage girls who experiment with drugs to quit (para 3.45).

26.     In neighbourhoods where young people are excluded from formal opportunities in terms of education and the job market, drugs and crime can offer alternative means by which to demonstrate status and achievement and provide financial rewards too (para 3.52).

27.    Local efforts to curb drug misuse are likely to be severely handicapped unless supported by wider schemes of urban regeneration, access to jobs and training, and other initiatives to combat social exclusion. We return to the question of deprivation in chapter 9 (para 3.54).

28.    The conclusions which can be drawn from the chapter are,

   • Family and peer networks are the most decisive influences on the development of drug use among young people, with, if anything, friendship being a more significant influence than that of the family. Practical efforts to enhance parents' capacities to discourage drug use should start in earlier childhood before the onset of adolescence (par 3.59).

   • In terms of intervention among friendship networks, peer education shows some promise among established groups of drug users in terms of fashioning harm reduction strategies but it is more difficult to conceive of primary prevention initiatives in these settings (para 3.60).

   • **It is better to engage popular culture and to deploy its language and imagery towards health promotion goals rather than try and combat the culture itself** (para 3.60).

   • The wider socio-economic context, while it does clearly shape and influence certain aspects of drug-related problems in modern Britain, also impinges on a variety of other policy issues with regard to employment, education and training, housing, and crime prevention. **That proposes the need for multi-agency strategies** (para 3.61).

   • **The prevention of drug-related harm is a matter which concerns the entire community and not just problem drug users and their families** (para 3.64).

# CHAPTER 4: COMMUNITY-BASED DRUG PREVENTION STRATEGIES: EVIDENCE AND REVIEW

29.    The chapter reviews a wide variety of prevention projects which have been attempted in community settings (para 4.1).

30.    Approaches involving the family fall into two categories: those that attempt to involve parents in actually delivering drugs prevention through the establishment of parent groups and those that have focused on working directly with parents or families in

order to prevent their children's drug use. To be effective interventions must involve more than just the young person and their close family. The extended family should be drawn in as well as a range of professional groups (paras 4.7 - 4.12).

31. Peer approaches come in many shapes and forms and there is as yet little that can be said about their effectiveness. Careful evaluations are needed in order to further our understanding of the different models of peer intervention and the likely mechanisms for influencing young people's drug use (para 4.14).

32. Approaches involving diversionary activity are popular at local community level. Well-conducted evaluations are rare but approaches targeted at high risk groups, which incorporate life and employment skills and are sustained over a considerable period of time, may offer hope of reducing drug use (paras 4.15 - 4.17).

33. Evidence from the US suggests that drug testing in the workplace can be very successful in reducing misuse. However in some settings there may be civil liberties objections (paras 4.18 - 4.20).

34. Considerable success has been demonstrated in harm reduction interventions for high risk groups (para 4.21).

35. Treatment and harm reduction approaches have been developed and promoted in Britain by community drug teams (para 4.22).

36. The involvement of the police in a multi-agency approach generally receives a good deal of support (paras 4.29 - 4.33). We consider the policing of drug markets in chapter 8.

37. Experience has shown that in some neighbourhoods drug problems can stimulate confrontational forms of community involvement. It has also shown the importance of convincing existing organisations in a neighbourhood to extend their scope so as to encompass drug issues (para 4.34 - 4.35).

38. Groups such as truants, young offenders and homeless youths may be at higher risk of experimentation with drugs and higher risk of problematic drug use (para 4.42). We explore the effects of homelessness in chapter 7.

39. **Some types of high-risk groups, such as young people looked after by local authorities and young offenders are probably best accessed and worked with through the institutions and agencies responsible for them (para 4.43).**

40. The community development model is one way of delivering drugs prevention at community level. The Home Office Drugs Prevention Initiative, which was first announced in October 1989, uses it. A review of the initiative in 1993 found that while there were signs that communities were taking an increasing lead in drugs prevention more attention needed to be given in the next stage to establishing what approaches worked effectively (para 4.45 – 4.46).

41. **Our conclusion from the review which Chapter 4 represents is that while we know little for sure about what works in terms of community-based drug prevention there is evidence that multi-component programmes hold out the most prospect of success** (para 4.64).

## CHAPTER 5: LOCAL DRUG PROJECTS AND LOCAL PREVENTIVE ACTION

42. Drug projects have grown up in a haphazard way since the 1960s and there are now a great number in existence (paras 5.1 – 5.8).

43. They are very diverse, delivering activity which fits into a continuum of treatment, harm reduction and prevention (paras 5.9 – 5.15).

44. While there has been an extraordinary growth in drug projects much of what they are doing remains hidden. **More information needs to be gathered about the processes and experiences with a view to establishing what is good practice. From this information policy makers should identify whether the most efficient and effective work is being done against drug misuse with communities** (para 5.9).

45. **Central guidance is required to help local projects set off in the right direction from the outset** and we offer some suggestions of what that guidance might comprise (paras 5.16 – 5.17).

46. **Treatment projects should ask themselves whether they should take on a wider prevention brief rather than treatment alone** (para 5.20).

47. **The role of Drug Action Teams will be central in helping to provide the necessary support for drug projects to develop successfully** (para 5.20).

## CHAPTER 6: DRUG PREVENTION AND THE ENVIRONMENT OF AWARENESS AND BELIEFS

48. The choices which people make about drugs, or anything else, are governed by awareness and beliefs - what they feel about something. The environment is as much about the surround of ideas as about physical structures. **This aspect of drug prevention has in the past too often been neglected or shrugged off as unapproachable but is of vital importance if further progress is to be made** (paras 6.1 - 6.2).

49. When it comes to drug misuse and values we think there is a complexity which must not be overlooked. Some values may appear insulting and unattainable for some people. The aim should be to adopt practices and foster an environment which enables individuals to attain the values which make them a part of society (para 6.6).

50. **If society intends to provide young people with an environment which helps them not to take illicit drugs (or abuse volatile substances), or to reduce the harms which they do, the climate of awareness and beliefs on alcohol and tobacco must be seen as part of that context** (para 6.20). We refer in paragraph 1.12 to the need for drug prevention policies to consider the place of alcohol and tobacco in the scheme of things.

51. The climate which influences individuals away from drugs is more likely to be engendered where people are truly informed, not just with facts but also with values - valuing themselves, valuing the community and valuing other people (para 6.21).

52. The media helps to shape the environment of ideas in which we all live and **we recommend that journalists should have access to a source of authoritative and consistent advice which not only responds to requests but also pro-actively engages journalists on the subject of drugs prevention** (para 6.22 - 6.23). The Welsh Drug and Alcohol Unit has already established such a mechanism.

53. **Employers should, if they have not already, have a policy on drugs and alcohol. This need not necessarily be elaborate but consideration should have been given to the issues involved** (para 6.29).

54. The particular difficulties of women drug misusers can be all too easily overlooked. **Women should be actively involved in the planning, development and provision of responses to drug misuse** (para 6.32).

55. Rather than deplore the music and dance culture in which young people exist we believe that **the places where young people congregate should be used for drug prevention activity** (para 6.40).

56.     Building on the Health Education Authority's earlier work **continued attempts need to be made to target specific messages at specific groups with more emphasis being put on distinguishing between them** (para 6.54).

57.     **We remain unconvinced that, as yet, sufficient attempts have been made through the HEA to reach young people in the ethnic minorities, women and older drug misusers and suggest that greater efforts should be made** (para 6.55).

58.     We question whether it is sensible to confine drug prevention messages to the health consequences of taking drugs. **We give some examples of other approaches, involving social unacceptability, which might be considered** (para 6.61).

59.     The local media seem to be more receptive to and more interested than the national media in carrying stories on or favourable to drugs prevention. **We suggest that Drug Action Teams, and others, engage the local media** (para 6.66).

60.     In England around 50% of all Drug Action Teams have decided to tackle alcohol misuse alongside drugs misuse - it is a requirement of Drugs and Alcohol Action Teams in Wales. **We would like to see all Drug Action Teams in England and Scotland seriously consider dealing with them, and volatile substance abuse, together** (para 6.68).

61.     **We recommend that personal social health education should be on the national curriculum** (para 6.70).

62.     **Given the desirability of avoiding exclusion from school except in the last resort there is a need for teachers to be adequately trained in how to deal with drug-related incidents** (para 6.71).

63.     **Children who are not attending school deserve targeted prevention action** and we suggest who might undertake it (para 6.73).

64.     **We recommend that renewed reliance should be put on the Youth Services in providing drugs education** (para 6.74).

65.     Most families, most of the time, will act as bulwarks against drug misuse. **But not all children are in such family surroundings and we believe that especial attention should be given, in terms of drug prevention and early intervention measures, to the situations where they are not** (para 6.78).

66. Professionals who work in "family" situations which render children more vulnerable to drug misuse should have some drugs training. Schools should be made aware of the possibility that children with problems may be part of families with drug related problems and should know where to seek advice (para 6.78).

67. **As children get older it is probably friends who have the greatest influence over their awareness and beliefs. This use of this characteristic in the cause of drug prevention needs to be considered further.** Peer approaches should not be regarded as a panacea (paras 6.82 - 6.83).

## CHAPTER 7: DRUG PREVENTION AND HOUSING

68. Poor housing or lack of access to affordable housing is in many instances a contributory factor in drug misuse (para 7.2).

69. **We suggest a "social contract" as a basis for local housing policies.** There is a public responsibility to meet the housing needs of drug users rather than reject them. That however must be balanced by the reasonable expectation that drug misusers will honour their side of the contract and not disrupt, disturb or threaten the neighbourhoods in which they are housed (para 7.5).

70. **We strongly caution against policies which lead to a concentration of drug users on any particular estate and suggest that it would be worth local authorities exploring the scope for greater use of the voluntary and private sectors for housing drug-misusing individuals** (para 7.9).

71. **For housing purposes we suggest that the test for dealing with a drug misuser should be whether the misuser's behaviour impinges unreasonably on the community in which he or she lives** (para 7.10).

72. **Where a misuser's activities do not interfere with the normal life of the community we suggest that an attempt should be made in the first instance to introduce the misuser to the local helping services** (para 7.11).

73. **Where a misuser's behaviour does impinge on the community we suggest that several types of action should be taken.** If dealing is occurring the police should be informed. If the nuisance is something less than that we suggest that the

target should be the anti-social behaviour of the misuser. There might still be a need to involve the police but behaviour might also be altered through putting the misuser in touch with the local helping services. At the same time it might be appropriate for the local authority to lay down, in the form of a contract, what behaviour is and is not acceptable. If after a period the misuser does not comply thought may have to be given to further sanctions (para 7.12).

74. **The ability of a housing authority to put misusers in touch with helping agencies points to a need for prior arrangements for co-operation to have been made between them at local level.** Social services may sometimes also need to be contacted (para 7.13).

75. **We suggest that eviction should be an action of last resort.** Before then there may well be scope for intervening so as to improve a misuser's behaviour. Such intervention is likely to be less costly than the process of eviction (para 7.15).

76. **Where individuals and families have been treated for their drug misusing problems and need housing afterwards, it is important that the progress which has been made in that treatment or rehabilitation is not negated by inappropriate or delayed housing allocation** (para 7.16).

77. While some problems brought on by drugs in a neighbourhood may require immediate and strict law enforcement to return it to some form of normality, in the longer term there is likely to be a need for different policies involving all the local services and the local community, including local young people (para 7.21).

78. **Local authority housing departments and housing associations should ensure they have policies in relation to drug problems. The policies should be stated and public and conveyed to tenants' associations and other relevant bodies** (para 7.24).

79. **The concept of designing out crime** both to reduce criminal activity and the fear of it is well-understood and **is particularly relevant in the context of drugs misuse** (para 7.26).

80. **Funders should not be too prescriptive and inflexible in their demands for output measures from community organisations and groups which seek money to help play a part in drug prevention** (para 7.30).

81. The homeless, who are a broad category and comprise a heterogeneous population, have particular problems of drug (and alcohol) misuse. In comparison with the general

population there is amongst the homeless a greatly increased prevalence of misuse for every category of drug. A young person who becomes homeless is likely to enter an unsupported environment where many people are using many different types of drugs and whether drugs will probably be freely available: it is difficult to envisage a situation more encouraging of drug misuse. **Any measures which deal more adequately with the root causes of homelessness, or get people out of this state sooner rather than later, are in our view likely to contribute significantly to the prevention of drug misuse** (paras 7.34 - 7.41).

82. While there is a need to address the basic problem of homelessness we also believe that appropriate help should meanwhile be targeted at the drug misusing homeless population. **Where a significant problem of homelessness exists within an area, DATs should ensure that responses are developed to meet the need of homeless drug users.** Intersectoral pilot projects and sharing of the experience would provide useful insights (paras 7.42 and 7.43).

83. The fact that Section 8 of the Misuse of Drugs Act 1971 makes it an offence for the occupier to suffer or permit the smoking of cannabis on premises has some unfortunate inhibiting effects on the support which can be provided to some drug misusers. The provision should be reviewed (para 7.44).

84. **The traditional role of housing managers,** which tends to be confined to the mechanics of housing allocation and management, **should be broadened through training so that they have more regard for, and understanding of, the problems to which drug misusers can give rise and a knowledge of where advice and help for drug misusing tenants can be obtained** (para 7.46).

85. **An identified person in the housing department should be responsible for housing policy for drug misusers** (para 7.47).

86. **Housing should be taken into account at the strategic level when dealing with drug misuse locally and the local director of housing should be on the Drug Action Team** (para 7.48).

87. **A mechanism should be found for sharing good practice between housing departments** (para 7.49).

88. **The way housing benefit regulations operate for young people seem to exacerbate drug misuse problems and they should be reviewed by the Government** (para 7.50).

## CHAPTER 8: DRUG MARKETS

89. **Interventions directed against established open drug markets will probably not eliminate them completely. In our view however, where such markets exist they should be dealt with rather than a blind eye turned** (para 8.18).

90. Drug markets have varying effects on the environment. Some of those effects will be very damaging to the community but the majority of transactions go unnoticed by the community at large taking place in pubs, clubs and behind closed doors (for example, from private homes) (paras 8.1 - 8.2).

91. In accordance with ACMD's report on Police, Drug Misusers and the Community (1994) action against drugs markets should be taken in the wider context of community safety (para 8.4).

92. A drugs market's characteristics are, like any other market, formed by the type of good which is being sold, who is buying, and who is selling and will constantly adjust to changes in circumstances (paras 8.5- 8.15).

93. **Any intervention directed at a market will lead to benefits and harms which should as far as possible be foreseen and always evaluated** (para 8.18).

94. Not to take action against blatant dealing must have a symbolic importance which should not be disregarded. It suggests a "don't care" attitude which can only affect the climate of beliefs adversely (para 8.20).

95. Experience from the United States suggests that when displacement of a drugs market occurs the effect is not total but that some dealing stops (para 8.25).

96. **In considering action against dealers police forces should bear in mind that some smaller scale sellers are often also misusers for whom it will be appropriate to try and secure help from treatment agencies** (para 8.26).

97. Local drug services and the police need to develop a common purpose and shared agenda for community strategies and we see an important role for DATs in helping to establish these and the wider partnerships which are required (para 8.27).

98. There are certain conditions which appear to sustain open markets and we refer to the Home Office report "Tackling Local Drug Markets" which was published in February 1997 which contained some detailed suggestions for tackling drug markets through treatment services, enforcement and situational prevention (para 8.30 - 8.33).

## CHAPTER 9: DRUGS AND SOCIAL DEPRIVATION

99.   We look at the meaning of the term deprivation and suggest that **if deprivation is related to drug misuse it is likely to be in a subtle and multiple way** (paras 9.1 - 9.12).

100.   We suggest that the basic proposition that the individual's social situation can have a significant relationship with their health and social adjustment is well supported. And we argue that with deprivation so widely relating to the individual's health and behaviour it would be surprising if drug misuse were found to be immune to this influence (para 9.18).

101.   We suggest that different drugs and different modes of drug use are likely to show very different types and intensities of relationship with socio-economic status (para 9.19).

102.   We conclude that Britain in the 1980s seems to have been in an unhappy sense recapitulating the American experience, and discovering that when heroin is widely available and geographical clustering of deprivation exists, the two factors are likely to make a connection (para 9.30).

103.   Some insights can be gained from examining the relationship between deprivation and volatile substance abuse. A recent report points to a statistical relationship between deprivation and VSA deaths. Deprivation accounts for 45% of the variation in VSA deaths, which leaves 55% to unexplained reasons (paras 9.32 - 9.35).

104.   We feel confident in asserting that deprivation relates statistically to types and intensities of drug use which are problematic and we are impressed by the strength and variety of evidence which supports that conclusion (para 9.45).

105.   **We further assert that on strong balance of probability, deprivation is today in Britain likely often to make a significant causal contribution to the cause, complications and intractability of damaging kinds of drug misuse. We believe that for purposes of public policy this is a conclusion which now provides a basis for further policy guidance while to take the sanguine view that the relationships are "only statistical" would be wrong and deny a crucial insight needed to inform further policy development** (para 9.49).

106.   We believe that **Drug Action Teams should, where there is presumptive cause for concern, assess and respond to significant relationships between drug misuse and deprivation which may exist within their own localities. Local surveys should be conducted either through agency identifications or sample interviewing, with drug problem prevalence related to personal or community indicators** (para 9.51).

107.   That kind of evidence should be used for accurate targeting of environmental prevention strategies of the many different kinds identified in other chapters of this report. **We are thus calling for strong new initiatives at local level drawn up within an awareness of the importance of the deprivation connection. Resource allocation formulas should include a measure of deprivation.** We are not suggesting that prevention resources within a locality should be targeted exclusively at areas of deprivation (para 9.52).

108.   We believe that **every DAT should consider these aspects of the local problem and include suitable responses within their overall action plans** (para 9.52).

109.   We also believe that **when areas are identified where drug misuse and deprivation have made a strong connection, such evidence must be seen as relevant to the planning and targeting of local drug treatment services as provided by both statutory and non-statutory agencies. We recommend that evidence should be given over time by DATs of tangible progress on this front** (para 9.54).

110.   **Where concentrations of poor housing contribute to and perpetuate social deprivation, it will be strongly supportive of drug prevention if such housing problems can be targeted and ameliorated in the ways we suggest in chapter 7** (para 9.55).

111.   **Within the Government's welfare-to-work programme a focused intervention at a national level is needed to identify best practice in employment generation and re-training for drug misusers and promoting their locally targeted implementation** (para 9.57).

112.   **We want now and in the future to see deprivation given its full and proper place in all considerations of drug prevention policy, at both the local and strategic levels, and not let slip from sight** (para 9.59).

## CHAPTER 10: THE RESOURCES AVAILABLE TO SUPPORT COMMUNITY ACTION ON PREVENTION

113.   This chapter is intended to be practical by highlighting some of the resources that might be tapped to assist with drug prevention in the community (para 10.3).

114.   **Drug Action Teams, Drug Prevention Teams and other agencies should keep in mind the scope for the use of volunteers.** We provide some ideas for the matters which should be considered in deciding whether to engage them and some organisations which should be able to give assistance (paras 10.4 - 10.9).

115.   Competition for funding is great. We describe some of the public and private sources -
       national, local, European - of money for drug prevention work (paras 10.10 - 10.19). If
       the Single Regeneration Budget remains in being, **we believe that in considering
       bids for Single Regeneration Budget funding the Government Offices for the
       Regions should require bidders to consider whether drug prevention should
       form part of the bid - it need not necessarily do so but should only be rejected
       after consideration**.

116.   There is much which has been done, and is being done, in the field of drug prevention.
       **It would be a mistake not to build on existing experience** and we have provided
       a list of organisations from whom advice and assistance can be sought (paras 10.20 -
       10.26).

## CHAPTER 11: THE RELEVANCE OF THIS REPORT TO THE INDIVIDUAL

117.   In this chapter we provide a final short rounding off of the report which describes
       what the individual should expect in terms of an environmental surround to help
       protect them from the harms of drug misuse.

118.   Drug misuse is a problem with linked personal and social origins. Our contention in
       this report is that while the individual has personal responsibility for healthy decision
       making, **there is a societal responsibility to construct and keep in repair a
       social, psychological and physical environmental surround which supports
       the individual's capacity to stay away from drug misuse and the harms of
       drug misuse and helps them pull out of damaging drug misuse**. The task is
       difficult but must be addressed (para 11.13).

*Chapter*

# 1 THE AIMS OF THE REPORT

*The purpose of this report is to look at prevention from an environmental perspective and on that basis make recommendations which will contribute to and strengthen the many ongoing efforts at drug prevention now being made in this country at national and local level. Within the total mix of policies environmentally based approaches should be given greater emphasis than they have been accorded in the past.*

## INTRODUCTION

1.1     Looking from an environmental perspective this report aims to inform the development of policy on the prevention of drug misuse in ways which we think are feasible and to provide advice on the practical implementation of policy. In so doing it will build on previous reports from ACMD. Relevant documents include an earlier overall analysis of drug prevention strategies (1984)[1], and more recent statements relating to drug misuse in schools (1993)[2] and to volatile substance abuse (1995)[3]. A range of other ACMD reports, including reports on drug misusers and the criminal justice system[4], and AIDS and drug misuse[5,6,7], also bear directly or indirectly on present concerns.

1.2     Later in this chapter we will return to a detailed consideration of the meaning to be given to "prevention" and "environment" as key terms. However, it will be useful at the outset to outline the essential nature of the perspective which will be central to this report's thinking. The problems of drug misuse have multiple determinants. Two prime dimensions which have, for instance, often received attention are the drug supply (leading to national and international policies imposing controls on particular substances), and the beliefs of the individual (leading to policies involving school-based or public drug education).

1.3     While in no way denying the importance of contributions which stem from those ways of seeing the drug problem, this report will explore the significance of a perspective which argues that why people choose to use drugs, go on using drugs or quit drug use, are issues which cannot be adequately understood without taking the environment in which they live into the reckoning. Adequate prevention strategies must, we will argue, be more willing to face up to the powerful influences, for better or worse, which are exerted on drug taking by the environment. Drug supply is a necessary pre-condition for drug misuse. However it is the individual who is the ultimate agent who does or does not make the personal decision to misuse drugs and his or her personal capacity to make sensible and healthy choices will be weakened or supported by the world which surrounds them.

1.4     It may make the position which we will be developing more readily intelligible if we take as an example the child in a classroom. The availability of drugs for that child is a highly important issue with which control strategies must continue to grapple.

Education which responds to the child as an individual sitting that day in the classroom and actively involves him or her in debate as to how to make informed and healthy choices will also provide a valuable, continuing, component to drug prevention. But the drug supply will never be totally eliminated and meanwhile that child exists outside the classroom in a multi-layered family, socio-cultural, economic and physical environment which is likely radically to impinge on his or her ability to deal with the fact of drug availability. Prevention should be a multiple activity with environmental responses more often and more strongly represented in the total mix of activities. The nature and extent of these activities will be dependent on the level of misuse and will need to address prevention both in terms of reducing the risk of an individual engaging in drug misuse and reducing the harm associated with drug misuse.

1.5    The intention of this report is to explore the meaning of the environmental perspective in relation to many different aspects of drug misuse problems and their prevention, to test the factual base for the positions which are taken, and to review experiences. But what must again be stressed is that the fundamental goal of the report is to serve practical ends. To return to the example of the child in the classroom, how is greater awareness of the environmental dimension to be used so as to put in place policies which render it less likely that this child will now or later in life be harmed by drugs? We return to this question in the final chapter of the report.

## CONTEXTS

1.6    The nature and prevalence of drug misuse is necessarily part of the context and is the subject of a separate chapter in the report (chapter 2). But here it is sufficient to note that drug misuse in the United Kingdom ranges across a wide variety of drugs, with nearly half of all people in the 16-19 age group having ever used a drug and about 20% having done so in the last month. Misuse is not confined to the young although its extent diminishes with age.

1.7    An important formal element of context is provided by recent policy statements issued by Government. The most significant documents are the Government's drug strategy for England, "Tackling Drugs Together - A strategy for England 1995-1998 (May 1995)", and the corresponding statements for Scotland - "Drugs in Scotland: Meeting the Challenge" (October 1994) - and Wales - "Forward Together" (October 1995). The Department for Education's circular on "Drug Prevention and Schools" (May 1995) is also very relevant, as is the Government's White Paper "Health of the Nation" (July 1992). We believe that the recommendations which will evolve from the present report are closely aligned with the overall thrust of current government policies on drug misuse as developed in these documents and the Government's wider policies. The report is written on the assumption that Drug Action Teams (and in Wales, Drug and Alcohol Action Teams) which were established by the Government's drug strategies will continue in being. We believe that they should because an environmental response to drug misuse demands action across the range of interests which they represent.

1.8    This report seeks to build on the experience, insights and energies of many types of drug prevention activity which are today going on in this country. The government's

Drugs Prevention Initiative, which has established Drugs Prevention Teams in various parts of the country, has over recent years substantially contributed to this accumulating, community-based experience which we refer to again in chapter 5. A highly important part of our context is therefore what other people have learnt about drugs and the environment, and what they have to tell. That proposes the need to consult widely and build on principles of partnership and working together.

1.9    ACMD is a body primarily concerned with practical policies and their application in the field, and throughout our work we have borne that practical expectation in mind. However and without going in a too academic direction, we saw it as essential to acknowledge as one aspect of context the national and international research base. The report will therefore seek to set out in plain language the ways in which research can help clarify the relationships between drugs and the environment, and what research has to tell about the efficacy of different policy interventions. It is important to identify the gaps in knowledge as well as what is known.

## DRUG MISUSE AND THE MEANING OF "PREVENTION"

1.10    In this section we will outline the meaning and scope of the term "prevention" as a concept fundamental to this report. Everything said here derives from and supports previous ACMD perspectives.

1.11    Prevention must embrace multiple and complementary levels of activity. These levels include prevention of initiation into drug misuse, those which discourage continued use or offer a way out of misuse through treatment, and interventions which aim to reduce the harm done by drug misuse. These approaches are in no sense contradictory. As recognised in "Tackling Drugs Together", the most effective approach is likely to be one which deploys a balanced mix of prevention policies, and tackles both the drug supply and the demand side.

1.12    Prevention must encompass measures directed at multiple drugs, used in isolation, simultaneously or in sequence. The concept of prevention employed here acknowledges that different drugs are used in different ways and with different patterns and intensities and with different routes by different people and with different levels of risk. Prevention is not about one, simple, monolithic entity called "drugs". ACMD's prevention approach is concerned with the totality of drugs covered by the Misuse of Drugs Act (and has also embraced volatile substance abuse). When setting up drug prevention policies consideration will often need at the same time to be given to the place of alcohol and tobacco in the scheme of things. By way of analogy in its report on drug education in schools ACMD (1993)[2] took the view that health education should embrace use of both licit and illicit substances.

1.13    Prevention should be concerned to relieve the harm done not only to the drug misuser him or herself but to other people besides. Such harm may for instance be done to the family who are bearing the brunt of a young person's behaviour, to the children of adult drug misusers, to the person's sexual partner whom the drug misuser infects with hepatitis or HIV, to the victim of drug-related crime, or to the community at large by damage to comfort and amenities.

1.14    Prevention should target all groups in the population. Prevention should sometimes give priority to strategies which respond to children and young adults as representing vulnerable sections often with high drug misuse exposure, but the needs of older population sectors should also be acknowledged. Drug misuse is a problem both in urban and rural areas. Prevention strategies should be sensitive to the position of ethnic and minority groups and to females as well as males.

## THE MEANING OF "ENVIRONMENT"

1.15    The discussion of prevention in the previous section is meant to consolidate an agreed, familiar perspective. Where we immediately enter into rather new territory for ACMD is when it comes to an attempt to define the meaning of "environment". The suggestions we make below aim to provide a working framework for the immediate task of this report.

1.16    The approach which we have favoured is to view the environment as an interactive whole - as the world in all its complexities in which the individual lives, and through which that person moves, not only being influenced by it but also influencing it themselves. Family, school, work and leisure environments, and peer group influences are part of this whole, as is homelessness. Friendship networks, intimacy, and social support are important at all ages. Cultural beliefs and expectations permeate the environment and for many people include spiritual values. Quality of housing and other aspects of the physical environment, and whether the setting is rural or urban can be relevant. The degree of access to education, gainful employment, welfare support, medical care, childcare and justice are further significant aspects. The economic and commercial climate will bear in many ways on the quality of the complex mix of social, cultural, interpersonal and physical factors caught up in this one word.

1.17    The environment can encourage or oppose drug use partly through greater or lesser physical access to drugs, the presence of drug markets and knowledge of them, the number of dealers and the level of enforcement. In addition, the environment comprises prevalent, normative attitudes towards drugs which make these drugs more or less attractive and acceptable to the individual. And there is no doubt that some individuals regard drug taking as attractive and not unduly risky - a normal part of their existence - while others would never take such substances. The influence of the environment affects the choices which individuals can and do make.

1.18    In many of its elements the environment as described above will be easily sensed by the individual as having an effect on their lives - their school, their friends, their family influences, the view from the window, the streets which they walk down, the places where they spend their leisure are for most people the realities that the word "environment" will conjure up. It is in developing prevention strategies within that immediate kind of context and within the individual's community that we see environmentally orientated prevention policies as having most to offer. Within the overall perspective attention must however also be given to the possible influence of larger, less direct and often less easily amenable aspects of the environment such as the impact of economic cycles, national levels of unemployment, levels of deprivation and so on.

1.19   It will be apparent from the preceding paragraphs that it is possible to identify two broad potential kinds of influence bearing on drug misuse - first, the micro-environment, comprising the more immediate aspects of an individual's interpersonal environment such as family, friendship networks, the school and workplace and, second, the macro-environment comprising broad social, economic and cultural factors.

1.20   While this is a convenient distinction, and one which we use in chapter 3, it is a distinction which often breaks down. For example, where should the individual's neighbourhood be located? On the one hand it will be the arena within which many macro-economic forces will be experienced, such as the local patterns of employment and the nature of available housing, but on the other it will be the place where some of the most important interpersonal influences - local peer groups above all - will operate. The school and the workplace are similarly difficult to place within the micro/macro division.

1.21   It would be naive to suppose that what happens to the larger socio-economic fabric will be influenced by local drug prevention efforts or recommendations by an ACMD report, and we have no intention of going in that direction. But if the facts suggest that macro-level factors influence drug misuse that needs to be stated.

## THE INTENDED READERSHIP

1.22   The statutory responsibility of ACMD is to give advice to Ministers, and we hope this report will help to contribute towards the development of government drug policies as they continue to evolve.

1.23   We also intend this report to be useful to those who work directly with drug misusers and carry local responsibilities for prevention of drug misuse. We hope that the report will be relevant for people working in all manner of drug agencies and of interest to administrators and planners at local level and particularly to Drug Action Teams and Drug Reference Groups in England and their equivalents in other parts of the United Kingdom. We hope that our recommendations will be seen as useful by those many people who hold general community-based, intersectoral responsibilities. Drug prevention, we believe, must very much be the concern of generalists as well as specialists.

## LAYOUT

1.24   Having in this chapter set out the aims of the report we move in chapter 2 to see what is known about the nature and extent of drug misuse in the United Kingdom. Then in chapters 3 and 4, drawing on experience here and abroad, we consider the environmental factors which influence drug misuse, and the community-based strategies which are being used to counter it. These three chapters review the available material and provide references for the readers who are interested in pursuing them.

1.25   In the following chapters, 5-9, we examine what is currently going on in terms of community-based prevention, pick out a number of themes which we think are particularly relevant - the environment of awareness and beliefs, housing, drug markets, and deprivation. In chapter 10 we suggest some sources which might be tapped to support community-based prevention. It is largely from these later chapters that our recommendations emerge. In the final chapter we describe what an individual should expect from the environment around them to help protect them from the harms of drug misuse.

# 2 THE NATURE AND EXTENT OF ILLICIT DRUG USE IN THE UNITED KINGDOM

*Pulling together information from multiple sources this chapter provides as best possible a description of the current extent of drug misuse. No one statistic can adequately represent the overall picture, but in general we conclude that drug misuse though far from universal in this country is widespread and has probably been quite steeply escalating since the late 1980s.*

## INTRODUCTION

2.1 This chapter provides information on the extent and the nature of illicit drug use in the UK. In considering an environmental response to drug misuse it is necessary to understand who is taking drugs, which drugs they are taking, with what frequency and so on. These matters are all part of the context of drug misuse and it is the aim of this chapter, so far as is possible, to set them out. Drug prevention policies in the United Kingdom should be designed with an awareness that drug misuse today is diverse widespread and in some areas an enormously common problem.

2.2 The question of how many people are using illicit drugs is deceptively easy to ask but notoriously difficult to answer. To provide an answer to this question it is necessary to combine information from a wide range of sources; however, the picture produced by this process can only ever be an imperfect approximation of the real state of affairs. There has never been a comprehensive national survey of drug misuse prevalence within the UK.[1] The difficulty of establishing accurate information on the prevalence and nature of illicit drug use is not, however, about the lack of such a survey but about the very nature of the activity being looked into. Illicit drug use is a hidden and stigmatised activity, the details of which many individuals are unwilling to reveal to others, particularly those whom they perceive as representing official authority. Drug use is also an activity which for the most part occurs outside the domains of the health care and criminal justice systems. As a result, our knowledge of the world of illicit drug use, and our ability to estimate the number of people using illicit drugs, is less complete than we may judge to be desirable.

2.3 The sources of information drawn upon in this chapter include the Home Office Addict Notification System[2] (which was wound up with effect from 1 May 1997), information on the numbers of individuals prosecuted under the Misuse of Drugs Act,[3][4] the Regional Drug Misuse Databases[5] and data from various sources on morbidity and mortality amongst drug users. This chapter also draws upon the results of a number of recent large scale surveys that have collected information on illicit drug use, including the 1996 British Crime Survey,[6] the 1996 Scottish Crime Survey,[7] the 1994/1995 Northern Ireland Crime Survey[8], the 1992 OPCS national survey of psychiatric morbidity[9] and a survey of drug usage and drug prevention sponsored by the Home Office - commonly known as the Four Cities Survey,[10] a number of more locally based surveys that have reported data on levels of drug use amongst young people, and finally some recent work attempting to estimate the prevalence of illicit drug use using capture-recapture methods- the latter techniques statistically model the size of the drug using population on the basis of a detailed analysis of the overlap between various different agencies lists of drug users (for example, drug users in contact with the police may be compared with drug users in contact with health and social care agencies).

2.4    It is important to recognise that each of these data sources present only a limited picture of the extent and nature of illicit drug use. In the case of the official data sources (for example, addict notification, regional drug misuse databases, criminal justice data) it is widely recognised that these data refer only to certain sections of the drug misusing population, principally those whose drug use has led them into contact with drug services or the criminal justice system. In the case of social survey data there is a reliance upon individuals' willingness accurately to report the details of their drug use. In the case of drug misuse prevalence estimates using capture-recapture methods, these techniques are at a relatively early stage of development and to date have been successfully applied only to a small number of areas. All of these data sources are limited in certain ways; nevertheless they represent the best data available at the present time.

## DRUG ADDICTION (DEPENDENCE)

2.5    Traditionally, information on the extent of addictive drug use was provided in the Home Office addict notification system – although in practice this system for the most part registers opiate or cocaine addicts who have approached the treatment system. As can be seen in Figure 1 below the numbers of both new and renotified addicts have doubled over recent years.

2.6    In 1996 a total of 43,372 individuals were notified as addicted of which 18,281 were new cases. The male to female ratio was broadly 3:1 and the average age of newly notified addicts was 25.9. Addiction to three of the most widely consumed drugs

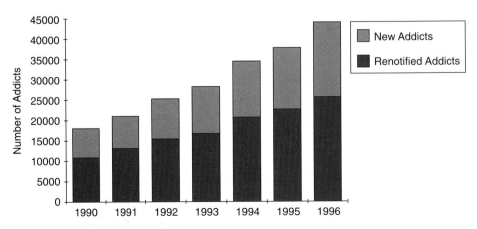

Figure 1. Drug addicts notified to the Home Office, United Kingdom, 1990-96

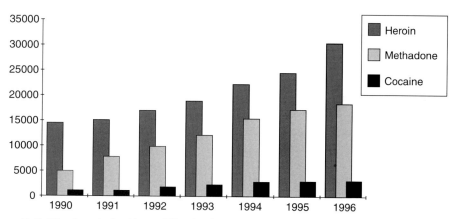

Figure 2. Notifications to the Home Office by drug, United Kingdom 1990-1996

makes up the bulk of cases included in the Home Office Index: heroin, methadone, and cocaine – with a steady increase in all three of these being recorded over the last seven years (see Figure 2).

2.7     The shortcomings of the addict notification system are well known; not all individuals who are addicted will be in contact with medical practitioners, equally not all practitioners passed on the details of addicted patients to the Home Office.[11] As a result of these shortcomings, it is not possible on the basis of the notification system to estimate how many people in the UK may be addicted to drugs. Information in this area can be gleaned, however, from the OPCS national survey of psychiatric morbidity which obtained data on levels of dependent drug use amongst approximately 10,000 adults in the UK in 1992. Drug dependence in this study was defined in terms of the individual self-reporting one or more of the following over the last twelve months: needing to use an increasing amount of the drug or drugs to achieve the desired effect, feeling dependent upon one or more of the drugs used, having tried unsuccessfully to reduce their level of drug use, and having experienced withdrawal symptoms. This definition is broad and may lead to inflation in prevalence estimates and we would therefore caution that when considering the results of the OPCS survey it is wise to bear in mind the definitional basis. The survey examined dependence on a range of commonly used drugs such as cannabis, amphetamines, LSD, heroin and cocaine, and also included solvents and the use of drugs that may have been prescribed, such as valium, but not alcohol.

2.8     Table 1 below summarises the percentages of the study population that were classified as having been drug dependent in the last 12 months.

**Table 1. Percentage of people dependent on drugs in last 12 months -**

OPCS Psychiatric Morbidity Survey

|         | 16-19 | 20-24 | 25-29 | 30-34 | 35-39 | 40-44 | 45-49 | 50-54 | 55-59 | 60-64 |
|---------|-------|-------|-------|-------|-------|-------|-------|-------|-------|-------|
| *Males* | 7.9 | 11.1 | 2.6 | 2.8 | 1.3 | 1.6 | 0.2 | 0.5 | 0.2 | 0.4 |
| *Females* | 5.6 | 2.9 | 1.9 | 1.4 | 1.3 | 0.3 | 0.5 | - | 0.9 | 0.7 |
| ***All*** | **6.8** | **7.0** | **2.3** | **2.6** | **1.3** | **0.9** | **0.4** | **0.2** | **0.5** | **0.4** |

Code:- no estimate

2.9    It is possible to combine data from the OPCS survey with data from the 1991 census to provide an estimate of the total number of people in England and Wales who were dependent on illicit drugs (Table 2).

**Table 2. Estimated number of people in England and Wales that were dependent on drugs in preceding year by age and sex**

| | | | | | thousands | | | | | | |
|---|---|---|---|---|---|---|---|---|---|---|---|
| | *16-19* | *20-24* | *25-29* | *30-34* | *35-39* | *40-44* | *45-49* | *50-54* | *55-59* | *60-64* | *Total* |
| *Males* | 105 | 204 | 51 | 50 | 21 | 29 | 3 | 7 | 3 | 9 | 482 |
| *Females* | 72 | 55 | 38 | 25 | 22 | 6 | 8 | - | 11 | 9 | 246 |
| *Total* | 177 | 259 | 89 | 75 | 43 | 35 | 11 | 7 | 14 | 18 | 728 |

Code:- no estimate

2.10    In 1992 approximately 728,000 individuals in England and Wales met the study's criteria for having been dependent on drugs in the last 12 months. The fact that this estimate is dependent on the operational criteria which have been employed should again be emphasised – a stricter definition or exclusion of cannabis might easily halve the estimate.

## DRUG USERS IN TOUCH WITH SERVICES

2.11    Both the Addicts Index and the OPCS survey refer to addiction/drug dependence. Additional information on drug users is also provided by the Regional Drug Misuse Databases in England, Wales and Scotland which collate information on problem drug users who present to services.

2.12    For the six month period ending 31 March 1996 there were a total of 28,856 individuals recorded on the databases. It should be noted however that there are guidelines on the type of agency contact that would warrant inclusion in the databases, in particular contacts made during outreach work or at needle/syringe exchanges are

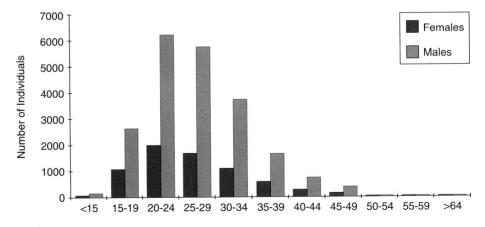

Figure 3. Individuals starting agency episodes in the period 1/10/95 - 31/3/96 by age and sex - Drug Misuse Databases - England, Wales and Scotland

excluded. Heroin was the main drug of misuse of 50% of those recorded on the Regional Drug Misuse Databases between 1995/1996, followed by methadone 16%, amphetamines 9%, cannabis 7%, benzodiazepines 5% and cocaine 4%. As with the addict notification system, men outnumber women 3:1 in the returns. In part this probably mirrors the fact that more men than women are using illicit drugs; however, it probably also reflects the fact that for a range of reasons, including the greater stigma attached to drug use by women, drug agencies are more accessible to males than females. The relatively small numbers of those aged under 20 is probably a reflection of this age group tending to have little contact with drug services.

2.13    Data from the databases also illustrate regional variations in prevalence of individuals receiving treatment for their drug misuse. Figure 4 (on page 12) shows differences in the level of drug agency contacts for the UK with the exception of Northern Ireland (which does not operate a Regional Drug Misuse Database). Some of the apparent variations in levels of drug use revealed by the databases refer to differences in the rigour with which drug agencies pass on information to the databases.

2.14    Figures 5 and 6 (on pages 13 and 14) contrast the reported route of use of heroin and amphetamine across regions and show something of the variation across the UK in the pattern of drug use for those individuals in treatment. Proportionally amongst those using heroin as their main drug, injecting is more widespread in parts of Scotland and in the South East Thames area than elsewhere in the UK; similarly amongst those using amphetamines as their main drug, injecting is proportionally greater in the Trent, North Western and South Western areas of England. The pattern of drug misuse in Wales is quite different from that discerned in England with cannabis and stimulants being the main drugs of misuse in Wales up to 1995 with heroin in 'third place', whilst heroin is the most widely reported drug of misuse to the databases across England.

2.15    Within any one of the large geographical areas covered by the Regional Drug Misuse Databases there are likely to be local differences in the nature of drug misuse. For example, from the Welsh Drug Misuse Database,[12] amphetamine use was more common in South Wales, whereas heroin use was more common in North Wales. There is very little contemporaneous collection of data on local patterns of drug use with which to identify evolving changes in drug use.

## CAPTURE-RECAPTURE ESTIMATION OF DRUG MISUSE PREVALENCE

2.16    Recent developments have been made in the use of capture-recapture methods to estimate drug misuse prevalence. These methods are based upon identifying the overlap between various statutory and non-statutory agencies' samples of drug misusers. The size of the overlap between samples allows a statistical model to be created with which to estimate the size of the wider drug using population. Such methods are particularly helpful in correcting for the under-ascertainment within official data sources. This approach has been applied to date in only a limited number of areas within the UK. In Glasgow[13] these methods have been used to estimate the size of the drug injecting population to be approximately 8,494; in Liverpool[14] the number of people using opiates or cocaine was estimated as 2,344 and research in

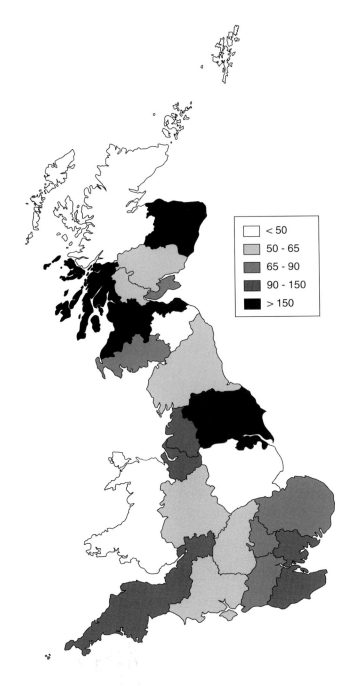

| | |
|---|---|
| ☐ | < 50 |
| ▣ | 50 - 65 |
| ▨ | 65 - 90 |
| ▩ | 90 - 150 |
| ■ | > 150 |

Digital boundaries for England and Wales © OPCS, © OS and © GDC 1991.
Digital boundaries for Scotland; source: GRO(S) © Crown copyright 1991.

Figure 4. Number of individuals Starting Agency Contact per 100,000 population aged 15-54

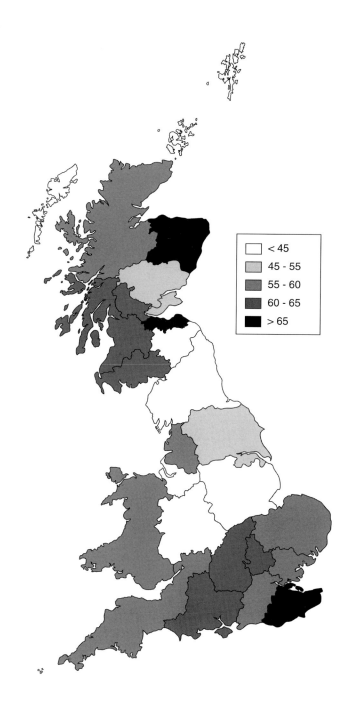

Figure 5. % of those using heroin as main drug who are injecting heroin

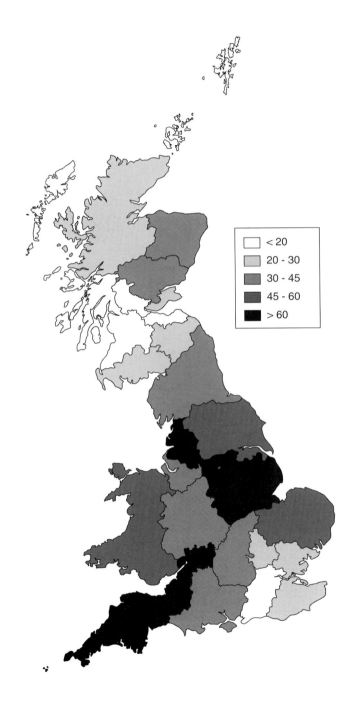

Figure 6. % of those using amphetamine as main drug who are injecting amphetamine

Dundee[15] has estimated the number of individuals using injectable drugs as 2,557. Although these methods have primarily been applied in urban areas, they were used to estimate that there were 8,351 serious drug users in Wales[16]. In addition to drug injecting, serious drug use was defined to include the non injectable use of heroin and crack-cocaine.

2.17   To put these estimates in context we need to compare the figures with those from official sources. To obtain the above Dundee estimate, for example, data from the local drug treatment agency, the local police, the HIV test register and from local GPs were merged with all double counting being removed. This process identified a total of 855 individuals from which it was possible to estimate that there were 2,557 people who were using opiates or benzodiazepines in Dundee. This figure contrasts markedly with the number of new cases in Dundee (106) notified to the Scottish Regional Drug Misuse Database for 1994/95. Similar analysis in the Chester area in 1993 identified 397 individuals in contact with a wide range of agencies which resulted in an estimated 1,027 opiate users in that area,[17] as opposed to 230 addicts notified to the Home Office.

## PREVALENCE OF ILLICIT DRUG USE: SOCIAL SURVEY DATA

2.18   Important data on the prevalence of illicit drug use have been provided by a wide range of national and local surveys. By definition, surveys rely upon individuals revealing information on the nature and extent of their drug use; however, while some individuals will be prepared to disclose the details of their drug use in this way, others will not. Moreover the obstacles to accurate self-reporting may be greater in the case of those drugs carrying greater social stigma, (for example, heroin) than for those drugs that are seen as rather more commonplace.

2.19   Table 3 summarises the data from the 1996 British Crime Survey and the 1996 Scottish Crime Survey on the percentages of people aged 16 to 59 reporting having ever used particular illicit drugs.

**Table 3.  Percentages of males and females that have ever used different drugs. Scottish Crime Survey 1996; British Crime Survey 1996**

*Ages 16-59*

| | SCS 1996 | | BCS 1996 | |
|---|---|---|---|---|
| | *Males* | *Females* | *Males* | *Female* |
| Cannabis | 23 | 15 | 27 | 18 |
| Amphetamines | 9 | 6 | 11 | 7 |
| LSD | 8 | 3 | 7 | 3 |
| Psilocybin | 8 | 3 | 7 | 3 |
| Ecstasy | 5 | 3 | 5 | 2 |
| Cocaine | 4 | 2 | 4 | 2 |
| Crack Cocaine | 1 | 1 | 1 | * |
| Heroin | 1 | * | 1 | * |
| Methadone | 1 | 1 | * | * |
| Code | * less than 0.5 | | | |

2.20    In this table we can see that in the case of cannabis and amphetamines higher levels of use were identified in the British Crime Survey than the Scottish Crime Survey. In the case of LSD, and Psilocybin use, however, slightly higher levels of use were found amongst the Scottish males. Table 4 presents the corresponding figures for drug use within the preceding 12 months.

**Table 4.  Percentages of males and females that have ever used different illicit drugs in the preceding 12 months. Scottish Crime Survey 1996; British Crime Survey 1996**

*Ages 16-59*

|  | SCS 1996 | | BCS 1996 | |
| --- | --- | --- | --- | --- |
|  | *Males* | *Females* | *Males* | *Female* |
| Cannabis | 11 | 6 | 11 | 7 |
| Amphetamines | 4 | 3 | 4 | 2 |
| LSD | 2 | 1 | 2 | * |
| Psilocybin | 2 | * | 1 | * |
| Ecstasy | 3 | 1 | 2 | 1 |
| Cocaine | 1 | 1 | 1 | * |
| Crack Cocaine | * | * | * | * |
| Heroin | * | * | * | * |
| Methadone | * | * | * | * |
| Code | * less than 0.5 | | | |

2.21    It is important to stress a cautionary note regarding such comparisons since the two surveys did not use exactly the same methods to collect data on drug use. In the British Crime Survey, respondents keyed in their answers to drug use questions themselves using a hand held computer, whereas in the Scottish Crime survey respondents completed the drug use questions of a paper and pencil survey, placing their answers in a sealed envelope. It is at least possible that this difference may have influenced the level of drug use reported in the two studies.

2.22    Both the Scottish Crime Survey and the British Crime survey present data on the misuse of temazepam and tranquillisers such as valium. In the Scottish Crime Survey 3% of females and 5% of males had ever misused temazepam, while in the British Crime Survey 3% of both males and females had ever used drugs in the 'temazepam etc.' category, which also includes valium, which had not been prescribed by a doctor.

2.23    The crime survey which was undertaken in Northern Ireland in 1994/1995 used the same format as the 1994 British Crime Survey[18]. Almost 2,200 people aged between 16 and 59 completed the drugs section, again using a hand held computer. Lower levels of drug use were found in this survey, for example 24% of men and 16% of women had ever taken any drug. As in the British Crime Survey, drug use was more common among younger people, for example 46% of those aged 18 to 21 had taken drugs; 51% of males and 38% of females in that age group. Cannabis was the most commonly used drug, experienced by 12% of all respondents and 24% of those in the 18-25 category.

2.24    Table 5 provides broad estimates for the total number of people in England and Wales who have ever used specific drugs based upon the 1996 British Crime Survey.

**Table 5. Estimated number of people aged 16 to 59 in England and Wales that have EVER used particular drugs   (Adapted from BCS 1996)**

|  | thousands |
|---|---|
|  | Mean estimate |
| Cannabis | 6,582 |
| Amphetamines | 2,632 |
| LSD | 1,461 |
| MDMA | 1,023 |

2.25    Table 6 provides estimates for lifetime drug use for Scotland based upon the 1996 Scottish Crime Survey.

**Table 6. Estimated number of people aged 16 to 59 in Scotland that have EVER used particular drugs   (Adapted from SCS 1996)**

|  | thousands |
|---|---|
|  | Mean estimate |
| Any drug | 679 |
| Cannabis | 560 |
| Stimulants/Hallucinogens | 330 |
| Opiates | 41 |

2.26    In addition to the national crime surveys there have been a number of smaller studies that have looked in particular at levels of illicit drug use amongst young people. The focus upon young people in such work derives in part from the fact that young people are known to be at particular risk of using illicit drugs.

## SUBSTANCE USE AND YOUNG PEOPLE

*TOBACCO, ALCOHOL AND SOLVENTS*

2.27    This chapter is principally concerned with the nature and extent of illicit drug use within the UK. In focusing attention upon young people it is important to also look at the use of tobacco, alcohol, and solvents, since early use of these drugs has been shown to predict later use of illicit drugs.[19] Balding and colleagues' survey of over 23,000 schoolchildren[20] identified 16.1% of boys and 21.7% of girls aged 14–15 as regular smokers in 1995. Adelekan and colleagues carried out a study of 2,888 11 to 16 year olds from Blackburn, Lancashire,[21] amongst whom 29.1% of boys and 27.6% of girls had ever smoked. A survey of 758 schoolchildren aged between 11 to 16 in Dundee, Scotland,[22] found that just over half (52.6%) had ever smoked.

2.28    Many of the studies on young people have identified significant proportions consuming alcohol. In Balding's survey, 25.9% of boys and 15.3% of girls aged 10–11 had consumed an alcoholic drink within the preceding week, rising to 60.6% of boys and 56.2% of girls aged 14–15. In the Dundee study 43.7% of schoolchildren reported having been drunk in the past. Most recently there has been concern over the availability of a number of alcoholic drinks, which in aspects of their marketing, and in some cases their sweet taste, may particularly appeal to young people - these drinks include a variety of white ciders and fruit wines. It has been shown that many of these drinks are being widely consumed by those under 16.[23]

2.29    A number of the studies in this area have also explored the use of solvents; a longitudinal study of over 700 young people in the north west of England[24], for example, found that 13% of 15-16 year olds had ever used solvents, with 3% having used solvents in the preceding month. Deaths associated with the use of solvents comprise an important proportion of all deaths in young people; for example over 6% of deaths of 15-16 year olds in 1991 were attributable to solvents.[25]

## ILLICIT DRUGS

2.30    Table 7 below summarises the results from four recent school surveys of drug use carried out in various parts of the UK, including a school based survey carried out in Northern Ireland.[26] The largest of these surveys, by Miller and Plant[27], identified over 40% of 15 and 16 year olds reporting past experience of having used an illicit drug.

### Table 7.  Percentages of young people who have ever used illicit drugs

| | Miller & Plant (1996) | | Parker (1995) | N. Ireland (1994) | | Barnard (1996) | |
| Age | Male | Female | All | Male | Female | Male | Female |
|---|---|---|---|---|---|---|---|
| 11 | | | | 4 | 1 | | |
| 12 | | | | | | 13 | 10 |
| 13 | | | | 15 | 10 | 29 | 18 |
| 14 | | | 36 | | | 41 | 33 |
| 15 | 44 | 40 | 47 | 25 | 22 | 59 | 55 |
| 16 | | | 51 | | | | |
| 17 | | | | | | | |
| 18 | | | | | | | |
| 19 | | | | | | | |
| N | 4092 | 3630 | * | 1994 | 1940 | 374 | 378 |

* The Parker study was longitudinal, studying more than 700 young people over three years.

2.31    The consistent finding across all of the studies in this area is that with increasing age there is an increase in the proportion of young people who have used illicit drugs. Within a number of areas the majority of young people will have used illicit drugs by their mid-teens. Where these studies have distinguished between males and females, they have tended to find drug use more widespread amongst younger males compared to younger females.

2.32    Of particular interest in the table above are the results from the Northern Ireland survey which suggest that the pattern of illicit drug use amongst young people in Northern Ireland is lower than that occurring elsewhere in the UK but nonetheless at a significant level - 25.0% of boys and 22.4% of girls at age 15 reporting some use of illicit drugs. In addition to the studies included in Table 8 above, Smith and Nutbeam have reported the results of a survey carried out amongst a large sample of 15 to 16 year olds in Wales.[28] In this study, young people were asked to describe the drugs they had ever used as well as those they had used in the last month. Of the 2,239 young people questioned 21.4% reported having used at least one of the following drugs in the past (solvents/glue, cannabis, amphetamine, LSD, magic mushrooms, anti-depressants, cocaine/crack and heroin), and 10.6% reported having used one or more of these drugs in the last month. Balding's survey identified around 10% of 12-13 year olds reporting past experience of having used an illicit drug (including solvents), rising to about 30% at age 14-15.

2.33   The distinction between current use and past use of illicit drugs is likely to be important for young people whose use of illicit drugs may be highly fluid. In Adelekan's Blackburn study, by age 15, 26.3% of the young people had tried at least one illicit substance. However in terms of the 15 year olds' current drug use, 8.8% were using magic mushrooms or LSD, 7.2% were using cannabis, 3.2% were using amphetamines, and 0.8% were using tranquillisers. The difference between the figures for past and current use reminds us that simply because a young person has tried an illicit drug does not mean that he or she will necessarily develop a pattern of long term use.

2.34   Over the last few years within the UK the use of MDMA (Ecstasy) and other drugs appears to have become closely associated with the dance culture. Whilst there has been considerable anecdotal and press coverage of the link between dance events and various forms of drug use, in fact there is a lack of reliable research data with which to estimate either the numbers of young people attending dance events or the proportion of attenders using different drugs. A recent survey of 135 participants in the Glasgow dance scene[29], however, found that in terms of drug use over the last year 95.6% had used cannabis, 87.4% had used MDMA, 78.5% had used LSD, 77.0% had used amphetamines, and 39.3% had used temazepam. Whilst MDMA is the drug that was most widely used at dance events, it was clear that depressant drugs such as temazepam would often be used following rave attendance as a way of "coming down" after a night's dancing. Drug use associated with the dance culture is neither confined to specific dance events nor to a specific drug.

## IS ILLICIT DRUG USE ON THE INCREASE IN THE UNITED KINGDOM?

2.35   To provide a clear cut answer to this question it would be necessary for the level of drug use to be measured in the same way amongst a representative sample of people at regular time intervals. Such nationally representative prevalence research has not occurred across the UK, but an identical methodology has been used for England and Wales in the last two British Crime Surveys. In the absence of such information there is a need to look at the broad trends in the available information. On this basis the evidence for an increase in the prevalence of illicit drug use since the 1980s is considerable.

2.36   Addict notifications, shown in Figure 1, have more than doubled from 1990 to 1996; similarly there has been a steady increase in the number of persons found guilty or cautioned by the police for drug-related offences (Table 8 below). These figures also include people who were dealt with by compounding, which is a payment of a penalty in lieu of prosecution for cases involving the importation of small quantities of cannabis for personal use.

### Table 8. Persons found guilty, cautioned or dealt with by compounding for drug offences, by drug 1990 - 1995

United Kingdom

| | 1990 | 1991 | 1992 | 1993 | 1994 | 1995 |
|---|---|---|---|---|---|---|
| Total Persons | 44922 | 47616 | 48927 | 68480 | 85693 | 93631 |
| Cannabis | 40194 | 42209 | 41353 | 56390 | 72393 | 76694 |
| Amphetamine | 2330 | 3532 | 5653 | 7622 | 8546 | 10364 |
| Heroin | 1605 | 1466 | 1415 | 2164 | 2971 | 4219 |
| Cocaine | 860 | 838 | 913 | 1671 | 1804 | 2073 |
| LSD | 915 | 1200 | 1428 | 1891 | 1878 | 1268 |
| MDMA | 286 | 559 | 1516 | 1577 | 1881 | 3281 |

Totals cannot be obtained by adding up the columns because the same person may be dealt with for more than one drug and other drugs are excluded

2.37   The available data on drugs seizures, summarised in Table 9, show a similar increase between 1990-1995.

### Table 9. Seizures of controlled drugs, by drug

United Kingdom

| | 1990 | 1991 | 1992 | 1993 | 1994 | 1995 |
|---|---|---|---|---|---|---|
| Total Number | 60859 | 69805 | 72065 | 87485 | 107629 | 114539 |
| Cannabis | 52856 | 59420 | 57663 | 69707 | 88540 | 91325 |
| Amphetamine | 4629 | 6821 | 10570 | 11719 | 12970 | 15443 |
| Heroin | 2593 | 2640 | 2968 | 3677 | 4480 | 6468 |
| Cocaine | 1805 | 1984 | 2365 | 2954 | 2992 | 3654 |
| LSD | 1859 | 1636 | 2474 | 2529 | 2289 | 1155 |
| MDMA | 399 | 1735 | 2399 | 2336 | 3574 | 5513 |

Totals cannot be obtained by adding up the columns because each seizure can involve more than one drug

2.38   An increase in addict notifications, in the number of persons found guilty or cautioned in relation to drug offences, or in drugs seizures, does not automatically mean that there has been a similar increase in the prevalence of illicit drug use - each of the changes could relate to alterations in the operational practice of the various agencies involved, e.g. medical practitioners, police and HM Customs, rather than to a genuine increase in the level of illicit drug use. And, for the last few years, the evidence from the British Crime Survey is rather different (Table 10).

### Table 10. Percentage of people aged 16 to 29 ever having used drugs. British Crime Surveys 1994, 1996

| | | EVER | | LAST YEAR | |
|---|---|---|---|---|---|
| | | BCS 94 | BCS 96 | BCS 94 | BCS 96 |
| Males | Cannabis | 40 | 42 | 25 | 25 |
| | All Drugs | 50 | 50 | 28 | 29 |
| Females | Cannabis | 28 | 31 | 16 | 17 |
| | All Drugs | 36 | 39 | 19 | 20 |
| Total | Cannabis | 34 | 36 | 20 | 21 |
| | All Drugs | 43 | 45 | 23 | 24 |

2.39    In this table we can see that between the 1994 and the 1996 British Crime Survey there have been some modest increases on the part of the 16-29 age group in the use of drugs ever. This extended perspective is not however so well suited to measuring recent changes as use within the last year. Any last year increases were so small as not to be statistically significant (that is, they could have happened by chance). In other words, the picture is more or less one of stability. Indeed, with an even narrower focus, on just the 16-24 age group, the population reporting use of any drug within the last year stayed constant at 29%.

2.40    Regionally, the British Crime Surveys for 1994 and 1996 indicate a North-South divergence within England, with signs of a reduction in London, coupled with increases in the North (and the Midlands). Drug use patterns in the North may be lagging behind those further South. Certainly information from the Regional Drug Misuse Database for the North West - recording people presenting for treatment - points to increases not so much in the period 1988 to 1990, but in more recent years (Figure 7).[30]

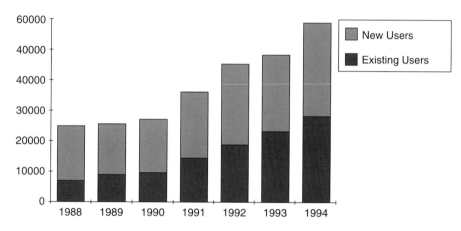

Figure 7. Number of Drug Users (from the University of Manchester Drug Misuse Research Unit, Drug Misuse Database)

2.41    None of these data prove beyond doubt that drug use has increased within the UK. Despite this it is plausible that there has been an increase. It is quite likely that since the late 1980s something approaching a doubling in several types of drug use may have occurred. Whether those upward trends are still continuing or continuing at the same rate, only time will tell.

## MORBIDITY AND MORTALITY

2.42    It is well known that users of some types of drugs are at increased risk of death compared to their non-drug-using counterparts. Oppenheimer and colleagues reported that heroin addicts in their 22 year cohort study had a mortality risk 11.9 times greater than the general population.[31] Within Glasgow by comparison Frischer and colleagues have recently shown that injecting drug users were 22 times more likely to die than their non injecting peers.[32] One of the largest increases in mortality risk has been identified in a study of over 2,000 injectors followed for 36 months in Oslo; in this study the risk of death amongst injectors was 32 times that for the general population.[33]

2.43    Recent research in the UK has shown that from 1985 to 1995 there has been a marked increase in drug related deaths amongst young people (aged between 15 to 19)[34]. Over this period the death rates attributed to opiates and other narcotics amongst young people increased by 27% per year. In 1985 there were 17 deaths due to opiates whilst by 1995 this figure had increased to 67 deaths. In the case of deaths from other psycho-stimulants the increase has been at the rate of 23% per year from 8 deaths in 1985 to 32 deaths in 1995. These data underline the serious health consequences associated with drug misuse amongst young people and the importance of identifying effective drug prevention strategies.

2.44    In terms of the data on deaths due to drug dependence (Table 11), there has been a steady increase in the numbers of deaths recorded from 1991 to 1995, as well as deaths of reported AIDS cases in the injecting drug use risk category.

| Table 11. Deaths with underlying cause described as drug dependence or non-dependent abuse of drugs | | | | | |
|---|---|---|---|---|---|
| Type of drug | 1991 | 1992 | 1993 | 1994 | 1995 |
| Morphine type (ICD codes 304.0 & 305.5) | 97 | 155 | 139 | 258 | 319 |
| All types | 307 | 345 | 322 | 489 | 602 |
| Deaths of Reported AIDS cases (Injecting drug users) | 79 | 82 | 110 | 119 | 147 |

2.45    In 1995 there were a total of 602 deaths attributable to drug dependence. More recently there has been growing concern over the number of deaths amongst young people associated with the use of MDMA. The Institute for the Study of Drug Dependence have reported details on 53 deaths amongst Ecstasy users since 1990: that figure is thought however to underestimate the true extent of mortality associated with MDMA use due to shortcomings in the available information on drug related deaths within the UK.[35]

2.46    It is likely that the official data on drug-related deaths more generally under-report the true extent of mortality associated with a drug using lifestyle. Frischer, for example, combined data from a wide range of sources to identify 51 drug-related deaths in Glasgow in 1989; this compares to 119 cases of accidental death due to drugs officially reported in the whole of Great Britain in the same year.[36] More recently the General Register Office (Scotland) reported a total of 267 drug-related deaths in Scotland in 1996.[37] There is often, considerable uncertainty as to what constitutes a drug-related death. In the case of deaths associated in some way with the use of MDMA, for example, it is often far from clear whether the death has resulted from the drug ingested or to more situational factors associated with its use e.g. overheating or excessive water intake. Aside from such difficulties there is the further factor that some medical practitioners may be reluctant to cite drug abuse as a cause of death on a death certificate in order to avoid the increased stigma which may be attached to such a designation. In Northern Ireland, for example, only a single addict death was officially recorded between 1990 and 1994.[38]

2.47    There are similar gaps in the information available on morbidity associated with a drug using lifestyle. There is no systematic collection of information, for example, on drug users use of medical services. In part this is entirely understandable given that drug users suffer from a range of medical problems only some of which are related to their drug use. Information is available, however, in relation to HIV and hepatitis B and C amongst drug users within the UK. With the exception of London, Edinburgh and Dundee, low levels of HIV infection have been recorded amongst injectors in the UK. Some data in relation to HIV and hepatitis B for London[39] are contained in Table 12, but different studies have given different results and rates for HIV sero-prevalence. In London rates have been variously reported as between 3 and 8%. Studies which recruit outside agencies generally find the higher level.

**Table 12. Prevalence of HIV infection and hepatitis B core antibody among injecting drug users, London and the South East: 1993**

|      | Number Tested | % HIV infected |
|------|---------------|----------------|
| 1993 | 788           | 3.7            |
|      | Number Tested | % anti-HBc positive |
| 1993 | 787           | 33.8           |

2.48    In Edinburgh it has been estimated that approximately 20% of injectors are HIV positive[40] and in Dundee the figure is approximately 27%.[41]

2.49    Giesecke and colleagues have combined data from the Communicable Diseases Surveillance Centre with information from the National Survey of Sexual Attitudes and Lifestyles, which was carried out in 19,000 households in the UK, to estimate the number of HIV positive drug injectors in England and Wales.[42] [43] The estimates they provide are summarised in Table 13.

**Table 13. Estimates of the number of drug injectors and related HIV seroprevalence, England and Wales**

|                         | Estimated Population | Calculated seroprevalence | Estimated no. HIV positive |
|-------------------------|----------------------|---------------------------|----------------------------|
| Current injecting drug users |                 |                           |                            |
| London, Men             | 29000                | 8.1                       | 2350                       |
| London, Women           | 16000                | 8.1                       | 1380                       |
| Outside London, Men     | 39000                | 0.6                       | 230                        |
| Outside London, Women   | 18000                | 0.6                       | 110                        |
| Total                   | 102000               | 3.4                       | 4070                       |
| Past Drug Users         |                      |                           |                            |
| Men                     | 53000                | 0.6                       | 280                        |
| Women                   | 20000                | 0.6                       | 100                        |
| Total                   | 73000                | 0.6                       | 380                        |

2.50     Other workers have however offered lower estimates in the range of 2,400 - 2,500 for the prevalence of HIV positive drug using injectors or previous injectors[44,45]. In terms of known cases of HIV and AIDS attributable to drug injecting among people who have volunteered for testing (in contrast to the real number estimates given in paragraph 2.49), by December 1996 the cumulative total (dead and living) in the UK stood at 839 AIDS cases and 2,992 HIV infected persons.[46]

2.51     There is increasing concern about hepatitis C infection amongst injecting drug users.[47] Although the information here is not as complete as it is on hepatitis B, there are several studies reporting a high prevalence of hepatitis C in drug injectors. Most of the studies in this area are based on drug treatment agencies and therefore have small sample sizes, for example 67% of a sample of 99 drug injectors in the North East of England[48] and 84% of a sample of 272 drug injectors in Dublin, Ireland,[49] were found to be infected with hepatitis C.

2.52     Although prevalence data are not available on the broader health problems associated with drug use, some indication of drug users' contact with hospital services can be gleaned from hospital admission data. For example, in Scotland[50] there were a total of 946 hospital admissions due to drug use in 1990; by 1994 this figure had increased to 2,274. Many of these admission are likely to have had to do with non-fatal drug overdose amongst drug users. In a study of 438 heroin users in London Gossop and colleagues found that 9% had experienced a non fatal overdose in the previous year.[51] Reporting on Glasgow, Taylor and colleagues found that out of 1018 injectors surveyed 27% had experienced at least one non fatal overdose requiring medical assistance in the last year.[52] Recent research carried out in Sydney, Australia,[53] suggests that this constitutes a major health risk; out of a sample of 329 heroin users surveyed 68% reported a past overdose, 29% in the preceding 12 months.

## SOCIAL CORRELATES OF DRUG USE

### GENDER

2.53     It will already have been apparent from previous sections that the experience of illicit drug use varies considerably by gender. Female drug users tend to utilise drug services less frequently than their male counterparts. In part this is a result of the greater stigma which may be attached to drug use by females. In the case of young mothers there may be the added fear that official knowledge of their drug use may lead to concerns being expressed as to their ability to care for their children. Similarly, in terms of health risks it has been shown that female injectors may be at greater risk of HIV and other infections than male injectors. This is as a result of the relatively low level of condom use amongst drug injectors combined with the fact that female injectors are more likely to have male partners who are injecting drug users themselves than are male injectors to have drug injecting female partners.[54,55] Research has also highlighted the close association in many areas between female prostitution and drug misuse.[56]

2.54     Whilst it has often been assumed that the ratio of male to female drug users within the UK is approximately 3:1 there is increasing evidence that the actual picture on male and female drug use may be more complex. The 3:1 ratio, for example, whilst being borne out in both the Regional Drug Misuse Databases and the Home Office Addict Notification System is not demonstrated in the social survey data. In the 1996 British Crime Survey, for example, 8% of males had used drugs within the preceding month as opposed to 4% of females, perhaps suggesting a ratio of 2:1 for types of use which may include less problematic use. When exploring the use of individual drugs, both 3% of males and 3% of females had ever used temazepam. This narrowing in the ratio of male to female drug users was also found in the 1996 Scottish Crime Survey especially for those in the 16-19 age group. The basis for these gender differences is not well understood at present; what is clear though is the fact that the impact of gender upon drug use, including the ratio of male to female drug users, is complex. The gender ratio is unlikely to be fixed for all time.

## ETHNICITY

2.55    The influence of ethnicity on illicit drug use is an under-researched topic. Ethnicity is not a single dimension of experience but a composite of identity, beliefs, expectations, cultural history and language. Many of these components are liable to change over time across successive generations. In addition, there will also be a degree to which ethnicity overlaps with other social variables including, for example, unemployment, so that it becomes very difficult to identify the specific influence of ethnicity on drug use. A necessary first step in this direction is to establish accurate information on the extent of drug use within different ethnic groups. Data in this area are available from the 1996 British Crime Survey (Table 14).

### Table 14. Prevalence of drug misuse by ethnic group - BCS 1996

% Ever taken any illicit drug - Ages 16 to 59

|  | White | Afro-Caribbean | Indian | Pakistani/ Bangladeshi | All All |
| --- | --- | --- | --- | --- | --- |
| Cannabis | 23 | 18 | 10 | 8 | 22 |
| Amphetamines | 9 | 6 | 2 | 2 | 9 |
| Heroin | 1 | 1 | * | 1 | 1 |
| Crack | 1 | 1 | * | 1 | 1 |
| Any illicit drug | 30 | 23 | 14 | 12 | 29 |
| Code | * less than 0.5 | | | | |

2.56    In line with other surveys, whites had the highest level of cannabis and amphetamines use, followed by those in the Afro-Caribbean group. Such results indicate very clearly, however, the fact that drug use is not confined to any particular ethnic group.

## EMPLOYMENT

2.57    Over the last few years a number of studies have documented the epidemic of drug use that has occurred amongst some of the poorest social groups within inner city parts of the UK. Unemployment has been one of the factors cited as having an influence on the growth of drug use within some of these areas. Unravelling the relationship between drug use and unemployment is, however, a far from easy task. Data on this link are contained within the Four Cities survey (Table 15) and the 1996 British Crime Survey

(Table 16). The employed group in the Four Cities Survey includes those with part-time jobs; such people have however been excluded from the BCS table.

### Table 15. Prevalence of drug misuse by employment status - Four Cities Survey

|  | % Presently in employment | % Not presently in employment |
|---|---|---|
| Ever used any drug | 17 | 24 |
| Recently used any drug | 6 | 11 |

2.58    From this survey, those who are currently not in full-time employment were more likely to be using drugs or to have ever used drugs than those who are currently employed.

### Table 16. Prevalence of drug misuse in preceding year by employment status and age group - BCS 1996

|  | 16-29 | 30-59 | All |
|---|---|---|---|
| Employed full-time | 22 | 5 | 9 |
| Not employed | 27 | 5 | 13 |

2.59    The 'not employed' group in the BCS table (and the earlier Four Cities Survey table) includes students and home makers as well as the unemployed. Looking just at 16-29s who were unemployed, as many as 45% had reported drug use in the previous year: more than double the rate (22%) of those with full-time jobs. The OPCS Psychiatric Morbidity Survey also found that those who were unemployed were very considerably more likely to be drug dependent (Table 17).

### Table 17. Prevalence of drug dependence by employment status - OPCS Psychiatric Morbidity Survey

% prevalence in last 12 months

|  | Working full-time | Working part-time | Unemployed | Economically inactive | All |
|---|---|---|---|---|---|
| Drug Dependence | 1.3 | 1.7 | 8.3 | 2.3 | 2.2 |

2.60    The relationship between unemployment and drug use is likely to be complex with some drug use leading to unemployment and the experience of unemployment creating the condition within which drug use flourishes – particularly perhaps in the case of young people. Equally, the fact of being employed will for some people enable them to sustain a level of drug use which in other circumstances would be more difficult. The difference in definition between the psychiatric morbidity survey which looked at drug dependence instead of drug use is again reflected in the lower prevalence levels reported in Table 17. We return to a discussion of the link between drug misuse and unemployment in Chapter 9 where we consider deprivation.

### URBAN/RURAL DRUG USE

2.61    Paralleling the perception that drug use is concentrated within some of the poorest social groups there is also a perception that it is largely an urban phenomenon. The data from the most recent crime survey, along with the OPCS Psychiatric Morbidity

Survey, indicate that drug use is occurring within both urban and rural environments (Tables 18 and 19).

**Table 18. Prevalence of drug use by locality - British Crime Survey 1996**

Age 16-29

|  | Inner City | All Other | All |
|---|---|---|---|
| % taken any drug in last year | 25 | 24 | 24 |

**Table 19. Prevalence of drug dependence by locality - OPCS Psychiatric Morbidity Survey**

|  | Urban | Semi-rural | Rural | All |
|---|---|---|---|---|
| % currently dependent on drugs | 2.6 | 1.6 | 0.9 | 2.2 |

2.62    In the OPCS survey drug dependence was found to be occurring more widely within the urban locations than either the semi-rural or rural areas. However both studies indicate that drug use is not confined to any one area type. Our knowledge of the nature and pattern of drug use within such rural areas however is comparatively limited as a result of the urban focus of the majority of drug misuse research.

## CONCLUSIONS

2.63    In summary, it is almost certainly the case within the UK today that illicit drugs are more widely available and more widely used than at any time in the recent past. Illicit drug use is neither confined to any particular part of the UK nor to any particular social group. Within at least some communities in the UK, drug misuse, in one form or another, has become almost a commonplace occurrence. Nevertheless, frequent or habitual drug misuse remains a minority activity.

2.64    Drug use or misuse is not, however, the same thing as drug dependence. Our best estimate of the extent of drug dependence in England and Wales in 1992 places that figure in the region of three quarters of a million people; our best estimate of the number of people who have ever used cannabis in England and Wales places the figure in the region of 6.5 million people. The difference between these figures gives some indication of the fact that use of an illegal drug does not lead inevitably to drug dependence. Whilst that fact is very evident from the statistics it is equally the case that we do not know enough about those factors which influence the development of such dependence to confidently dismiss such widespread drug use as little more than experimental, one-off use. We need to be cautious in inferring anything about the likely rate of progression from drug use to drug dependence on the basis of past experience. We do not know what proportion of young people, for example, who are currently using Ecstasy will go on to use other illegal drugs and ultimately to develop a pattern of longer term dependent use. What is certainly clear is the fact that Ecstasy is only one of a wide range of drugs that are available within the dance scene and more widely the UK.

2.65   It is clear on the basis of this chapter that the nature and extent of drug misuse differs by region, by age, by sex, by ethnicity and by employment status. As a result there is unlikely to be a single approach to drug prevention which can be universally applied across the UK. There is a need instead to develop approaches to drug prevention which are sensitive to the diverse experiences of different social groups. Policy makers should not become dulled to the extent and nature of the problem or ignore its complexity.

2.66   It is evident from the data presented in this chapter that drug misuse is not confined to the unemployed. Nevertheless, it is equally clear that there is a close link between drug misuse and unemployment. In the 1996 British Crime Survey, for example, on the part of the 16–29 age group the level of drug misuse over the last year amongst the unemployed was twice that amongst those employed full-time; within the OPCS Psychiatric Morbidity Survey the level of drug dependence was six times higher amongst those who were unemployed than amongst those who were employed. These statistics do not, of course, resolve the direction of causality between drug misuse, drug dependence and unemployment; what they do show beyond a doubt however is the fact of the association between these three and the importance in our Drug prevention efforts of being sensitive to the wider social environment. Chapter 3 of this report looks in detail at the links between drug misuse and both micro and macro environmental factors.

2.67   We believe that the material that we have reviewed in this chapter points to the need to strengthen the research base on the nature and extent of drug misuse in several respects. What policy making and monitoring of policy effectiveness requires is the guaranteed, systematic availability of repeat national estimates of prevalence which use consistent methodology over time, with breakdowns by drug type, frequency of use, route of use, dependence, demographic characteristics of the user, and geographical distribution. Beyond that basic but vital kind of empirical data there is, however, also need for strengthened investment in policy-relevant social research of a more explanatory kind. For instance, we need sharper understanding of the extent to which drug misuse is a seamless and interactive whole or whether in reality it is a collection of rather distinct and discreet behaviours with different causes, consequences, and natural histories. Is the blanket term "drug misuse" really satisfactory for the policy analysis? Further, under this explanatory research heading, we would like to see greater investment in studies which determine, partition and quantitatively estimate the relative contributions made to the causes of any type or intensity of drug misuse by, say, environmental factors, personal factors and the drugs supply and availability of drugs.

*Chapter*

# 3 ENVIRONMENTAL FACTORS AND DRUG MISUSE

*This chapter explores evidence on what factors within the environment are likely to bear on the individual's choice to use or not to use drugs. Research amply confirms the importance of a range of factors on this choice.*

## INTRODUCTION

3.1    While in chapter 2 we examined what the available data tell us about who is taking drugs, which drugs they are taking and with what frequency, and so on, in this chapter we review what is known about the environmental influences which bear on the individual.

3.2    In chapter 1 we discussed what we meant by "environment" and pointed to the possibility of distinguishing between the micro-environment, the more immediate aspects of an individual's interpersonal environment, and the macro-environment, comprising broad social, economic and cultural factors. We use these two concepts in this chapter.

3.3    The chapter is organised into four sections. The first begins with a broad outline of how one might expect various aspects of the micro-environment to have a bearing on an individual's pattern of drug use and its development. This is followed by a section which offers a more detailed examination of family and peer group influences. The third section examines what research tells us about the macro-environmental context, and the fourth explores the inferences for this report.

3.4    Although an attempt has been made to reflect wherever possible the main directions indicated by relevant research, this chapter is not intended as a comprehensive research review. The list of references and works cited in the text should therefore be regarded as illustrative rather than exhaustive. One further limitation which should be noted is that, reflecting the overwhelming emphasis of the research base, this review will concentrate almost entirely on drug use in adolescence and, to a lesser extent, young adulthood. This focus has often been justified on the grounds that drug using styles find their origins predominantly in adolescence. It nevertheless remains true that this bias is a central weakness in our understanding of the development of patterns of drug use and misuse through early adulthood and beyond. Drug misuse is not only an issue among the young.

## THE MICRO-ENVIRONMENT

3.5    A general account of a drug using 'career' from initiation into drug use, through experimentation , a 'recreational' phase of occasional use, and the possibility of this pattern becoming consolidated into a continuing period of regular and possibly problematic or compulsive drug use, would require attention to a number of features within the individual's immediate environment. This section will provide a brief sketch of these issues.

## ACCESS

3.6     Access to any substance is a fundamental and necessary requirement of an individual's external environment before any other consideration in the development of a drug using career. Where licit drugs such as alcohol and tobacco are concerned, access can be significantly influenced by such factors as price, taxation, licensing regulations, etc. The availability and provision of illicit drugs depends however upon ill-charted local, regional, national and trans-national networks (markets) with a truly global reach.

3.7     Access to illicit drugs is most likely at the initial stage to be provided by friends. This is well-researched and well-evidenced. In the light of the decisive role of friendship networks in disseminating drugs, it is difficult to conceive of any effective form of conventionally conceived drug enforcement policy to control access at this level - quite simply, how might one be expected to police friendship? One possible site of action currently being explored is 'peer education', although this is among existing drug users (rather than among not-yet-users) and seems to be largely directed towards harm-reduction goals, that is secondary rather than primary prevention.[1]

3.8     The role of friendship and peer networks, which will later be discussed in more detail, also touches upon an individual's attachment to wider sets of values and pursuits such as youth cultures and subcultures. For example, it might be a young person's attraction to a particular style of music (the lyrics and imagery of 'psychedelic' music in the 1960s, or varieties of 'rave' dance music in the 1990s) which make them more or less likely to try a particular drug for the first time.

3.9     Attention to the meanings and interpretations of drug use even *prior* to actual drug use is a fundamental aspect of the environment. We need to regard human subjects as living in a symbolic and cultural realm in addition to a biological realm where drugs attract or repel. This symbolic aspect of the environment is powerfully embodied in the institutions of the news media, film and television, the visual arts, music, and other aspects of popular culture. Given the immediacy of these global networks and markets upon individuals, it points to one of the difficulties in defining the 'environment', and more specifically clearly demarcating a difference between the 'micro' and 'macro' environments.

3.10    'Access' to drugs therefore involves both material access, but also access in a cultural and symbolic realm - in other words 'being accessible' to the promised or intended meanings of drugs. Another way of stating this is to say that drug choices will be influenced as much by fashion as by pharmacology, and fashions can and do change.

3.11    An interesting contemporary example of this is that there appears to be an ebb in the crack/cocaine epidemic in New York, but only among young people. This is revealed by the Drug Use Forecasting (DUF) programme which since 1987 has involved the routine anonymous urine-testing of a sample of people arrested for largely non-drug offences.[2] With as many as two-thirds of arrestees testing positive overall for cocaine in

Manhattan in the late 1980s and early 1990s, a recent analysis of DUF data has shown that while older age cohorts continue to test positive for cocaine there has been a spectacular decrease in younger age cohorts from 78% of those born in 1968 to a low of 10% of those born in 1975 and 1976.[3] The trend was first noticed in New York and ethnographic fieldwork from the same research team suggests that this decline results from young people in high-risk inner-city neighbourhoods reaching their teens in the late 1980s and early 1990s who saw the negative effects of crack smoking and chose not to use drugs in this way.[4] A decline of cocaine use among young people has subsequently been noted in other urban centres such as Los Angeles, Chicago and Detroit[5] and researchers describe the phenomenon as 'strong evidence of a passing cocaine fad among youths'. If so, it is one of the few areas of good news in drugs research in recent years.

## EXPERIMENTATION: PERSONALITY FACTORS AND INTER-PERSONAL INFLUENCES

3.12    Properly speaking, personality factors are outside the remit of this chapter since they involve issues 'internal' to the individual. However, given that large areas of biology, psychology and sociology view the individual personality as dependent on external environmental factors - for example, family environment, social class, culture and ethnicity - these must at least be mentioned. Family influences will be considered in more detail in the next section.

3.13    Personality factors will undoubtedly influence an individual's choice whether or not to try a drug. A predisposition towards *risk and excitement* might be one such factor. On the other hand, a willingness to *share in the experiences of others* within peer and friendship networks might also be influential. One should bear in mind that some persons inclined to take risks (for example, rock climbers) might be disinclined to consume drugs on a regular basis because of their attachment to physical fitness and a sporting lifestyle.[6]

## CONTINUING USE

3.14    In order to be motivated to continue to experiment with the use of any drug, the individual must learn to use the drug appropriately and to *experience its effects as pleasurable*. This may depend partly on genetic predisposition, which influences whether drug use is pleasurable[7] and to a large degree on contact with a peer/user network already socialised into these practices and understandings. This dependence on an existing system of interpretation and meaning with regard to drug effects was first articulated fully by Becker[8] with regard to marijuana. It was for these reasons sometimes misunderstood as only relevant to so-called 'soft' drugs with high degree of 'plasticity' in their pharmacology.[9] One of the most persuasive contra-indications of this assumption is the Preble and Casey study of the street life of heroin addicts in New York,[10] where the constant routines and hustles of 'taking care of business' are shown to offer sources of meaning and motivation even more powerful than the effects of the drug itself. More recently in the context of the British heroin epidemic of the 1980s, directly similar lifestyles have been noted.[11,12] Becker's essay on 'Becoming a Marijuana User' is therefore a position with much more widespread application which suggests the need, further discussed below, to view peer networks as being less concerned with 'pressure' than with the *interpretation and meaning* of drug effects and lifestyles.

3.15    For drug use to continue beyond experimentation, access to the substance must be maintained. Moreover, it must be maintained at an 'effective price', that is not only in terms of monetary price but also in terms of costs such as 'search time' and other potential forms of inconvenience. Raising the effective price (particularly in terms of search time) is potentially one of the most useful ways of erecting barriers between initiation and regular use for a drug such as heroin, since the novice user is less likely to be prepared to endure too many inconveniences in pursuit of a novel drug as compared with the habitual user. This was first suggested as a strategic aim for drug control policies by Moore[13] in his book "Buy and Bust", and it is a position with a variety of possible criminal justice applications in terms of harm reduction goals.[14,15] As Kleiman's review[15] makes clear, moreover, the likely effectiveness of these policy options varies considerably for different drugs and their associated lifestyles.

3.16    Another form of non-monetary 'cost' to the individual would be if the form of drug consumption contemplated or undertaken were to be highly socially stigmatised or to be associated with highly stigmatised groups of people or other socially stigmatised experiences. This is one of the ways in which particular forms of drug use can, and do, move in and out of fashion. The per capita decline in cocaine use in the USA since the early 1980s, for example, was undoubtedly a consequence of cocaine use becoming unfashionable among the middle class.[16] More recently, as already indicated, there is evidence from the US Drug Use Forecasting (DUF) programme that crack-cocaine use is declining among younger people in New York and that part of the reason for this decline is the growing unfashionability of crack-cocaine among the young in New York City.

3.17    The impulse to continue using drugs beyond an 'experimental' or 'recreational' phase is not uncommonly ascribed to one degree or another of 'dependence' or 'addiction'. The phenomenon of drug dependence has been conceptualised in a variety of different ways, most of which fall outside a review of environmental influences since they imply physical or psychological states. In one admittedly extreme theory of addiction, however, primacy is placed on the activities and routines associated with drug consumption as inducements to compulsive use.[17] Without wishing to adopt such a radical position, as suggested earlier a review of environmental influences will necessarily lean in the direction of an emphasis on the role of friendship networks; neighbourhood and family life; the ways in which drugs are found to be compatible or incompatible with daily routines and lifestyle; whether or not an effective means of access to the drug can be maintained or is regarded as desirable; and the extent to which drug use is condoned or stigmatised within a person's social circle. And none of this is to contradict the fact that different drugs are in a pharmacological sense different, with differing properties for reward and reinforcement.[18]

## *LIFESTYLE*

3.18    Another way of stating these relationships at this point in a general account of transition from experimentation to regular use is in terms of *lifestyle*. This will include monetary cost, but more equally will encompass whether or not a pattern of regular drug use is compatible with other features of an individual's valued life commitments. Here there are two potential pathways.

3.19    Some drugs will be either integrated into an existing lifestyle, or rejected by either the individual or peer network because of their incompatibility with an existing lifestyle. Certain drugs (for example, cannabis and alcohol) are in all probability more easily integrated with a range of otherwise quite diverse (including conventional) lifestyles which no doubt accounts for their popularity. Others, such as heroin, will be found more broadly to be incompatible.

3.20    Correspondingly, some drugs will be found so attractive in terms of their effects that even though initially incompatible with adopted lifestyles, they will have lifestyle transforming potential. Heroin and cocaine will be such an influence for some people and networks, so that life becomes increasingly organised around the daily routines associated with the drug culture. Even so, research indicates where cocaine use is concerned among non-clinic samples that many users who have experienced increasingly heavy levels of consumption at a point in their drug using careers will at some future point either rein in their use levels or quit.[19,20] The motivation for reducing the level of drug consumption will tend to be organised around considerations such as lifestyle and identity, and environmental influences. For example, drug use might be experienced as enveloping the individual and hindering other interests and pursuits; or friends and family will put pressure on an individual to quit.

*SELF-RECOVERY*

3.21    Studies of self-recovery by drug users have also shown that shifts in identity and lifestyle, together with changes in an individual's environment, were commonly involved in transitions and pathways out of addiction.[21,22] These will sometimes depend upon access to formal welfare supports, together with the encouragement of friends, partners, children, parents and other people regarded as significant. One of the most dramatic demonstrations of environmental impact on drug using patterns was provided by the study of the return of heroin using Vietnam veterans to the USA, when the change of environment facilitated a return to abstinence for large numbers of these and forced a major reconsideration among professionals who had previously regarded opiate addiction as a largely irretrievable condition.[23]

3.22    Self-recovery studies certainly do not support the view that a drug user has to reach 'rock bottom' before being motivated to quit. Environmental factors provide important encouragements, particularly in terms of interpersonal influence. Even where the financial burden of continuing use might be a consideration, this will be likely to mean that the individual already has other more valued financial commitments, such as family.

## FAMILIES AND FRIENDS: KEY ISSUES IN THE MICRO-ENVIRONMENT

3.23    The brief sketch offered above indicates some of the ways in which transition points in an individual's pattern of drug use will be influenced by various factors in the human environment. What research consistently shows, however, is that the key influences are those of the family and peer group, and this section will examine these in a little more detail.

3.24    There is a large volume of research on juvenile delinquency which examines both family and peer influences, often together, and which sometimes pays attention to both drug use and delinquency. It is almost entirely from North America, suffers from having no common theoretical or methodological base, and has been criticised in some quarters as being disjointed and contradictory.[24] Elsewhere, it has been strongly argued that it is a research tradition which demonstrates clear areas of common agreement.[25,26]

3.25    Possibly reflecting its North American origins, a major preoccupation within this body of research has been concerned with examining what connections might exist between drug misuse and delinquency. The causal connection is a vexed issue which divides a number of substantial research undertakings.[25,27] A common assumption is that it is drug misuse which leads directly to criminal involvement, although this is by no means given uniform support by the research literature.

3.26    A directly contrary viewpoint which is given a large degree of support is that involvement in crime frequently precedes involvement with drugs, whereas others posit a two-way interaction between drugs and crime. Finally, there is an increasingly stated view that the frequently observed drugs-crime connection is a consequence of the co-existence of crime and drug misuse among some groups within a general deviant syndrome or lifestyle.[28] However, it is difficult once more to extract 'micro-environmental' influences of family and peers from the wider environmental contexts of neighbourhood, poverty and social exclusion.[29,30]

3.27    The interactions between different factors and variables can always be assumed to be complex. In other words, there is general agreement that no single causal mechanism is at work in terms of either the onset or continuation of drug use (and delinquency) and therefore no 'magic bullet' cure in terms of environmental intervention. There is nevertheless widespread agreement that both family influences and peer influences are key aspects of the environment which will have a significant impact on an individual's drug use - although questions of initiation, experimentation, occasional use, and problem use have often not been distinguished with sufficient clarity. Research which employs categories such as 'lifetime use' or 'ever used a drug' are of little use, for example, if one wishes to understand how persistent and problematic patterns of drug consumption are influenced by families or peers.

3.28    Allowing for shortcomings such as these, what the available research does appear to indicate, with varying shades of emphasis, are significant areas of interaction between family influences and peer influences. Before offering a few illustrative examples of how these might work, however, it will be useful to make some general observations about common assumptions on both family and peer influences.

*THE FAMILY*

3.29    Where family influences are concerned, there is a long tradition which traces delinquency (and by association drug use) to the broken home. More recently, this has been shown where delinquency studies are concerned to be a confused and potentially misleading set of assumptions.[31] In reviewing a range of earlier studies, Wells and Rankin came to the conclusion that there was no common definition of 'broken home' in these studies, and that it acted as an umbrella concept to imply a variety of quite different aspects of household structure and family functioning. The crucial difference is between family structure (e.g. the lone parent household or a re-constituted family) as against family process (e.g. a conflict-ridden marriage or the absence of affection and/or control in a two-parent household). Reviews of the research indicate that while the 'broken home' has been commonly identified as a feature in the onset of deviant behaviour, it is often associated with other factors,[32] and might have little independent influence.[26]

3.30   On balance, it seems that family process is more important than family structure in predicting deviant conduct in young people, and that warmth, affection, consistency, and parental supervision are the most reliable indicators of effective parenting. Alcohol studies have also indicated that the children of parents with alcohol problems are not only more likely to be heavy drinkers, but more likely to develop problems.[33] Research on drug using parents is much less extensive, but points in a similar direction.[26] However, alcohol studies have also suggested that people from abstinent or low prevalence drinking cultures (and hence family backgrounds) seem particularly liable to develop problems if they do drink.[33] It is, however, perhaps unwise to extrapolate from alcohol studies since, unlike illicit drug use which is largely a minority pursuit, drinking is a dominant feature of European and North American cultures.

## FRIENDSHIP AND PEER GROUPS

3.31   If the role of the family has been a major consideration in understanding the onset of drug use, a preoccupation with the role of peer influences has been just as influential, if not more so. While some studies have suggested that rejection by peers can be associated with deviant behaviour, it is the association with drug-using peers which is much more commonly viewed as a factor in youthful drug use.[26] As stated by one authority in the field: 'Peer related factors are consistently the strongest predictors of subsequent alcohol and marijuana use, even when other factors are controlled'.[35]

3.32   It is indisputable that friendship networks are invariably the means by which people are introduced to drugs, and that among young people the first steps in a drug using career might involve exploration among a group of friends. This is supported by a wide range of evidence, including British research on opiate use.[12,36,37] The role of friendship will also be a continuing feature of an individual's drug using career, including any future likelihood of quitting and cessation. In one study of untreated self-recovery from heroin addiction, for example, one-third of the sample gave friendship - fear of hurting or losing a significant person, encouragement to quit, family commitments etc - as a motivating factor.[22] Similar issues have been identified in cocaine studies.[20]

3.33   What is less clear is that the commonly used expression 'peer pressure' is a particularly useful concept for understanding the onset of drug use among young people. The notion of 'peer pressure' (described even more forcefully by some researchers as 'peer coercion'[38]) implies some form of external pressure in which the individual is a passive and even unwilling victim. Rather than viewing peer influences as external, it is more appropriate to understand young people as being immersed within peer networks of friendship and/or youth subcultures. As already suggested, a young person's prior attachment to a style of music might be a predisposing factor both in the choice of friends and the inclination to try certain kinds of drugs. Equally, as indicated by McKeganey and Barnard's ethnographic field study of needle-sharing in Glasgow,[39] this high-risk practice was better understood not as consequence of pathological motivation but as the expression of some of the most positive aspects of the local culture such as solidarity, friendship and preparedness to help others in times of need.

3.34   The emphasis on friendship as 'peer pressure' reflects a major difficulty in so much of the social discourse around drug-related issues - whether mass media, policy formulation, or academic debates - namely the absence of any notion of volition or desire. Health education discourses in particular have often been cleansed of any reference to the possibility that people might use drugs because they find them pleasurable.[11,37] Reflecting the same tendency to view the drug user as a passive victim of circumstance, there is a constant resort to the use of the term 'pusher' which does not accurately describe the dynamics of consensual drug markets, or to the alleged involvement of foreign and alien influences in drug-dealing networks.

3.35   One formulation which attempts to avoid the unhelpful implications of the term 'peer pressure' is that offered by Oetting and Beauvais who develop the concept of a 'peer cluster' as the central focus for the dissemination of drug habits and preferences.[40] Pointing to the way in which the term 'peer pressure... implies either a general attitude in an entire age cohort toward drugs or... that an innocent youth is being coerced into taking drugs by a "pusher" or by deviant companions', they contrast their own concept of peer cluster as 'small, cohesive, marked by closely shared attitudes and beliefs'. 'The youth in a peer cluster', they add, 'is not an innocent victim, but is part of the cluster, helping to shape its attitudes and behaviours, equally a recipient and a source of drug encouragement.' This is similar to Kandel's dual emphasis on the way in which young people select friends on the basis of their similarity to themselves, while at the same time peer networks involve a process of socialisation, and friends have a tendency to become more like one another in attitudes and behaviour. In these more active formulations of the influence of friendship networks on drug use, individuals can both influence and be influenced by their peers - although as noted by a recent research review, we still have an inadequate understanding of how adolescent friendships come to be formed and broken, and in particular the dynamics of how young people come to associate with drug using peers.[41]

## AN ILLUSTRATION OF FAMILY-PEER INFLUENCE AND INTERACTIONS

3.36   As already indicated, since the 1970s a number of major North American longitudinal and cross-sectional surveys have explored risk factors for drug misuse and delinquency, with a marked tendency to arrive at agreement that the family and friendship networks are among the strongest predictors. A thorough review of this body of research is beyond the scope of this chapter. Rather, following the preliminary discussion of some of the key issues above, what is offered is merely illustrative of the complexities which this research points to - complexities not only in the interpretation of the research evidence, but also in the practical implications which might flow from it.

3.37 The work of Kandel and associates has already been mentioned. One striking feature of this work is that while considerable stress is placed on poor and inconsistent family management strategies as precursors to drug problems among young people, the influence of peer group associations is found to be an even stronger predictor.

3.38 Another longitudinal follow-up study which attached considerable importance to the adolescent peer group was the US National Youth Survey initiated in 1975 among 1,700 young aged 11-17 years.[42,43] A variety of measures were tested in relation to delinquent behaviour and drug use, including social frustration, conventional bonds to the family and school, involvement with delinquent peers, and prior delinquency and/or drug use. The most effective predictors were found to be involvement with delinquent peers and prior involvement in either delinquency or drugs, albeit with many subtle variations. For example, involvement with delinquent peers was a better predictor of delinquency than prior delinquency; whereas prior marijuana use was a better predictor of current marijuana use than peer involvements. Similarly, prior hard drug use was generally a better predictor of current hard drug use than delinquent peer involvement, although this held true only for males and not for females.

3.39 In their 1985 publication, "Explaining Delinquency and Drug Use", an attempt was made by these researchers to develop an ambitious integration of a number of contrasting theoretical approaches from sociology, criminology and social psychology. These were social learning theory which stresses the effects of reinforcements for conventional or deviant behaviour; strain theory which places an emphasis on social exclusion, restricted opportunities and frustrated ambition as a cause of deviance; and control theory which assumes that all human beings experience frustration and unfulfilled needs, and that it is attachment to conventional values and institutions which restrain the "natural" impulse to delinquency.

3.40 What was perhaps most striking from this approach, is that low levels of bonding to the conventional social order (i.e. involvement with family and school, and attachment to conventional norms and aspirations) did not in themselves predict either delinquency or drug use. However, where there was both involvement with delinquent peers *and* a low level of conventional bonding, this was highly predictive - even when controlling for prior involvement in delinquency or drugs.

3.41 The National Youth Survey thus concluded that 'delinquency is embedded in the adolescent peer group context' and that the adolescent friendship network should be a key site of preventive interventions. The authors did not discount attempts to build stronger attachments to school and family, to increase stakes in conformity, and to encourage conventional beliefs. Nevertheless, these would not, according to their analysis, immunise young people against the effects of involvement with delinquent peers, and might well prove more costly as well as being less effective. The authors also warned against methods of group work with young people which involved bringing together delinquents or drug users, since in their view this would exacerbate the peer group influence.

3.42 One possible line of direction flowing from studies such as that by Elliott and his colleagues is that although family influences appear to have a low direct influence on adolescent drug use, parental monitoring might remain the most effective means of influencing a young person's friendship network.[44] One further illustrative study which highlights the complexities in terms of empirical evidence and causal linkages, and hence difficulties in the effective implementation of practical strategies, is a recent longitudinal study of 6,500 high school students in California and Wisconsin which explores such an approach.[38]

3.43    While generally confirming earlier findings that parental monitoring and peer involvement can influence an adolescent's drug use, this study also examined whether or not these influences varied according to whether one was concerned with initiation into drug use or the transition to regular use. Young people were divided into three groups - non-users, experimental drug users, and heavy drug users - and the results were once again highly complex. For example, parental monitoring could help reduce drug consumption among already heavy drug using boys, but could not predict whether experimenters would desist or go on to become regular users. Among girls, on the other hand, parental monitoring predicted which experimenters would quit, but not which would go on to heavy use.

3.44    Where peer group relations were concerned, Steinberg et al. found that the more involved in drug use an adolescent might be the more involved his or her friends would be.[38] A further conclusion was that parental monitoring generally did not prevent young people from associating with drug using friends. If a young person used drugs, they would mix with other drug users irrespective of parental influence: 'over time boys tend to move towards their peers in substance use regardless of how vigilantly their parents monitor them'. For girls, these effects were somewhat different with girls tending to experience higher levels of monitoring irrespective of drug use status, but more likely to increase their drug involvement when poorly monitored.

3.45    In summary, high levels of parental monitoring could discourage both boys and girls from beginning to use drugs, help reduce levels of consumption among heavy using boys, and encourage girl experimenters to quit. Once young people had begun to use drugs, however, peer influences seemed more influential than parental behaviour (especially for boys) perhaps as young drug users sought friends with similar leisure patterns. Peer influences could however work both ways: young people with more drug using friends would be likely to increase their drug involvement, whereas those with friends less involved with drugs would be more likely to reduce their drug consumption. The bottom line of this research, and the associated work of Patterson[44], is that intervention programmes which aim to enhance effective parental monitoring should commence in the pre-adolescent years - that is, before the likely onset of drug experimentation. Steinberg and his colleagues admit, nevertheless, that theirs was a study conducted within a predominantly middle-class sample (as with the work of Kandel), and that 'we do not know whether this strategy is as effective in high-risk environments'[38].

## THE MACRO-ENVIRONMENT

3.46    If the family and friends can profoundly influence the development of drug use, consideration must also be given to wider environmental context of social, economic and cultural factors. We are familiar with a variety of inequalities in health which are associated with different aspects of social deprivation.[45] Crime rates also suffer from local and regional variations, and the British Crime Survey has consistently shown that the highest victimisation levels are found in the poorest neighbourhoods.[46] How do things stand where drugs and drug problems are concerned? We return in chapter 9 to a detailed consideration of drug misuse and deprivation, but in the context of the present chapter it will be helpful to enter a preliminary note on this issue.

## SOCIO-ECONOMIC BACKGROUND

3.47   Drug use, including problem drug use, is found in all sections of society. Nevertheless, complex evidence from a variety of different sources does suggest that socio-economic factors are associated in different ways with patterns and levels of drug use and misuse. The causal link, however, is by no means clear. The extensive review of largely US sources by Hawkins suggests that while some survey research has pointed to links between extreme economic deprivation, childhood conduct problems and delinquency this has not always been the case.[26] Indeed, some North American research has noted an association between modest cannabis and/or cocaine use and increased productivity levels and wage levels.[47] It is possible, of course, that these associations are the result of people with higher disposable incomes being better able to afford expensive commodities such as illicit drugs in moderate degrees. As another US study of heroin use, criminal involvement and employment status suggests, however, 'employment represents more than simply a source of income' and that employment status might interact in different ways (depending upon the nature of the individual's occupation) with involvement in drug subcultures.[48]

## SOCIALLY DEPRIVED NEIGHBOURHOODS AND URBAN CLUSTERING EFFECTS

3.48   If clear and unambiguous socio-economic variations in drug use are not always found at the *individual* level, it is equally important to recognise that they are consistently found at the *neighbourhood* or *area* level. This tradition of the area analysis of social problems was first formulated with any degree of sophistication in the work of the Chicago School of Sociology in the inter-war years which linked multiple problems of crime, ill health, and poverty in 'inner city' neighbourhoods in a number of ways. Some of the most notable of these Chicago studies of the spatial dimensions of social problems were concerned with juvenile delinquency,[49] mental disorder,[50] and opium addiction.[51]

3.49   Where drug misuse is concerned, post-war research in the USA has consistently found that the highest concentrations of drug-related problems are in the poorest urban neighbourhoods, from the earliest post-war heroin epidemics of the 1950s and 1960s in New York, Chicago and elsewhere[52,53] to the crack epidemics of the 1980s.[54,55] More recently, in the context of the British heroin epidemic of the 1980s, powerful confirmation was given to this trend through a number studies most notably in Merseyside,[36] in Glasgow,[56] in Nottingham,[57] and in South East London.[58,59]

3.50   The most likely explanation of these 'urban clustering effects' which gather together dense concentrations of multiple social difficulty - unemployment, poverty, housing decay, single parents households, lone pensioners, crime and drug misuse - is that they are a consequence of the mechanism of the housing market which brings together people who are experiencing a variety of otherwise unrelated problems in 'hard-to-let' housing estates.[60] Similar arguments about the influence of housing markets on local crime rates have been put forward in Britain by Anthony Bottoms and his colleagues.[61]

3.51    One consequence of urban clustering effects is that problems associated with a high density and visibility of drug misuse and drug dealing can become problems for the entire neighbourhood, including the majority of local residents who are not problem drug users. Establishing means to alleviate such neighbourhood difficulties will be in all likelihood a high priority for environmental approaches to the prevention of drug-related harms.

3.52    One further practical aspect of these connections is that in poor neighbourhoods where young people suffer exclusion from formal opportunities in terms of education and the job market, drugs and crime can offer an alternative means by which to demonstrate status and achievement.[62,63] Where low level drug dealing is concerned, this can involve significant monetary gains[64,65] although there has been little attention in Britain to the economics of retail level drug markets.[66] While estimates of the monetary scale of drug-related crime have sometimes been hugely inflated in Britain[67] it remains true that the size of this informal economy is considerable, and that it offers tangible rewards for those prepared to take risks and able to exercise sufficient entrepreneurial skill.[68]

3.53    Quite apart from monetary gains, success within such local networks is a means by which to claim respect, demonstrate authority and credibility, and sustain a meaningful lifestyle and identity - as first demonstrated in the everyday lives of New York street addicts by Preble and Casey[10] and more recently by similar ethnographic field research in the USA[65,68] and in Britain.[11,58] Identity focussed studies of the street life of drug users such as these have invariably centred on male users, but there are also ethnographic studies of female drug users which while stressing fundamental gender differences in daily routines such as the demands of childcare find directly similar lifestyle attractions in context of urban deprivation.[69,70]

3.54    In summary, Britain first came to experience widespread and serious problems of drug misuse amidst the economic downturn of the early 1980s which devastated the local economies of many industrial working class communities.[71,72,73] Subsequently, chronic drug-related problems have become established as a common feature of the social landscape in many neighbourhoods in this condition. Under such circumstances, local efforts to curb drug misuse are likely to be severely handicapped unless supported by wider schemes of urban regeneration, access to jobs and training, and other initiatives to combat social exclusion.

*CULTURE, ETHNICITY AND RELIGION*

3.55    Broad cross-cultural variations have often been observed in drug preferences, although these might well be largely of a traditional nature and a result of local patterns of plant-life and drug availability - such as the use of qat in Yemen and the Horn of Africa[74] - and thus of increasingly less relevance in an era of global drug markets. Where drug attitudes are concerned, religious attachment nevertheless remains an important influence as demonstrated by a survey among 13-15 year olds in England[75] - although whether drug attitudes are carried over into drug behaviours is always a problem in interpreting attitude surveys. In chapter 2 we saw that drug misuse is not confined to any particular ethnic group but that it was not possible from the data to identify the reasons for variations between ethnic groups or within them. Indeed, whatever variations might be established between cultural and religious groups, the idea of a 'drug-free' culture seems a remote prospect.

3.56    Within multi-racial and multi-cultural societies such as Britain and the USA, nevertheless, there are some observable differences. Variations in patterns of needle-sharing have been noted in the USA, for example, among whites, blacks and Hispanics.[76] In Britain, there is every indication that black people were significantly under-represented in the 1980s heroin epidemic although in this respect we are handicapped by virtue of the fact that the Addicts Index maintained by the Home Office did not incorporate a monitoring code for race and ethnicity. There is some local evidence nevertheless that black drug users might be less likely to inject drugs than white users[77] - although a monitoring code for the national index would again be helpful in this regard. A series of regional and national self-report studies have also consistently indicated that young Asians are less likely to report the use of illicit drugs than either young white people or those of African-Caribbean descent.[78,79,80] Outreach fieldwork among Asian drug users in Bradford, however, suggests that where patterns of drug use are concerned (as distinct from the scale of use) the behaviour of young Asians is directly similar to that of young whites and demonstrates few, if any, novel features - whereas among older Asians of Pakistani Muslim descent, among whom alcohol consumption is frowned upon, betel-nut chewing might be commonplace and habit-forming.[81]

3.57    More recent Home Office research, which is also drawn upon in chapter 2, has further complicated the picture with regard to drug use within the Asian community. One the one hand, Graham and Bowling point to some quite sharp variations within the Asian population, according to whether young people are of Indian, Pakistani, or Bangladeshi descent.[82] The most recent data from the 1994 and 1996 British Crime Surveys also confirms that Asians generally report less drug use than whites or African-Caribbeans.[83,84] Although the 1994 survey pointed to higher rates of heroin use among Pakistani and Bangladeshi respondents the 1996 survey results indicated that their level of heroin consumption was no higher than that of whites aged 16-59; comparatively young Pakistanis and Bangladeshis had lower rates of heroin use than equivalent whites and African-Carribeans.

3.58    Whatever differences might or might not be observed in terms of patterns of drug use among black and other minority ethnic groups in modern Britain, these will often be difficult to interpret because of differential access to helping agencies between ethnic groups. The under-representation of black people among populations of drug users known to agencies might, for example, be a consequence of the failure of agencies to make themselves accessible and meaningful to all members of a multi-cultural society. Just as drug agencies have had to change styles of working and presentation to make themselves more attractive to women drug users, there still remains much to be done to get away from the inherited traditions of drug agencies which were often created specifically to respond to the needs of white male opiate injectors. Research confirms that there is a tendency for drug users from black and other minority ethnic groups to see agencies as 'run by white people, for white people', although there are now also a number of useful examples of how agencies can change and implement effective anti-discriminatory and equal opportunity policies.[85,86]

## CONCLUSIONS

3.59    The human environment is highly complex. Nevertheless, where the micro-environment is concerned research emphatically demonstrates that the family and peer networks are the most decisive influences on the development of drug use among young people. If anything, friendship appears to be a more significant influence than that of the family. If so, practical efforts to enhance parents' capacities to discourage drug misuse and to monitor and supervise their offspring more effectively would have to commence in earlier childhood before the onset of adolescence.[38]

3.60    In terms of intervention among friendship networks, although 'peer education' shows some promise among established groups of drug users in terms of fashioning harm-reduction strategies1 it is perhaps more difficult to conceive of primary prevention initiatives. A powerful aspect of the environment of adolescents and young adults is the vast popular culture of music, video, dance and dress-style which encourages the consumption of a wide range of excitements and commodities including drink and drugs. Twentieth century popular music from the earliest forms of jazz and blues has often been embroiled in controversies about drug use,[87,88] and deeply felt anxieties about the effects of popular entertainments on the morals of young people have been expressed in Britain since the earliest days of Queen Victoria's reign.[89] The language and imagery of drug use has become deeply embedded within the contemporary popular culture. Attempting to fashion health education messages which combat this popular culture (which has huge commercial resources at its command) would seem fruitless. The challenge is probably how to engage with it, and to deploy its language and imagery towards health promotion goals - as the innovative Manchester Lifeline projects have done with devices such as strip cartoons directed first at HIV-risk among drug injectors and more recently issues connected with raves and dance drugs.[90]

3.61    The wider socio-economic context, while it does clearly shape and influence certain aspects of drug-related problems in modern Britain, also impinges on a variety of other policy issues with regard to employment, education and training, housing, and crime prevention. Such a complex and over-lapping set of goals and objectives would seem to insist on some form or other of 'multi-agency' strategy, although the often-invoked aim of improved inter-agency cooperation is not always easy to accomplish.[91,92] Where local multi-agency initiatives directed towards neighbourhood crime prevention have been carefully evaluated, although they show some promise and partial success, the outcomes are nevertheless mixed.[93]

3.62    One final set of comments need to be addressed to the question of causality in the various influences which have been discussed above. Where drugs and the environment are under discussion, it is no doubt the impact of the environment on drug consumption which is often taken as the focus. It would be wrong, however, to conclude without reminding ourselves that this linear and uni-directional model of causality is not always supported by research. Sometimes causal mechanisms have been identified working in the opposite direction, together with those which are interactive and multi-directional, while research has also sometimes contested whether causal relations exist at all between drug misuse and various social factors. It is commonly assumed that drug misuse causes crime, for example, although research has repeatedly demonstrated that a person's involvement in crime often precedes their involvement with drugs. The difficulties are well illustrated by a recent review of the research evidence on the commonly assumed relationship between intoxication and aggression.[94]

3.63    These considerations provide a common thread across this otherwise broad field of vision. In each area that has been examined, there are a set of potentially conflicting directions of causality:

- Family dysfunction causes drug use, as against drug use results in family dysfunction

- Unemployment causes drug misuse, as against drug misuse influences employment status

- Peer networks lead to drug use, as against drug use leads to association with friends with similar habits

- Lifestyle leads to drug use, as against drug use alters lifestyle

- Neighbourhood disorganisation encourages drug use, as against drug misuse results in neighbourhood damage

- Criminal involvement offers an inroad to drug use, as against drug misuse causes crime

3.64    These inter-related matters of causality have been most rigorously scrutinised in relation to the drugs-crime connection, although in the USA there have also more recently been discussions of the damaging impact of both drug epidemics and drug-control policies on inner-city neighbourhoods, their local economies, and prospects for urban regeneration.[95,96] Although disputes about causality will continue to be matters of considerable scientific interest and controversy, they are unlikely to be settled to everyone's satisfaction in the foreseeable future. The vast research effort on the still disputed drugs-crime connection in the USA, conducted over more than thirty years and including some highly sophisticated methodological work, suggests that questions of causality should be regarded as difficulties and confusions to be lived with rather than resolved. Where drugs and the environment are concerned, the likelihood that we are invariably dealing with two-way directions of cause and effect, reminds us that the prevention of drug-related harm is a matter which concerns the entire community and not just problem drug misusers and their families.

*Chapter*

# 4 CURRENT COMMUNITY-BASED DRUG PREVENTION STRATEGIES: EVIDENCE AND REVIEW

*Here we take a critical look at evidence on what types of community approaches can be shown to be effective. Some useful leads emerge, but research in this area is difficult and it is not possible at present to offer any one conclusive best buy.*

## INTRODUCTION

4.1 This chapter focuses on community-based drugs prevention. It is not presented as a full review of the literature but as a selective and critical account of the wide variety of prevention projects which have been attempted in community settings. A particular concern will be to develop a sense of what is evidence based.

4.2 The emphasis of this chapter is on drugs prevention outside the school environment. The drugs education literature has been extensively reviewed and discussed elsewhere[1,2] and drugs education in schools was the specific focus of a previous ACMD report[3]. Another area that is excluded is the media, which has tended to operate at a supra-community level. However, in both cases, where education or media approaches, or both, have formed parts of larger, more community-oriented programmes, they have been included.

4.3 The chapter is divided into three sections. The first concentrates on community-based projects and approaches: included here are approaches involving the family; activities-based projects; workplace approaches; community-based treatment and harm reduction; and local curtailment of supply. The second focuses on broader issues relating to targeting and models for delivery of community-based prevention: included here is a discussion of the need for projects that target minority and high-risk groups, and a summary of community development and multi-component models of drugs prevention. The last section draws some brief conclusions.

## (I) COMMUNITY-BASED PREVENTION APPROACHES

4.4 There is a wide variety of projects that could be included under each of the headings that follow. However, we will not attempt to describe and evaluate all these approaches in detail: interesting examples will be highlighted and discussed.

4.5 In general, the literature is often stronger on prescriptions, especially regarding principles of good practice, than on evidence of the impact of programmes. Different countries focus on different things. For example, North American work has generally aimed to impact on use of tobacco, alcohol and other drugs taken together, while the British effort has more often been devoted towards tobacco, or alcohol, or specific illicit drugs.

4.6    In common with many other fields of programme evaluation, much of the research can be criticised on methodological grounds, especially for its lack of control or comparison groups, inattention to attrition rates, and neglect of process and implementation issues.

## APPROACHES INVOLVING THE FAMILY

4.7    Two strategies can be identified: those that attempt to involve parents in actually delivering drugs prevention through the establishment of parents groups and those that have focused on working directly with parents or families in order to prevent their children's drug use. The work described here has all been undertaken in the USA.

### PARENTS GROUPS

4.8    There has been little evaluation of the impact of parents groups. Where the attempt has been made, it has proved difficult to produce conclusive evidence[4]. Where parents or other community groups become involved, they are effective in putting substance use on the agenda, acting as agents for change themselves (often in response to a personal or local social crisis) but they may lack knowledge and skills about what works in prevention. Parents groups' first response is often to re-invent the wheel, adopting methods which have been shown not to work (eg use of fear-arousal campaigns or information-only publicity).

4.9    Researchers[5] have aimed comprehensively to describe the parent movement in the USA using three related studies: a mail survey of a national sample; in-depth, on-site interviews with key parents, teachers, school administrators, community leaders and criminal justice system personnel in ten sites; and telephone interviews with community members and their children. Assessment of impact depended on reports from respondents, who cited increased community awareness, and other changes in the schools, judicial and treatment systems and in youth culture. The authors themselves refer to these as 'modest appraisals of group effects'. The main influence of parents groups seemed to be that 'community agencies generally felt supported by the parents groups' and 'the support of the groups provided agencies such as the schools and law enforcement with a "mandate" to "get tough on drugs"'. The major achievement appeared to be in raising community awareness.

### WORKING DIRECTLY WITH FAMILIES

4.10   Other approaches have focused on strengthening families. Here the aim is to train parents to be effective change agents. The Kumpfer and DeMarsh Strengthening Families Programme[6] aimed to impact on the family's role in socialisation. Parent-training programmes emphasised improving communications and family problem-solving techniques. DeMarsh and Kumpfer's model programme of parent training found evidence that parents could be assisted to develop more effective parental styles. Similarly a school climate that is positive can lead to increased involvement and bonding, they claimed.

4.11   Family therapy aims to reduce risk factors or to help those who are already substance misusers. Families and Schools Together (FAST) is a collaborative effort involving community agencies and parents as partners. It is a whole family approach and targets 'at-risk' elementary school children not yet involved in drug use. Some monitoring of the programme has taken place but there is no evidence as yet as to its long term effect. The designs so far have involved pre- and post-test measures and have measured features of the children such as attentiveness and conduct as well as anxiety (with measures linked to self-esteem and depression). Parents appeared to feel more positively supported and mothers reported improved family cohesion while the programme was running. The State of Wisconsin found preliminary findings persuasive enough to allocate $1 million to replicate the programme elsewhere in the state and the Office for Substance Abuse Prevention in 1990 distinguished it as an Exemplary Model Programme[7].

4.12   The conclusion of much work in the family therapy field is that to be effective interventions must involve more people than just the young person and their close family. The extended family should be drawn in as well as a range of professional groups.

## PEERS

4.13   While many peer approaches are based in school and are therefore beyond the scope of this chapter, others are based in community contexts, such as youth clubs or through outreach work. Since Tobler's meta-analysis (an analysis which combines the results of a number of studies) of American drug prevention programmes[8,9] which showed peer programmes to be the most effective type of a range of interventions, peer interventions have gained considerably in popularity both in the USA and in the UK. However, there is considerable confusion about what constitutes "peer" interventions, programmes or education. While some "peer" programmes targeted at young people are delivered by young people of exactly the same age-group, others are delivered by young adults[10]; and some "peer" projects involve adults providing information to adult peers. Furthermore, it would appear that some commentators have described programmes that focus on resisting peer pressure as "peer programmes": Tobler apparently included programmes delivered by mental health professionals, counsellors and teachers under her "peer program" rubric.

4.14   Given such confusion, there is little that can be said about the effectiveness of peer interventions. At least in the UK, descriptive, process-orientated evaluations, such as that carried out by Shiner and Newburn (1996)[10] on the Youth Awareness Programme in Newham, London, are needed in order to further our understanding of the different models of peer intervention and the likely mechanisms for influencing young peoples' drug use.

## DIVERSIONARY OR ALTERNATIVE ACTIVITIES

4.15   Respondents in surveys and interviews often cite boredom and lack of local facilities as a cause of young people's drug use or crime, or both.[11] A large number of local 'diversionary' projects have been set up with this common-sense idea in mind: that providing young people with activities as diverse as sports, art and craft, music or trips to the countryside will divert them from - or provide alternatives to - drug use. These projects have been run by youth workers, charities and concerned local people, and have the attraction of being comparatively easy to set up (provided the activity is a popular one). However, as has been pointed out, beyond such common-sense notions of filling empty leisure time, there is a lack of clarity about how such projects might impact on drug use.[12] For some projects, the activities act as attractors, ensuring that young people attend a particular youth centre, where they will also be exposed to drugs education. However, where drugs information is 'tacked-on' to a project, it may be very difficult to gain the attention of young people and may even endanger the activities component of the project: 'bolting on a drugs element to an inappropriate medium does not work. Sometimes it weakens an otherwise perfectly viable project'.[12] Another proposition is that 'activities themselves will inculcate and highlight positive lifestyles and divert them away from the negative behaviour and culture which fosters problematic drugs use and crime'. This may be expecting too much from what may often only amount to an hour a week playing football at the local youth centre.

4.16   More positively, a recurrent theme in the literature is that diversionary activities may have an impact if they include opportunities which enhance future employment prospects.[13] A meta-analysis of drugs prevention evaluations found that 'alternatives programs were found to be effective in increasing skill levels and changing observed drug behaviours'.[9] The programmes included were aimed at 'populations at risk of abusive or compulsive drug use' and were 'marked by individualized activities such as one-on-one reading, basic life skills, job preparation and/or physical adventure.'

4.17   In conclusion, while this area is marked by some conceptual confusion, it is an approach which is popular at a local community level. Well-conducted evaluations of diversionary projects are rare, but what research has been carried out suggests that approaches targeted at high risk groups, which incorporate life and employment skills and are sustained over a considerable period of time[12] may offer the best hope of reducing drug misuse.

## APPROACHES AT THE WORKPLACE

4.18   Employee assistance programmes aim at early identification and intervention. Drug-screening efforts concentrated in high-risk occupations focus on the individual. Many of these prevention activities are not the primary responsibility of drugs prevention workers but are incorporated into broader occupational health practices. Alcohol problems are often a focus of concern although drug misuse also increasingly receives attention.

4.19   Interventions at the workplace involve the testing of applicants for jobs or after an accident has occurred, as well as random testing in some occupations. These seem to have a deterrent effect. For example, according to a 1990 study, Southern Pacific Railroad reported a decrease in its accident rate between 1984 and 1988 after introducing drug testing in the workplace (not necessarily of all employees) and General Motors found less absenteeism and fewer disciplinary actions and accident claims.[14] The same study also found that 'the drug testing programme of the military has been exemplary. In the Navy [US] the most common drug detected was marijuana. The overall positivity rate has fallen from 48% in 1980 to 3% in 1987'. The study concluded that 'Overall drug testing has been viewed as successful in highly regimented situations such as the armed services or in highly focused applications such as pre-employment or probable cause testing'.

4.20    Drug testing in the work place is generally considered legitimate in employment settings where drug use may carry especially high risks (for instance, the driving of heavy goods vehicles, airline pilots or members of the armed forces). However, opponents raise civil liberties objections and would also question the cost-effectiveness. We return again to drugs in the workplace in paragraphs 6.28 - 6.31.

## TREATMENT AND HARM REDUCTION

4.21    'Prevention' often refers to the reduction of levels of drug distribution and consumption but it can also mean, rather differently, the minimisation of various forms of harm, including health, social, legal and financial harm.[15,16] The broad aims of community-based treatment are to ensure that as many users as possible are brought into contact with welfare or treatment agencies. A special sub-category of interventions are those aimed at high-risk groups, especially hidden populations such as injecting drug users and sex workers. Considerable success has been demonstrated here and it has been cogently argued that the harm minimisation strategies introduced in this country have contributed significantly to prevention of what would otherwise have been a more severe HIV epidemic.[17,18]

4.22    In Britain in the 1980s, community drug teams (CDTs) were developed and promoted. The aim was to bring the treatment of drug misusers into the mainstream and to provide training and support for generic or non-specialist workers. These developments built on the experiences of the community alcohol teams. CDTs were intended to be multi-disciplinary teams and had responsibility for a defined geographical area. Some developed forms of shared care with generalists like general practitioners. By 1991 there were 81 CDTs operating around the UK. While their aim was to move away from specialisation, in practice CDTs have formed another layer of drugs treatment services, operating a specialist service at the local level. The aim to involve a wider range of agencies at the boundaries between treatment and prevention has not been very successful. This is partly because there was a failure to learn from the research findings of the Maudsley Alcohol Pilot Project,[19] which had concluded that 'providing generic workers with an account of the size of the problem and exhorting them to respond' is not enough.[20]

4.23    Syringe exchanges have been shown to reach drug injectors not previously in touch with services and help them change their risk behaviour.[17] The monitoring research group described how some people were helped to sustain lower risk behaviour and others adopted it.

4.24    Increasing involvement of community pharmacists in Britain in provision not only of equipment but also of health education is a recent trend which deserves further evaluation, as does the role of mobile needle exchange schemes.

4.25    Outreach projects have moved outside conventional treatment and care settings and focused on risk behaviour as it occurs in particular settings.[21] Choices about sharing injecting equipment and safer sex in real situations are influenced by conditions in these settings, even by such mundane issues as availability of clean water.

4.26    It is notable that one setting where high risk behaviour is known to exist has been subject to relatively little prevention activity or research - that of the prison. Research by Turnbull and colleagues has recently focused on drug use, supply, services for drug users, injecting and HIV infection in prison populations. This study highlights practices among prisoners which carry high risks of infection.[22] In its 1996 report ACMD made recommendations on the measures which should be taken to reduce harms in prisons.[23]

## CURTAILMENT OF SUPPLY

4.27    This section will look at what information is available on strategies at local level which can counteract the availability of drugs. It begins with a consideration of what can be learned from crime prevention initiatives and then turns to the main strands of supply reduction: low-level enforcement and community action.

### CRIME PREVENTION INITIATIVES

4.28    There is some debate about how much can be learnt about drugs prevention from prior crime prevention research. There has been research on Priority Estates (a housing management improvement initiative) interventions and on Safe Neighbourhoods (estate-based crime prevention through a consultative and participative approach) but some of the conclusions drawn remain controversial. It is difficult to assess the impact of packages, and implementation varies greatly from area to area. Ethical issues are raised about non-intervention, (ie purposely not working in particular areas so that they can act as 'control' or comparison sites) which hinders comparison attempts, as does the unwillingness of funders to fund research into non-intervention. Assessing the impact of such broad initiatives is impossible with certainty, especially in a fast changing world where unemployment, other economic conditions and other policy initiatives will influence what is going on. However, in a context permeated by the idea that nothing works, the impact of some urban initiatives gives some ground for optimism.[24] Although the complexity of urban programmes makes analysis difficult and in many instances there has been little systematic monitoring and observation, Rock's review of crime reduction initiatives on problem estates such as those projects run by the National Association for the Care and Rehabilitation of Offenders and the Priority Estates Project, indicates promising new developments worth continuing. Changes in design, management, letting policies, use of civil law and community development can make a difference.

### LOW-LEVEL ENFORCEMENT STRATEGIES AND COMMUNITY POLICING

4.29    There is some support for efforts devoted to low-level enforcement strategies as a form of social control impacting on the environment itself. Strategies to reduce demand for drugs include low level enforcement tactics such as disruptive and inconvenience policing within a multi-agency approach.

4.30    Where drug users cause unacceptable annoyance to other citizens especially in residential areas, police may be encouraged to take action. This use of law enforcement as a harm reduction strategy has been observed in places such as Rotterdam and

Merseyside. A similar approach is the zero-tolerance strategy of the New York Police Department, which has been credited by some commentators with the recent reduction in the crime rate and improvement in the quality of life in New York - although competing explanations point to the waning of the crack epidemic, demographic changes and the increase in use of incarceration of drug takers. Similar approaches have been introduced in England, for example on the Kingsmead Estate in Hackney and in Southwark where the local authorities have been active in using the civil law to control anti-social residents. These efforts can be effective where the trouble makers are clearly identified as outsiders. They are more difficult to implement where a high proportion of local residents are involved in such behaviours. We return to matters of housing and policing drugs markets in chapters 7 and 8.

4.31    The involvement of police in a multi-agency approach receives a good deal of support, although viewed with continuing suspicion by some groups and neighbourhoods. The problem of assessing the impact of such strategies lies with the absence of reliable information about the base-line situation, especially with regard to illicit or disapproved activities. The issue of community resilience is addressed in some of the research.

4.32    The implementation issue is one of making strategic alliances with those groups which oppose the targeted activities and finding ways to outmanoeuvre those who are gaining from drug dealing. What this demonstrates is that the management of prevention interventions can be a deeply political process, requiring specific skills on the part of those involved. Multi-agency approaches need to determine which agencies to involve, who should take the lead, what goals they have in mind and what operational devices to utilise. Views remain mixed on where police effort is best directed - whether at the top dealers or at street level.

4.33    Operation Welwyn, a street level drug enforcement operation in Kings Cross, which involved establishing local partnerships, attempted to build alliances with the community. Collaboration was established between the Metropolitan Police, British Transport Police, two local councils, Islington Safer Cities Project, the local Family Health Authority and the Health Authority, and business and community representatives. Methods used included targeting and surveillance and intensive patrolling, and appeared effective. There were complaints that the problem had simply been displaced. But insofar as drug dealing was less overt this was in itself seen as a favourable outcome. We look at policing drugs markets in more detail in chapter 8.

*COMMUNITY ACTIVISM AND COMMUNITY DEVELOPMENT*

4.34    The community development approaches discussed more fully in paragraphs 4.45-4.52 are combinations of both top-down and bottom-up endeavours, but where the aim is to retain some professional guidance of what happens. In the 1990s, however, anti-drug activism has taken some new forms. Forms of independent, community-led action have included Block Watch, demands for police protection, confrontational activism, efforts to evict drug dealers, attempts to renovate or demolish drug houses, and marches and rallies.

4.35    Confrontational activism has been reported to be more common in less affluent, high-crime and minority neighbourhoods, where drug problems are on the increase. Research has found that drug problems stimulate confrontational forms of community involvement against drugs. A further lesson drawn is of the importance of convincing existing organisations in a neighbourhood to extend their scope to encompass drug issues.[25]

4.36    Early research concluded that most community anti-crime programmes do not work and that they are unlikely to originate in the low-income neighbourhoods where they are sorely needed.[26] However another attempt to evaluate the impact of these community initiatives concluded that 'all of the programs reduced fear of crime, three of the four programs enhanced social control and cohesion and two of the four programs increased resident empowerment and neighbourhood satisfaction and reduced signs of physical decay'.[27] This study showed residents of low-income neighbourhoods working effectively with each other and with the police. Further research in this area is thus desirable.

4.37    The damaging effects of drug-taking on the environment have also been the focus of community-based drugs prevention activity, especially with regard to the increase of crime and incivilities, such as open drug-dealing, emergence of street markets, disorderly behaviour, drug-specific litter (discarded syringes), and the take-over of parks and other areas by drug users. There is less attention to addressing the causative factors in the environment which seem conducive to drug-taking, such as unemployment (particularly of youth), boredom and alienation, lack of recreational opportunities (alternative sources of affordable fun) and so on. But community development strategies narrowly or widely interpreted do relate to this approach. At the widest level, urban initiatives such as Safer Cities or City Challenge, which aimed to impact on urban deprivation through increasing job opportunities, enhancing social and economic regeneration and improving the quality of life for residents, have been subject to evaluation studies.[28] The results are not conclusive, although the descriptive findings illuminate social processes and can aid policy debates.

4.38    Again, the research in this field is characterised by the higher extent of prescription than description. Furthermore, conclusions in this field have been hampered by lack of experimental design, comparable control groups, lack of data on mediating variables and the absence of process or implementation data. However, quantitative evaluation of the impact of community action is very difficult to undertake: because action comes from the community itself, programmes cannot simply be implemented in a particular site and their effects monitored. Moreover, it is difficult for researchers to study community action from its inception, unless they just happen to be studying a particular community as the process begins - research on the initial development of community action will, in all likelihood, need to be carried out retrospectively.

## (II) TARGETING AND MODELS FOR DELIVERY

4.39    This section deals with issues relating to targeting and mechanisms or models for delivering drugs prevention in the community. Many of the approaches referred to above have consisted of primary prevention approaches, targeted at a wide range of young people, but there are strong arguments for targeting drugs prevention more narrowly. Under the first heading of this section we address the issue of targeting. The rest of the section describes two models for the delivery of community drugs prevention: community development and multi-component approaches.

# TARGETING

## MINORITY ETHNIC GROUPS

4.40   There has been little evaluation in the United Kingdom of the impact of drugs prevention activities on mixed race and minority groups. There have been a few studies of the impact of programmes on Native Americans or African Americans in the United States but on the whole, the area is one which has been neglected. Culturally relevant interventions and culturally sensitive evaluation methods have yet to be developed, which is striking given the exceedingly high prevalence rates of drug misuse in African American children in the USA.

4.41   One model programme that has been developed in this field is SAFE (Substance-Abuse-Free Environment). This is a broad-spectrum family intervention aiming to empower through training in competence-based skills, provision of alternative activities and including a culturally relevant evaluation plan that involves feedback to the program. The studies that have been produced have valuable comments to make with regard to process issues.[29,30] For example, while SAFE 'awaits empirical evaluation and confirmation'[30] it has been designed to build on the findings of previous studies which highlighted the importance of involving parents and the family system in intervention efforts and recognition of the severe disadvantages experienced by African American children in impoverished areas. Project SAFE involves parent and child training (PACT), use of peers as leaders and community activities. PACT works closely with existing agencies like churches and community centres. The community activities offer music and athletics as an alternative to more negative pursuits. In the implementation and evaluation, great attention is paid to developing culturally appropriate projects and measures, for example by including in the evaluation a committee consisting of African American mental health professionals and educators. On the basis of their advice, some proposed research instruments were rejected. This cultural sensitivity is a distinctive aspect of SAFE. Another is its stress on provision of alternatives. And a third is the stress on linking young people, their families and the community. So far only anecdotal evidence is available about its impact.

## HIGH-RISK GROUPS

4.42   As stated earlier, the focus of much drugs prevention work is on young people in general. This may stem from the fact that only limited research has been undertaken on differences of class, race, gender, culture, language or religion. It may also be related to the dearth of research (especially in this country) on specific high-risk groups in specific contexts. From what is known about background factors associated with drug use, it could be expected that groups such as truants, young offenders and homeless youths may be at higher risk of experimentation with drugs and higher risk of problematic drug use. However, at present very little is known about the drug use of such groups. There is also a dearth of evaluative research that has focused on drugs prevention work with such groups.

4.43   However, there is a tension between targeting high-risk groups or individuals and community-based and particularly, community-led approaches. The (hopefully) wide ownership of many community approaches can make it difficult for them to target particular groups or individuals. Moreover, some types of high-risk groups, such as young people looked after by local authorities and young offenders are probably best accessed and worked with through the institutions and agencies responsible for them.

4.44    Avoiding the problems of targeting particular high-risk groups or individuals, some commentators have suggested that prevention efforts should target high-risk neighbourhoods.[31] In the USA, the Centre for Substance Abuse Prevention has targeted high-risk or vulnerable children and youth, but avoided singling out particular individuals by focusing on particular neighbourhoods, such as public housing or high density housing, which have high rates of social problems as measured by conventional indicators. However, there is limited research on these projects at present.

## COMMUNITY DEVELOPMENT

4.45    One way of delivering drugs prevention at the community level is through a community development model. This approach has been defined as follows:

"Community development focuses on the participation of local people themselves and encouragement of their own initiative, self-help and mutual help. The aim is that the community should define its own needs and make provision for meeting them and for fostering co-operative networks of people and groups in the community through the involvement of community development workers, using their skills in a non-directive way."[32]

4.46    The community development approach was promoted through the 1980s in America and Australia and came later to the UK in the form of the Home Office Drugs Prevention Initiative (DPI) in the late 1980s. The DPI, first announced in October 1989, was originally designed to promote drugs prevention in neighbourhoods most at risk from drug misuse. Twenty local drugs prevention teams were established with the aim of getting communities and agencies involved in drugs prevention and these teams supported a number of community development approaches, through resourcing and supporting neighbourhood-based practitioners, using community networks, creating new networks, initiating training and resourcing action-research. Implementation of these initiatives relied on the establishment of trust; close involvement of local people in devising strategies; accessibility and close liaison; provision of information and improving the knowledge-base of the community; and working in partnership with other agencies in the area.[33] A review of the work of the teams concluded that while there are signs that communities are taking an increasing lead in drugs prevention,[34] in the next stage more attention needed to be given to establishing what approaches work effectively. The second phase of the DPI aims to implement and closely evaluate a range of drugs prevention approaches, including community development projects and an integrated drugs prevention programme.

4.47    The British approach has been more clearly focused on areas of deprivation or high-risk areas than have the American or Australian. The assumption on which the DPI is based is that successful long term solutions to drugs problems will depend on all sections of the community pulling together. Local projects have had evaluations conducted and the Central Drugs Prevention Unit of the Home Office has published a series of reports on the findings, including an evaluation of community development approaches conducted in phase I of the initiative.[33]

4.48   It has often been a struggle to set up community intervention projects. Lack of funds, opposition and difficulties in getting agreement to proceed hinder developments, in spite of the sterling efforts of those involved. Projects can become overwhelmed by the enormity of the tasks, especially when they operate in impoverished communities.[35]

4.49   In the literature on these community development projects, much attention is given to process issues, stressing the value of sponsorship, participation in high-quality training, the prevention of programme drift and the value of integrating research and evaluation into practice. Key implementation principles stressed include: the value of a step-wise progression; the value of multi-component strategies; the importance of negotiating entry; the need for community support through sponsorship, leadership and the role of business; the importance of community ownership; and the importance of continuity. Sustained integrated approaches are thought to work best, involving the school, the media, parents and community organisations.

4.50   The findings to date refer mainly to *design* and *implementation* issues rather than to *impact*. In any case, it is thought unlikely that cause-effect can be demonstrated in a conventional way. What is emphasised is that the objectives of drugs prevention work must be clearly stated, for example, whether the aim is to reduce the general prevalence of drugs consumption, to cut back on overt drug dealing or the presence of drug markets in impoverished areas, or other aims.

4.51   Stress is also placed on the importance of defining tangible objectives, such as the reclaiming of public space and offering alternatives and new opportunities. Less tangible objectives may operate longer-term, such as building community infrastructure and improving the quality of life. Coalitions are seen as active agents for change.

4.52   In the USA, the core problems are seen as *community disorganisation* and *norms favourable to drug use*. This has been described in terms of 'Increasing poverty, lack of opportunities for youth and neighbourhood disorganisation leading to family deterioration appear to be related to increased illegal drug trafficking and increased drug susceptibility in high-risk youth'.[36] Over 250 community partnership demonstration and evaluation programmes are being implemented in the United States as well as other community partnership schemes funded by Foundations. The aim is, through involving the community in the action, to change norms and to create opportunities and skills, empowering through encouraging ownership of the problem. Risk assessment is the first step and action plans build on the community effort to produce a risk assessment. The evidence regarding long-term impact of many of these programmes in USA and elsewhere remains thin however, in spite of their inherent plausibility.[32,37]

## MULTI-COMPONENT PROGRAMMES

4.53   Another way of delivering community drugs prevention approaches is through multi-component programmes. Multi-component drugs prevention programmes involve the delivery of a number of drugs prevention approaches within a given community or area. They have gained considerable popularity in the USA, where some programmes have been shown to have a significant impact on smoking and marijuana use. Their development has stemmed from a number of influences. Perhaps most significant, are the broadly negative findings that have come from the numerous evaluations of school-based programmes. The difficulty of impacting young peoples' drug use through school has led researchers and practitioners to think about alternative contexts in which to deliver drug prevention. Another influence has been the developments in research and thinking on 'risk' and 'protective' factors. Research has repeatedly identified a number of factors that are associated with drug misuse, for example, poor academic performance, early alcohol use, smoking, neighbourhood disorganisation and poor parental supervision.[38,39] More recently, the importance of protective factors in preventing the onset of drug misuse has also been stressed. The identification of a range of such factors, many of which cannot be targeted through a school programme, has led to the design of multi-component programmes that attempt to impact multiple risk and protective factors across a number of contexts, many of them in the community. Lastly, the development of community heart disease prevention programmes which draw on a wide number of health promotion approaches have provided a model for the implementation of integrated, multi-component drugs prevention approaches.[40,41] These programmes have involved a combination of tactics, including face-to-face intervention, involvement of mass media, training of public health and social care personnel to prioritise issues in contacts with patients or clients, public policy change (for example, with regard to advertising), and resistance skills training. Evaluation of such interventions have shown that face-to-face work is a necessary part of a successful programme and that programmes based on the dissemination of information alone are less likely to be effective.

4.54    A number of different combinations of approaches have been applied in such multi-component programmes: school-based and community-based education and information campaigns have been delivered by teachers, researchers, peer-groups or through the media. Education and information and treatment may be workplace-based or leisure-based. Other techniques may involve parents and families. Special tertiary prevention (that is, approaches seeking to mitigate the effects of harmful drug use) may include outreach work. There are also community development approaches and use of policing and the criminal justice system.

*EXAMPLES OF MULTI-COMPONENT PROGRAMMES: PATHE AND THE MIDWESTERN PROJECTS*

4.55    Project PATHE is a project focusing on high-risk, low socio-economic status young people. Techniques employed included: co-operative learning; life skills courses; peer counselling; peer leadership programmes; sports and hobbies; school pride days; after-school tutoring; and musicals. The result of the first year of operations indicated positive reductions in substance use in comparison to a control school.[42] The evaluation emphasises the value of stressing protective factors, as much if not more than, risk factors: protective factors are identified as optimism, empathy, insight, intellectual competence, self-esteem, direction or mission and determination and perseverance. The coping or life skills associated with these attributes are emotional management skills, interpersonal social skills, interpersonal reflective skills, academic skills, self-esteem, planning skills and life skills and problem-solving ability. The researchers state that 'Resilient individuals have been found to have significantly more of these characteristics and skills'.[36]

4.56    The Midwestern Prevention Project is another, multi-component programme worth highlighting. This project has operated in fifteen areas (communities) of Kansas City and has been extensively evaluated.[43] Four channels of influence were used: the school, the family, the media and community organisations. Methods included resistance skills training, focusing directly on young people and training the trainers - teachers, parents, community leaders and youth workers. Research, which incorporated a control group, has shown a significant impact of the programme on tobacco and cannabis use four years after implementation.[44] The programme also appears to have been equally effective with high- and low-risk adolescents.[45] While these evaluations appeared positive, further work is needed to assess how the project develops beyond the initial 'honeymoon' period, other issues of implementation, community ownership, access to hard to reach groups and change over a longer period.[44] Researchers claim that the Midwestern project 'because of its comprehensiveness, the scientific rigor of its evaluation methodology, the use of state-of-the-art prevention methods and the strength of its behavioural outcome data ... provides the best model of a community-based approach to substance abuse prevention currently available and the most persuasive evidence that this type of prevention strategy is effective'.[46]

4.57    However, this study and others like it have shown most effect in reducing use of tobacco, alcohol and marijuana. The extent to which these methods may be generalised to other illicit, particularly hard, drugs remains unanswered. There is also a disconcerting slippage in terminology in a number of these articles from consideration of substance use to conclusions about substance misuse.

## ISSUES RELATING TO MULTI-COMPONENT APPROACHES

4.58    Community efforts have aimed to reinforce non-using norms among parents, school personnel, local business and community leaders. Sponsorship from the latter is thought to be important in gaining support for the intervention. However, most programmes to date have focused on 'low-risk', 'white', 'middle-class', young people[47] and there is a need to design and evaluate drugs prevention approaches which target young people from different ethnic groups and social backgrounds, in different risk-related contexts.

4.59    The prevailing wisdom in the field regarding the best routes forward has been summed up as follows: prevention interventions need to be targeted to the intended audience; prevention interventions need to be based on the best known aetiological (causative) factors; more aetiological research is needed; increased prevention effectiveness research is needed; cost-effectiveness and cost-benefit analyses should be conducted; and preferred prevention strategies are those that co-ordinate local community involvement, including messages that stress healthy lifestyles, target high-risk youth, and are enduring naturalistic prevention programmes.[42]

4.60    On the other hand, a rather different conclusion has been that the contribution evaluation research is making to improving substance abuse prevention is wanting, mainly due to faults in the methodology - lack of control groups and inattention to attrition rates. 'Not only are the findings predominantly negative ... but the recommendations for where to go from here are extremely weak'.[48] A major theoretical flaw in these programmes, the researcher argues, has been to attribute risk to the characters of individuals rather than to see these as attributes of the environment. Instead of focusing on individual skills, programmes should instead get community residents involved in community development activities to impact these risk factors, he argues.

## (III) CONCLUSIONS

4.61   It is very easy, faced with limited research evidence about the effectiveness of particular approaches, to conclude that they do not work. However, in such circumstances, great care must be taken to differentiate the failures of *evaluation* from the failures of *interventions*. Community-based drugs prevention is extremely hard to evaluate and as this chapter has shown, very few studies have convincingly tackled the issue of the impact of such projects on drug use. This does not mean that the approaches do not work - it means the verdict is still open.

4.62   Much of this work is highly innovative and at an early stage of development. In some areas it may be too early to even attempt a rigorous, quantitative, outcomes-focused evaluation. An example of one such area is peer interventions, which are poorly defined and poorly understood. In such circumstances, evaluation has a crucial role to play in taking forward our understanding of such approaches through *qualitative* appraisal - describing the process, development and operation of projects and seeking to generalise about the possible mechanisms for impact and making recommendations for practice. This is not to duck the issue of what works. The ultimate aim must always be to assess the impact of drugs prevention programmes on drug use. Nevertheless, it must sometimes be recognised that we are simply not ready to do this yet.

4.63   Where research evidence is available - be it focused on process or outcomes - it is important that practitioners take it into account in designing new initiatives. However, it should be recognised that research can be more or less "available" - journal articles or long and technical reports are not likely to inform the work of "coal-face" community workers. It is therefore important that the findings of evaluations are made accessible, for example, through organisations like the Institute for the Study of Drug Dependence, whose address is given in paragraph 10.24.

4.64   While the overall conclusion must therefore be that we know very little for sure, there are nevertheless strong suggestions from the research of the types of approaches that are likely to prove must fruitful. Given the way that drug use (both legal drug use and perhaps increasingly, illicit drug use) are part of our culture, there has been a growing awareness of the need to tackle drug use in a multi-faceted, community-focused manner. It is not enough to attempt drugs prevention solely through a teacher in a classroom - school approaches need to be supported by community approaches. There is evidence that multi-component programmes that bring together in a co-ordinated manner, school programmes, parental programmes, local information campaigns and leisure and employment projects, while at the same time effectively harnessing the energy and enthusiasm of local communities and agencies, may prove the most successful.

# 5 LOCAL DRUG PROJECTS AND LOCAL PREVENTIVE ACTION

*The number of local drug projects has burgeoned in the last few years. Some order and direction needs to be given to the way they are set up and developed. Treatment projects should consider their role in the wider drug prevention setting.*

## INTRODUCTION

5.1    The preceding chapter reviewed what is known about the effectiveness of prevention projects in community settings. The review provided some useful indications of good practice, whilst acknowledging that there is a shortage of conclusive research evidence about effectiveness. In this chapter we look briefly at the historical background and seek to assess what is going on now - and there is a good deal. We then go on to identify how drug projects can be successful, identifying good practice pointers for local practitioners, before drawing some emerging conclusions for policy makers about how best practice should be nurtured and sustained.

## THE HISTORICAL DEVELOPMENT OF COMMUNITY RESPONSES

5.2    In most European countries organised responses to drug problems did not begin until the mid-to-late sixties and were in response to a recognition of a growing drug problem associated with youth and counter-culture movements. In the initial stages there appears to have been considerable difficulty in getting professional or community groups to take ownership of the problem. While communities were prepared to take part in prevention activities they viewed those who took drugs as being apart from the body of the community. The potential conflicts between community, institutional and professional interests has been little examined in recent years.

5.3    The initial wave of service development in the United Kingdom in the sixties saw the establishment, almost entirely in London, of a network of specialist drug clinics and residential programmes. In the seventies there was more expansion of residential programmes. The first non-statutory services were almost exclusively linked to Christian churches and were based in central London providing befriending, some basic welfare work and counselling[1]. The first community drug services developed with the Soho Project, Blenheim Project and The Community Drug Project in South London. Also the Association for the Parents of Addicts, subsequently renamed the Association for the Prevention of Addiction, was established and resulted in the development of a network of services in different parts of the country. A number of socially concerned individuals were involved in establishing ROMA, New Horizon,

Kaleidoscope, CURE, ISDD and Release, many of which continue today. As part of the network of community services some therapeutic communities were formed – Alpha House in Portsmouth, Phoenix House in London, Suffolk House in Iver Health and the Ley Community in Oxford.

5.4    Thus in the 1970s the non-statutory and community-based organisations formed an important part of the network of community services. Many of the services were distinctive and carried the characteristics of the individuals involved in establishing them. Those services have been described as having four distinct roles[1,2] – casualty caring, after care, education and agitation. The mid-eighties saw the establishment of new forms of parent action, usually as a result of heroin misuse, with parents being directly involved in establishing community services such as CADA and Drugline in South London and ADFAM and Families Anonymous as national organisations.

5.5    The 1980s also saw the development and burgeoning of "a new orthodoxy" of services which were largely characterised by being multi-disciplinary, community based and accessible.[3] This followed on the Advisory Council on the Misuse of Drugs' Report on Treatment and Rehabilitation[4] and the development of the Central Funding Initiative aimed at supporting the development of both statutory and non-statutory community based drug services.

5.6    The late 1980s saw the development of community drug services with a multi-disciplinary - health service, social service and probation service - input.[5] Such multi-disciplinary teams had a major emphasis on working with primary care services and supporting broader generic responses as a contrast to the previous model of specialist drug dependence units. There was a clear recognition that all agencies including housing, social services, criminal justice agencies and health agencies were dealing with problems of drug misuse but failing to do so in any co-ordinated manner and failing to galvanise the broader resources within the community. Much of the model was based on previous experience with the development of community alcohol teams and in both cases the challenge was to use the community teams to foster generic service response with a particular focus on primary care. Despite this intention all too often the community services focused mainly on direct client work and frequently ended up as a form of specialised service with limited levels of broader community links.[6]

5.7    In the discussion of this issue much of the literature is focused on the challenge of getting different professionals in the community to work together and to develop different ways to transfer basic skills to generic community workers. To date there is limited evidence that the diverse range of professionals in the community manage to link well together. Since their establishment, Drug Action Teams have addressed these kinds of practical issues. A recent evaluation[7] has examined how effective they have been in these tasks in England, concluding that they are bedding down well in many areas.

## WHAT IS GOING ON NOW?

5.8    It is not easy to obtain a comprehensive picture of what is being delivered by drug projects all over the country. There are a great number of local projects to tackle drugs problems. Some are funded under central Government programmes such as the Home

Office's Drugs Prevention Initiative, the Department of Health's Section 64 grants, or the cross-departmental Drugs Challenge Fund; or as part of wider programmes such as the Single Regeneration Budget Challenge Fund. Local drug projects are also supported by health and local authorities as part of local service provision, and many feature in Drug Action Teams' action plans. Some have been going on for a long time while others are comparatively new initiatives responding to new problems.

5.9     A great deal of what these different groups are doing, and their experience in doing it, remains hidden. Drug projects, in all their variation, are often characterised most by the strength of commitment, motivation and enthusiasm of the participants. It is often a struggle to set them up and maintain them – problems with funding, local opposition and difficulties in getting agreement to proceed may all have to be overcome. There is also an evident risk that local projects may proceed with high hopes but in ignorance of what has already been tried elsewhere (and failed or succeeded) or what may be known to be good practice. It follows, in our view, that much more information needs to be gathered about the processes and experiences of projects across the country with a view to establishing what is good practice. There is a demand for such information from Drug Action Teams (DATs) and a need for it to help local projects set up effective schemes. From this information policy-makers should identify whether the most efficient and effective work is being done against drug misuse within communities.

5.10    Attempts are being made to gather a better picture of what is going on in different areas of the country, defining, categorising and identifying good practice. For example, in 1996 SCODA undertook a mapping exercise on behalf of the Health Education Authority, which involved:

   • a census of 300 specific local drug education and prevention activities;

   • a survey and analysis of the roles of generic and specialised local bodies with a defined or substantive role in drug education or prevention work;

   • an analysis of the roles of national and regional agencies with a substantive role in facilitating drug education and prevention.

5.11    The results of the 1996 mapping exercise were to be published in November 1997 and will we understand be updated in 1998.

5.12    Capturing the learning from local experience of community-based drugs prevention activity is also the aim of the Home Office Drugs Prevention Initiative (DPI). As we noted in chapter 4 the second phase of the DPI, which runs from 1995-99, aims to implement and closely evaluate a range of drugs prevention action which local people can take in partnership with others in the community. The DPI has made and continues to make extensive use of independent research and evaluation in this task: the findings of some of the research projects in phase 1 have already been published in a series of Drugs Prevention Initiative Papers. But there has been a deliberate shift in phase 2 to a more organised programme of learning and development. The 70 plus projects now being funded and supported by the DPI teams as part of the DPI's national programme of work have been planned to answer a substantial set of questions about drugs prevention. Full findings will not be available till 1998-99 but some lessons are beginning to emerge which are reflected in paragraph 5.17.

5.13    We have so far in this chapter referred to local drugs prevention projects in a way which suggests that they might be regarded as homogeneous. This is patently not the case. They come in numerous shapes and forms. It is beyond the scope of this chapter to try and characterise all drugs projects but in the following two paragraphs we attempt to illustrate their diversity.

5.14    A drug project may consist of a group of parents working together against the drug problems in their neighbourhood. It may involve detached youth work, or centre-based activities for young people. The main objective may be to raise awareness or provide information. Some projects may deliver one-off interventions, while others aim to deliver longer term sustained interventions. Responding to local problems, drug projects may deliver activity which fits into a continuum of treatment, harm reduction, and prevention. A project may in many cases be a pilot for an approach which it is hoped may in the longer term become part of main-stream service delivery.

5.15    Following are some actual examples of drugs projects:

### Parents for Prevention in Birmingham

The aim of this project is to educate parents to help them feel more confident and assured about drugs enabling them to support young people; and to provide help for parents who are having to deal with their own drug misusing children.

### The Hathershaw Solvent Misuse Project

The project concentrates on volatile substance abuse while recognising that it cannot be isolated from other forms of substance misuse. They undertake detached youth work to build confidence and self-esteem; run projects, for example, to educate on drugs and solvents; take referrals of misusers from parents (and others); and provide advice and information.

### The Albion Nightshelter

The project provides a shared house for homeless drug addicts who have repeatedly failed de-toxification and re-habilitation. They have the support of a drug counsellor and a housing adviser. Abstinence is not a requirement of residence but commitment to change is. The intention is to provide stable housing before addressing drug misuse and related issues.

### West Sussex Rural Youth Mobile Project

The project provides a youth service, information, and a social venue in villages with little or no active youth provision. It puts drug education in the context of general health education, and aims to get young people involved in activities which divert them from drug misuse. Another aim is that once the bus stops visiting the young people should establish their own meeting place and activities.

### Taff Ely Drug Support (TEDS)

TEDS is a voluntary agency that provides a wide range of services including counselling, outreach, home detoxification and rehabilitation, needle exchange (static and mobile) and aftercare. The project works with all age groups and has a harm reduction philosophy. Prevention and education work is an integral part of the service provided.

**North Edinburgh Drug Advice Centre**

This group grew out of a community response in North East Edinburgh. Originally known as SHADA (support, help and advice for drug addiction), it began as a volunteer-led project. It now provides a range of services including counselling, support and welfare benefit advice for the whole range of people affected by problematic drug misuse in the north of the capital.

5.16 We have referred in paragraph 5.8 to the fact that there are already in existence a great number of local projects in the United Kingdom to tackle drug problems. This is a remarkable phenomenon in itself showing the strength and ability of local - often voluntary - organisations to take action locally. The fact that so many have grown up so quickly suggests a real and strong demand for them to respond to local problems, problems which are not being met by official responses. While noting this extraordinary growth we believe that the time has come to bring some order to the scene through the sort of work which is being done by SCODA and the DPI, to which we referred in paragraphs 5.10-5.12. As soon as possible there needs to be central guidance which helps local projects set off in the right direction from the outset. In the next section, on the basis of current understanding, we give some idea of what we think guidance might comprise.

## WHAT MAKES A PROJECT WORK?

5.17 It is not possible to establish common good practice guidelines for every kind of drug project. For example, delivering effective local information for young people is a different proposition from developing a local support, counselling and befriending service for parents, or an arrest referral scheme. But there are some broad guidelines which we believe apply:

• *Identify realistic targets:* All projects should identify specific, realistic and measurable objectives. Many local projects set themselves broad over-ambitious aspirations, e.g. "to reduce young people's drug misuse" which are both beyond the scope of a single project and impossible for the project to measure. It is much better to find out what it is possible for particular interventions to achieve and then to set realistic targets which can be achieved. For instance, it is clear from the research literature that providing information about drugs on its own can increase knowledge but is unlikely to change behaviour, so a leaflet or local campaign could aim to increase knowledge about drugs, but would not thereby expect a dramatic change in behaviour. It can make good sense to be as tightly specific as possible in identifying target groups for interventions. Age, gender (or sexual orientation), ethnicity, and lifestyle, and the locations in which the target population is found, can all be significant in whether a prevention approach is effective or not. Consideration should also be given to whether the project touches on confidentiality issues which need to be addressed. The question of whether the target population can easily gain access to the services which are being provided by the project will need considering too.

• *Secure Funding:* Good projects need to obtain resources and local support if they are to survive. They require resources in the form of access to advice and training, for example, but the most immediate requirement, and that which is argued for and discussed most often, is the direct provision of funding. To attract funding from any source in today's world, a project needs to be able to put together a decent bid. In the process it is likely to have to demonstrate good management practice, an ability to forward plan, and an ability to manage change. It should be mindful of health and safety requirements in going about its work. Within the DPI's programme, work is being done which aims to increase investment in drugs prevention projects. A number of small local groups and potential funders have been consulted : based on that consultation, training is being provided to equip projects with the skills and knowledge to access further funding and with the skills necessary to enable them to manage change and growth that further funding often brings with it. SCODA is currently taking forward a national programme to identify a wider base of sources of funding for drugs projects and to better equip drugs projects to access that funding. These are obviously useful exercises. Looking from the other side funders should consider whether there is a uniqueness which justifies funding a project which would not otherwise qualify and, as we have said in paragraph 7.30, they should not be too prescriptive or inflexible in their demands for output measures.

• *Ensure a continuity of partners, and support from a network of agencies:* Two main types of network have been identified, those of the professional agencies and service providers, and those of the people living in the area - tenants or residents, members of community groups, religious groups or other associations. Relationships should, as appropriate, be established with them. The local Drug Action Team will be a chief source of support whose co-operation and assistance should be secured. There needs to be continuing commitment from these networks for the resourcing of the work of the project. Those resources may usefully come in the form of dedicated workers, volunteers, training, advice, the servicing of local forums or networks, or in other kind, as well as, or rather than, cash grants to the project.

• *Be aware of the context of the work:* While keeping a tight focus on the project's objectives, it is important that other aspects of the problem are not ignored. For example, a project focused on reducing young mothers' tranquilliser use should not ignore the stresses that might lead them to use tranquillisers in the first place, or a project aiming at reducing young people's 'recreational' drug use may need to take account of the lack of alternative avenues for recreational activity. Such awareness will help when the project works with other local agencies, which may be focused on precisely these other aspects. Awareness will help to gain the trust and co-operation of these other agencies and ensure that all are 'talking the same language'. Addressing the problem from different perspectives will maximise the possibility of success.

• *Monitor and evaluate:* Monitoring progress is an essential part of good practice. Projects can and must monitor themselves by keeping a record of what they do. They should also undertake self-evaluations. These are important tools in keeping partnerships involved, by enabling success and milestones reached to be recognised and built on; it is also essential for developing the work. Questions which should be asked include, has action resulted in desirable outcomes, or should the project change course, does what has happened so far suggest that the nature of the problem may be different from how it seemed at first? If some degree of external evaluation can be undertaken so much the better. It may be possible to learn useful lessons from other local projects and Drugs Reference Groups may provide a means by which to share those lessons.

- *Obtain the trust of local people:* Careful consultation is important, starting with an initial assessment of the local situation, and devising an appropriate strategy, involving local people throughout. The drugs work should relate to wider community concerns and consideration might be given to linking drugs prevention activity to work which is being done to address those wider concerns.

## CONCLUSIONS

5.18    This short (and limited) review of the history and current position of drug projects across the country has shown the rather haphazard but very rapid way in which drugs services, based on projects have developed. It is clear that much good work has been and still is being done, and that it is possible for one-off local initiatives to develop into mainstream services. But current arrangements do not guarantee that good work will be maintained or good practice spread.

5.19    The challenge for policy makers now is to devise a system which provides some direction to the development of drug projects. It would in our view be a mistake to allow projects to go on proliferating in the way they have in the past without being guided on the processes which they should go through and given a steer on what is most likely to be effective. At the same time we would not wish to see innovation and local initiative stifled; and there needs to be an acknowledgement that lessons learned from one place may not automatically transfer to another because the circumstances are so different.

5.20    In order to nurture and sustain local drug projects, whether in isolation or as part of a wider programme to address local problems, there is a need for training and other resources and a high level of support from local services. There is a need for investment in partnerships and the incorporation of professional capacity if effective work is to expand and continue. Treatment projects should ask themselves whether they should take on a wider prevention brief rather than treatment alone. We see the role of Drug Action Teams as central in helping to provide the necessary support for these developments.

*Chapter*

# 6 DRUG PREVENTION AND THE ENVIRONMENT OF AWARENESS AND BELIEFS

*What people and communities believe about drugs is as much part of the environment as is the physical surround. We argue that attitudes to tobacco and alcohol are part of this context of ideas and that DATs should consider the merit of dealing with all substances together. The media as well as intentional health education are among the factors which shape the relevant climate.*

## INTRODUCTION

6.1 The choices which people make about drugs, or anything else, are governed by awareness and beliefs - what they feel about something. The issue is one which we believe deserves attention - the environment is as much about the surround of ideas as about physical structures.

6.2 At the outset we should say that in this chapter the term "awareness and beliefs" is not supposed to be a restrictive concept. It will include to a greater or lesser extent other attributes such as attitudes and values. Our thesis is that how people value themselves, whether they think they can control their destiny, how they think they fit in with society, and so on will influence whether they take drugs. We are dealing here with the basis for an environmental aspect of drug prevention which has in the past too often been neglected or shrugged off as unapproachable but which is of vital importance if further progress is to be made.

6.3 We considered the extent to which we should introduce the concept of shaping the values of individuals into this chapter. In this we were informed by the consultation document issued in November 1996 by the National Forum for Values in Education and the Community which was set up by the School Curriculum and Assessment Authority (SCAA) to make recommendations on values in education and the community.

6.4 It is very difficult to say how the values of an individual are formed. School education may have a part to play in their establishment but the greater influence probably comes from family and friends and to some extent from the society in which the individual lives.

6.5 In the process of trying to shape values it appears that individuals may have very different starting points. Indeed it would be surprising if from within the pluralistic society in which we live everyone emerged with the same values. However, we think it is a reasonable expectation on the part of the individual that he or she should not be excluded from being a neighbour, having the respect of others and respecting themself - that is, being part of society. Those who feel let down by society and see no means of improving their lot may well feel that society has one set of values for the well off and one for them. They would regard it as insulting if you suggested they should aspire to those general values.

6.6     The point is that when it comes to drug misuse and values we think there is complexity which must not be overlooked. Some values may appear insulting and unattainable for some people. On the other hand we think that at a general level values remain important as a touchstone of a civilised society. The aim should be to adopt practices and foster an environment which enables individuals to attain the values which make them a part of society.

6.7     It is not society's role to dictate what an individual's beliefs should be but we do believe that the environment of awareness and beliefs should be sufficiently strong to enable an individual to make healthy and informed choices. In terms of drug prevention this means reducing initiation into misuse and reducing the harms of misuse. In this chapter in common with previous ACMD reports we have adopted the word "misuse" to cover harmful and experimental, or occasional use, unless the context makes it plain otherwise rather than adopt the convention of regarding harmful taking as "misuse" and other taking as "use".

6.8     In reaching the conclusions in this chapter (and others) we have been mindful of the content of the reviews which are the subject of chapters 2, 3 and 4 and have also taken evidence from people with a knowledge of these matters. On the basis of that input and our own discussions we have reached certain conclusions. They cannot be based on incontrovertible evidence because it does not exist but that does not mean that nothing can be said. We hope that what we say here will at the least serve as a starting point for debate.

6.9     We see awareness and beliefs operating at several levels, or in different layers. These layers do not have clear lines between them but overlap and interact. They do nonetheless provide useful preliminary ways of mapping this field of awareness and beliefs. In this chapter we will use the following model.

6.10    First, there is the layer of what the large society around us believes. Its beliefs are not uniform but contradictory and varied. Some parts would want to see drug misusers punished rather than treated while other parts would like to see drugs legalised, arguing that resultant crime would reduce. And there are sections of society which regard their drug taking as use rather than misuse - that is, as a normal and not anti-social activity. Parliament and policy makers' views will be at odds with some part of society's but it will be theirs which at the official level prevail. Second, there is the layer of neighbourhood. As with the wider society there will be differences of belief within the community. Third, there is the layer of the family, whose beliefs are bound to be an influence on the action of the members who comprise it. And fourthly, there are the beliefs of individuals themselves and the immediate world in which they move outside the home.

## SOCIETY

6.11    This report is only concerned with United Kingdom society, but the United Kingdom is not isolated from the rest of the world and is inevitably influenced in its attitudes and beliefs towards drugs by the international community. This is well illustrated by the

United Nations Drugs Conventions which control certain drugs and to which the United Kingdom and many other countries are signatories. It is from these Conventions that the UK laws on drugs derive, and these, of course, set the tone and are the embodiment of society's attitude towards drugs misuse.

6.12     It is society at large, with policy makers as its agents, who determine how the misuse of drugs should be regarded. There will be conflicts of ideas within society and those ideas are likely to vary with time. For example, most people would wish to see the status quo retained and all currently illicit drugs to remain illegal but the proportion drops among young people from non-affluent areas, although even then it remains at about half. Even persons who have taken drugs do not necessarily believe they should be decriminalised or legalised. Among those who would like to see change there is only really support for decriminalising cannabis.

6.13     Society's main current response is a combination of education, treatment and criminal processes and the debate around the balance between them seems to us to be healthy. The Advisory Council would not pretend that it would ever be possible, or necessarily desirable, to have a society, the beliefs of which were entirely uniform on drug taking, but we believe that there are steps which can be taken to change, to some extent, society's larger "awareness and beliefs" environment in the cause of drug prevention.

6.14     It is sometimes suggested that drug taking in this country is a normalised activity. That as a general proposition is misleading. Nationally among younger people (16-29) around 45% have taken a prohibited drug some time in their lives but only about 15% recently (in the last month), implying much lower levels of regular misuse[1]. There are also regional variations in the prevalence of drug taking, to the extent that in some localities and in some groups it may be regarded as normalised. There is much less taking among older people. The drugs taken and the settings of misuse vary too. It thus follows that in thinking about drug prevention it is wrong to consider people as a homogeneous whole. They will, for whatever reasons, all have different starting points - non-takers, experimenters, frequent misusers - and there is no sense in regarding them as if they were all the same. Prevention activity in relation to awareness and beliefs needs to be targeted just as much as any other drug prevention activity.

6.15     For many young people alcohol, tobacco and illicit drugs inhabit one and the same world rather than constituting separate domains. The possible influence on their illicit drug-taking behaviour which is exerted by the climate of ideas on licit drugs needs therefore to be considered. There is clear evidence from US data that early use of licit drugs increases the risk of developing patterns of illicit drug use at a later stage[2]. The majority of people who have used illicit drugs have previously used tobacco and alcohol. Similarly those who have never smoked or consumed alcohol rarely report use of illicit drugs. Alcohol and cigarette smoking have been found to be the most powerful predictors of marijuana use for both females and males and the relationship strongest where the cigarette smoking had begun before the individual was aged 17.

6.16     In Britain some of the strongest evidence for the association between alcohol use and illicit drug use is contained in the 1996 British Crime Survey.[1]

6.17    The table below shows a strong association across all age ranges between drug misuse and alcohol consumption:

**Percentages of respondents consuming different levels of alcohol who have used drugs ever or in the last month, by age groups**

| | Alcohol use level | | | | |
|---|---|---|---|---|---|
| | Never | Light drinker | Moderate drinker | Heavy drinker | Average |
| Drug use | | | | | |
| Ever/ | | | | | |
| Lifetime | | | | | |
| 16-29 | 20 | 37 | 55 | 70 | 45 |
| 30-59 | 12 | 19 | 29 | 36 | 22 |
| All | 14 | 24 | 37 | 49 | 29 |
| Last Month | | | | | |
| 16-29 | 6 | 9 | 18 | 31 | 15 |
| 30-59 | 1 | 2 | 3 | 6 | 2 |
| All | 2 | 4 | 7 | 15 | 6 |

Note: Heavy drinkers for the purposes of this study comprised those consuming 2+ units a day; moderate drinkers those on one or more units a day (but less than two); light drinkers were those on less than one unit a day. The proportion of respondents in each category was: heavy drinkers, 16%; moderate drinkers, 17%; light drinkers, 56%; non-drinkers, 11%. Those who did not know their alcohol consumption or refused to disclose it have been excluded. Source 1996 BCS (weighted data).

6.18    Numerous other studies in Britain have identified the fact of simultaneous use of tobacco, alcohol and illicit drugs by young people. In one survey[3] in 1994 of 48,297 young people aged between 11 to 16, it was found that at age 15, 22% of boys and 27% of girls were classified as smokers, 62.3% of boys had consumed alcohol compared to 58.3% of girls, and 24.7% of boys and 20.3% of girls had consumed cannabis.

6.19    Considerably higher percentages of tobacco, alcohol and illicit drug use have been identified in research carried out in specific cities. In a 1996 survey[4] of 758 school children surveyed in Dundee, for example, it was found that at age 15/16, 68.2% of pupils had smoked, 70% had drunk alcohol on at least one occasion and 56.7% had tried at least one illicit drug.

6.20    Furthermore, alcohol is as much a "dance drug" as ecstasy or amphetamines. Young people live in a society which heavily advertises alcohol and tobacco, and where they are readily and lawfully accessible, and the advertising of "alcopops" has on occasion seemingly been targeted at young people and has at times veered towards open encouragement of drunkenness. To establish causal connections between use of one type of psychoactive substance and another is notoriously difficult, but our conclusion is that if society intends to provide young people with an environment which helps them not to take illicit drugs (or to abuse volatile substances), or to reduce the harms which they do, the climate of awareness and beliefs on alcohol and tobacco must be seen as part of the context. The guidance which the then Department for Education issued in May 1995 on drug prevention, sensibly in our view, covered them all. So has guidance issued by the Scottish Office Education Department.

6.21 To reduce illicit drug misuse we believe that individuals need to be engaged in the decisions which they take. By this we mean that individuals need to feel there is a purpose to the decisions which they take and that they are realisable. The aim is for society to alter the climate in which those decisions are made so as to make the misuse of drugs less acceptable and thus influence individuals away from them. That climate is more likely to be engendered where people are truly informed, not just with facts but also with values - valuing themselves, valuing the community and valuing other people. In recent years drinking and driving has become much less acceptable than it was which we see as an interesting parallel in terms of change of attitude with what we are proposing should be the aim for society's attitude towards drug misuse.

## THE MEDIA

6.22 The media undoubtedly helps to shape the environment of ideas in which we all live. The national news media effectively sets its own agenda and, because there is only so much space or time for news, reports on drugs more often approach the subject from a crime and law enforcement angle. It makes a better news story than reports on prevention.

6.23 We see little scope for changing the emphasis to any great extent - although the experience of the "Scotland Against Drugs" campaign may prove us to be unduly pessimistic on this score - but we do believe that there is a case for ensuring that journalists have ready access to reliable drug prevention information on matters helpful to drug prevention. We therefore recommend that consideration should be given to establishing a source of authoritative and consistent advice which not only responds to requests but also pro-actively engages journalists on the subject of drugs prevention. In Wales, the Welsh Drug and Alcohol Unit have developed a media strategy in consultation with the national broadcasters. This strategy indicates where the media can access expert knowledge and advice, makes recommendations on the language used in storylines and reports, and provides ideas as to how the media can support the national strategy 'Forward Together'. There is a comparison to be made between our recommendation here and the suggestions in the Report of the Working Group on the Fear of Crime, chaired by Michael Grade, which was published at the end of 1989. It suggested, among other things, that the police, because they were the main source of information on crime, were in a particularly good position to offer the media stories of a positive nature. We are not proposing that a police model should be used for drug prevention but simply making the point that expert and unbiased briefing for journalists on drug issues should be more readily available. The Institute for the Study of Drug Dependence (see chapter 10) is a source of information which should be capable of performing that function.

6.24 It would be wrong to suggest that all coverage given to drugs by all sections of the media is detrimental to reducing drug misuse. We are aware of examples of magazines carrying good material which has had positive results which we applaud. We would like more articles and stories whether in magazines, newspapers, or on television and radio to carry more pro-prevention messages than they currently do. We also see scope for including in journalists' training elements on drugs misuse and prevention, and the effect which the media has on the climate of acceptability of drugs. It might be possible to incorporate it into the GNVQ and SNQ (Scottish National Qualification) journalism courses. The GNVQ course in health and social care might also usefully include reference to the role of the media in reporting drug misuse.

## THE INTERNET

6.25    The Internet is increasingly becoming part of people's lives as access to it becomes more available whether through facilities at home, work, school or elsewhere. Like television, magazines and newspapers it is a source of information. Undoubtedly there is information about drugs on it which is irresponsible. On the other hand there seems to us to be scope for putting the Internet to good use in the cause of drug prevention.

6.26    It enables enquirers to seek information anonymously (a feature which has been found to be wanted by young people[5]) and can operate interactively, both of which may encourage people to use it. Material can be tailored, for example, in terms of the language which is used, to suit target audiences. These attributes are ones which we understand are already being used by some sites on the Internet devoted to drug prevention. Over time we have little doubt that there will be technical developments which will enable it to be used even more innovatively than it is now.

6.27    In short, we believe that the Internet provides a powerful medium for the dissemination of drugs prevention messages which should be exploited. We include against the names of the organisations listed in chapter 10 Website references for those organisations which run them.

## WORKPLACE

6.28    The attitude of employers can also play a part in influencing awareness and beliefs. The need for some employees not to take alcohol and other drugs, because of the nature of their jobs has long been recognised. In the transport industry this has been taken to the stage of making it a criminal offence for certain workers to be unfit through drugs (or drink) while working. We saw in chapter 4 that, subject to civil liberties objections and questions of cost effectiveness, testing was generally regarded as legitimate in high risk settings.

6.29    We feel that all employers should have a policy on drugs and alcohol. The policy will depend on the nature of the work, its setting, the size of the organisation etc. It need not be elaborate but some consideration should have been given to the issues involved.

6.30    It would be reasonable to expect any sizeable organisation which has a stable workforce to have some form of health or pastoral care system which embraced drugs, alcohol and tobacco. We see this as not only of benefit to the individual but, notwithstanding the cost, also of benefit to the employer in terms of a healthier workforce.

6.31    Whether the policy should include any form of testing must be a matter of judgement for individual employers in consultation with their employees. Testing might take place after an accident, randomly, or as part of the selection process for a job. It is essential that whenever a test is done and it is positive that there is a clear policy in relation to the individual concerned. Our firm belief is that in the range of responses there should, where appropriate, be one which provides support and assistance to the employee who is misusing. We understand that the Health and Safety Executive will shortly be issuing new guidance on drugs in the workplace.

*WOMEN*

6.32  We think the place of women in the environment of awareness and beliefs deserves a special mention. Drug misuse among them tends to be more hidden than it is in the rest of the population and, because their drug taking is seen as explicitly going against their conventionally perceived role as nurturers and providers, there is a tendency for them to become cut off from the norms of society. This assumption that their drug taking is somehow less acceptable than the same activity in men should be challenged. In order to do so service providers should ensure that they do not fall into the trap of stereotyping women drug misusers and that women are actively involved in the planning, development and provision of responses to drug misuse.

*YOUTH*

6.33  Young people, while being part of larger society, belong to a society (which includes many subsets) of their own. They mostly associate with friends of the same age, they go to the same places as other young people, and as a body they will often have concerns that the older generation do not always share, for example, on the environment and their employment prospects. Similarly their attitudes on drugs are quite likely to be at variance with older people's and generally less condemnatory. They are more likely than adults to regard drugs as an accepted part of life even if they do not misuse them themselves. But even among youth there will be variations in beliefs towards drugs. While some may favour decriminalisation of some drugs, others will not.

6.34  The lives of young people are surrounded by influences in which drugs are involved.

6.35  Popular music deserves particular mention since it is regarded by some as a malign influence in encouraging people to take drugs or, at least, in making it a respectable activity. This is not a new view. Indeed we saw in chapter 3 that deeply felt anxieties about the effects of popular entertainments on the morals of young people have been expressed in Britain since early Victorian times.

6.36  Instances of popular music referring to drugs in an equivocal or favourable way can be traced back to the 1920s in US jazz and in subsequent years right up to the present. We would not condone the practice but believe that the position as it is today should be kept in its historical context.

6.37  In the 1970s in the US some attempt was made to ban certain songs from the airwaves but the attempt was found to be impracticable. As it is, we understand that since about 1990 records produced in the US have employed "explicit lyrics" stickers. A similar system is now operated in this country by the British Phonographic Industry (BPI) to advise purchasers and parents that a recording contains explicit lyrics; and broadcasters will sometimes refuse to play on the air material they regard as offensive. The BPI's sticker system does not apply specifically in relation to drugs but applies to swearing and sexual content, based on accepted standards of taste and decency.

6.38  The question then arises of whether the degree of regulation, such as it is, which is currently applied in relation to drugs, is adequate. Our view is that it is not feasible to go further and is probably undesirable. While the larger reputable record companies may be willing and able to use a sticker system the way recordings can and are made and distributed by ever smaller organisations makes complete regulation an impractical proposition. The cost of operating a regulatory mechanism, like a board of censors, say, would be prohibitive. We also suspect that references to drugs in songs probably have little direct impact on drug taking among the people who listen to them. (We think it is highly regrettable that we can only speak in terms of "suspicions". There is a sad lack of research to provide information on the influence of popular music on individuals. In its absence opinions are formed on the basis of views and anecdote which we believe is not good enough. More research is required to fill the gap and to identify what young people are doing, where they are going and in what numbers in their leisure time.)

6.39    Thus while the lyrics in themselves are not, we suggest, something about which we need be very concerned we feel that in drug prevention there is a need for an awareness of the music and dance culture in which young people exist. Its existence is nothing new although its shape and pervasiveness changes with time. It may be right to suppose that the misuse of drugs affects the type of music which is popular at any one time and not the other way round.

6.40    Rather than simply deplore this culture, which every succeeding generation is tempted to do, we believe that it should be used as a resource for drugs prevention. In practical terms we suggest that thought should be given locally to reducing opportunities for dealing where young people congregate and using these places for prevention messages. The places which we have in mind and might be considered for such measures would include dance clubs, concert venues, and record shops although there may well be others too. Some Drug Action Teams and drugs services already work with clubs and pubs to encourage prevention messages. The London Drug Policy Forum in December 1996 issued a code of practice on health and safety at dance venues, "dance till dawn safely"[6] , which we commend, and the Scottish Office have issued guidelines for Scotland.

6.41    There is an availability of books and magazines and information on drugs which is much greater now than in the past. We would regard some of the material as good and some of it as bad. It is often aimed at a young market. The places where it is available should be considered as possible sites for drug prevention efforts.

6.42    Sport is also very much part of young people's existence and there is a ready acceptance of alcohol consumption with some sports and indeed prominent sponsorship of some sports by drinks companies. This very open acceptance of alcohol is part of the wider drugs, alcohol and tobacco context to which we referred in paragraph 6.20. The bodies which are responsible for governing them have anti-drug policies, which cover both psychoactive drugs and performance enhancing drugs such as anabolic steroids, but reports of drug-taking among sportsmen still appear. Sometimes the offender is sacked and other times he is taken back into the fold on the basis that he will undertake treatment and become abstinent - there is an inconsistency in these two approaches which the young may find difficult to make sense of.

6.43    Style also plays a greater part in most young people's lives than it used to, whether in terms of hairstyle or body shape or in terms of the clothes which they wear. Drug associations can be found here too with some drugs being used in an attempt to improve the look of the body (rather than for improving sporting ability) and in drug images being used in the design of clothes.

6.44    In short, young people (and older people too although they may be less aware of it) live in a society which acknowledges and accepts drugs to some extent, a state of affairs which arises from environmental factors.

6.45 Young people in tertiary education form a sector of their own. Many of them will be living away from home for the first time and if there is a pro-drug culture at the institution any vulnerability which a student has may be accentuated. This vulnerability might manifest itself in terms of initiation, continued misuse or more dependent misuse.

6.46 Surprisingly there appears to be very little information on the prevalence of problems of misuse in tertiary education and they may be no better or worse than other similarly aged populations. But it does seem to us to be an environment to which more attention should be given in the cause of drugs prevention. We do not think we can here give a detailed analysis of the measures which might be taken - that could possibly form the content of a separate report in its own right - but local services, student unions, university authorities and student health staff should have on their agendas drug education and prevention measures. We understand that the Committee of Vice-Chancellors and Principals have taken some first steps by issuing information on drug misuse.

*THE OFFICIAL RESPONSE*

6.47 As we have said earlier drug prevention has in the past tended not to take on the environmental perspective of awareness and beliefs. It has tended to centre on the individual and how they might reduce harm to themself rather than attempt to shape their values, although the one is likely to influence the other.

6.48 The Department of Health's publicity campaigns have perhaps come closest to attempting to influence attitudes. These started in 1985 with the "heroin screws you up" campaign which emphasised the social consequences of drugs misuse. It was followed in 1986 with another campaign which again concentrated on heroin and which aimed to show how to refuse drugs on offer without losing face. In 1987 heroin continued as the drug of focus but the main purpose was to warn existing misusers of the dangers of spreading the HIV virus through sharing injecting equipment.

6.49 In 1988 and 1989 the campaign shifted so as not to be specific to any single drug. In the 1990 campaign the key objective was to deter those at risk from taking drugs at all and to discourage experimenters with drugs and occasional users becoming more heavily involved with drugs. It also warned of the dangers of losing control through misusing drugs.

6.50 1991 and 1992 saw the introduction of solvent misuse to the campaign and the production of two booklets. The aim was to raise the awareness of parents of children between 8 and 16 years. The central campaign was supported by locally-based campaigns. The 1994 campaign had the theme "talk to your child about drugs before someone else does" and was backed up with a new leaflet.

6.51 It is difficult to assess just how effective these campaigns have been in influencing awareness and beliefs. It is probable that they have had some effect although without stemming the rise in drug misuse. However lessons have been learned during the course of the campaigns which have, for example, pointed to a greater degree of success when there has been a local focus, a focus on parents, or a focus on reducing harm rather than advocating abstinence.

6.52 The aim of the Health Education Authority's 1995-96 campaign, undertaken on behalf of the Department of Health, was to replace some of the myths on drugs with facts to enable young people to make decisions based on sound information. In pursuing that aim the HEA tried to support local activity so as to give the campaign a "bottom up" as well as a "top down" approach.

6.53    There was careful preparation for the campaign. This involved a national survey of 5000 11-35 year olds and some in-depth research of children and their parents, and careful consideration of the vehicles which might be used for the messages. Among those used were magazines, television and radio which are known to reach large proportions of young people. But in addition the HEA targeted young people in their social settings by putting the helpline number (which is not only for use in a crisis) on the caps of bottles in clubs, on postcards left in pubs, clubs and wine bars and by putting information on record shop bags.

6.54    We very much favour these attempts to reach young people by different means and in different settings. As we have said earlier, different age groups, non-users, occasional misusers and regular misusers will be receptive to different messages and different modes of delivery depending on their existing awareness and beliefs, their age, etc. Continued attempts need to be made to target specific messages at specific groups with more emphasis being put on distinguishing between non-users, misusers and polydrug misusers, and even between problematic and non-problematic misusers. The way to achieve this may be through very localised activity. Given the links between drug misuse and alcohol consumption, pubs, off licences, clubs and the like would appear to be obvious locations for targeting.

6.55    We remain unconvinced that, as yet, sufficient attempts have been made to reach young people in the ethnic minorities, women and older drug misusers. Greater efforts in these areas are needed.

6.56    There is obviously a limit to the breadth which the HEA's campaign can have at any one time but we would expect it to broaden and develop with time, which it is showing signs of doing.

6.57    Much of the activity undertaken by the HEA in England had been paralleled in Scotland by the work of the Health Education Board for Scotland (HEBS). Mass media campaigns have been mounted since autumn 1995 with a focus on parents and young people respectively. The parents campaign has concentrated on encouraging parents to develop their "know-how" in terms of engaging in dialogue with teenagers. Television advertising has been supported by extensive distribution of the HEBS publication The Facts of Drugs: A Parent's Guide. The teenager campaign has been more drug specific but has underlined the unpredictable nature of illegal drugs. Again this has been complemented by publications which in addition to giving "health warnings" have provided information on the legal aspects of drug misuse.

6.58    Other HEBS activities have included the production of It's My Life, a video based pack distributed to all secondary schools and community centres, targeted at pupils and parents, support for a community based demonstration project and the production of an information dataset on drug misuse in Scotland. Information on drug misuse is also available through HEBS Web Site. All of the activities have been based on, or relate to, an extensive research or needs assessment project undertaken in 1994-95.

6.59    The credibility of the messages is enormously important if the awareness and beliefs of individuals are going to be influenced. The HEA's messages are very largely health based predicated on a survey finding that 61% of misusers said they would stop misusing if there was evidence of a health risk. This figure seems to us improbably high and a reflection of the difference between what people say they will do and what they actually do. Another aspect of the messages which we should like to mention is the balance to be struck between the desired feelings generated by taking the drug and the undesirable health consequences. For those who misuse the drug in question and know its effects absence of any mention of the desirable effects is likely to reduce the credibility of the whole message. This reinforces our earlier suggestion that messages may need to have a very specific target. We would also advise caution in the use of slang to describe particular substances. The slang is likely to change from place to place and with time so that to avoid confusion and possible ridicule it is important to retain the proper name as well as any slang terms which are used.

6.60    We understand that evaluation of the HEA's 1995-96 campaign has led to some interesting conclusions, two of which we will mention here. First, the mass audience of information programmes does not take sufficient account of the different people who form the mass audience and, second, the obvious one that providing people with information does not necessarily lead to attitudinal or behavioural change. The first underlines our views on targeting and the second suggests that the provision of information should be but one part of a wider continuing drugs prevention effort. Stepwise learning and not forgetting what has gone before are important elements in formulating drugs campaigns.

6.61    We have remarked in preceding paragraphs that the HEA's messages are essentially about the health consequences of taking drugs. The question arises of whether this is enough. We live in a society which makes the production, supply and possession of these substances unlawful on the basis that they cause social problems so why shouldn't the messages say that drug taking is socially unacceptable as well as unhealthy? This approach might go beyond the HEA's brief but we think it is a question that deserves further consideration. If messages concentrate too much on the health consequences it is comparatively easy for the drug taking individual to dismiss the risks as small. Other approaches might involve the risks of jeopardising relationships; that it is irresponsible to break the law (and being caught and convicted could have knock-on consequences in terms of job etc); that taking drugs supports drug trafficking and all that goes with it; that to take drugs and get out of control may be to recklessly expose oneself (and others) to danger and expect others to pick up the pieces; that violence is sometimes associated with drugs; and that regular use can lead to debt. That is, that the individual has a responsibility to themself and other people. Another approach might be to point to the risks of being ripped off - any drug transaction involves illegality and is not subject to the safeguards which apply to most consumer goods and you cannot be sure of what you're getting.

6.62    In Scotland, the Scotland Against Drugs Campaign was established in May 1996 with funding of £1 million. It has the support of all the political parties in Scotland and an Advisory Council, with broad membership interests, and encourages support from business and the media amongst others. The campaign aims to raise awareness of the drugs misuse problem in Scotland and to promote and facilitate a cultural shift in the attitude towards drugs.

6.63    Activities have included an advertising campaign targeted on two groups - young people (both users and non-users) and older Scots; a schools survey of drug misuse followed by an interactive television debate; and a shop-a-dealer event. The work of the Campaign builds on the recommendations of the Ministerial Drugs Task Force Report[7].

6.64    Funding of £2m was made available to the Campaign in 1997-8 whose work continued to be aimed at harnessing the support and partnership of business and the media and attracting the involvement of local communities and individuals behind efforts to tackle drug misuse in Scotland.

## NEIGHBOURHOOD AND COMMUNITY

6.65    While the previous section has looked at the level of wider society's attitude towards drug misuse this section will look at the level of local community. This level lies somewhere between societal level and individual level and will itself be affected by both. That is not to suggest that all communities are the same. They come in many different shapes, sizes and forms.

6.66    In the previous section we said that we saw limited scope for changing the national news media's emphasis in the approach it takes to reporting on drugs issues. Experience suggests however that local media may be more receptive and more interested in carrying stories on or favourable to drugs prevention. We suggest that Drug Action Teams (DATs) should engage the local media so as to achieve coverage for drugs which supports prevention. The effort is likely to need to be sustained not only by DATs but by the police, doctors, health educators and others, if media coverage is not to slide back into concentrating on crime and law enforcement activities. The Central Drugs Co-ordination Unit has distributed to DATs a useful guide on handling the media. Many DATs now have media strategies and protocols, and others have included the subject in their action plans.

6.67    The attitude of the community towards drug misuse will undoubtedly have a bearing on an individual's own beliefs and actions. The community's beliefs are likely to be shaped by the wider society of which they are part and also by rather more immediate influences. These might be the nuisance caused by dealers and misusers or indeed the absence of any evidence of misuse. Where drugs misuse in the community appears to be implicitly condoned by a blind eye being turned towards it we believe that efforts should be made to change the acceptability. There are many examples of this being done in the UK. The initiators might be the police, the local authority, tenants' associations, or other groups or a combination of these. In chapter 5 we looked at some of the things which can be done at local community level to improve the environment in the cause of drug prevention.

6.68    Also significant at local level is the attitude which is taken to the use of alcohol. It is part of the spectrum of misused substances. In Wales alcohol is an essential part of every team's remit which also includes volatile substance abuse. But that is not the case for DATs in England and Scotland. We are aware that in England around 50% of all DATs have decided to tackle alcohol misuse alongside drugs misuse and, given the similarity of some of the aspects of that misuse, we regard it as a sensible approach. We also believe there is a case for all DATs in England and Scotland to take on volatile substance abuse too - at present about 70% do. We would like to see all DATs seriously consider dealing with them all together.

6.69    Religion is part of the local make-up of influences. Different faiths will have different levels of influence on their adherents. It is not clear whether the attitudes to drugs which are formed by people of particular faiths are a result of their religious beliefs or a consequence of the way in which they live because they are members of a particular faith. It is probably a combination of both. And while some religions may help protect their members from drug misuse membership of a religion does not guarantee absence of drug misuse. Adherence to other particular beliefs, which would not normally count as membership of religion, might also serve to protect some people.

6.70    The school might also be regarded as being part of the neighbourhood and community. Our report on Drug Education in Schools,[8] set out ACMD's views on how that should be approached and we are glad that recent Government policy has to a great extent taken on our recommendations. There is a further recommendation which we would like to add to those earlier ones and that is that personal social and health education (PSHE) should be included as part of the statutory national curriculum. We feel we are supported in that recommendation by OFSTED's 1997 report into drug education in schools[9] which found that, overall, drug education through a personal social education programme was more coherent and effective than through a tutorial system. It would also allow other, broader issues such as citizenship and parent education to be offered to young people through the school curriculum as part of the preparation of young people for adult life. However, a substantial change such as this will require significant long term support, including appropriate teacher training at initial and in-service levels.

6.71    In that same publication there is reference to some evidence of an increase in the last year of drug related incidents in schools. In order to maintain a low level of exclusions and given the desirability of avoiding such a course of action except in the last resort, there is a need for teachers (in particular head teachers) and school governors, and members of school boards in Scotland, to be adequately trained, both in initial and in-service training programmes to identify and manage situations effectively. It is very important that the pupils who are excluded are subsequently and immediately given the help and support they require.

6.72    The Department for Education and Employment Schools Circular 4/95, "Drug Prevention and Schools" states that head teachers must retain the responsibility for deciding how to respond to particular incidents but "the fact that certain behaviour could constitute a violation of the criminal law should not, in itself, be taken as automatically leading to an exclusion of a pupil". The circular goes on to say that schools will want to develop a repertoire of responses, incorporating both sanctions and counselling, reflecting the different kinds of drug related offences, such as possession of an illegal drug, individual use and selling or sharing drugs with other pupils. There will, in many instances, be pressure from parents to attempt a hard line approach, in the belief that in so doing, children are being "protected". The statutory responsibility of a school has to take into account both a pupil's educational and personal needs, as well as the school's needs to take appropriate disciplinary action.

6.73    Children who are not attending school are a particular worry and deserve targeted prevention action. This might be undertaken by education welfare officers, pupil referral units, the social services dealing with young people in care, or the youth service in its various forms.

6.74    The youth services have a contribution to make to drug education which is acknowledged in a 1997 OFSTED report.[10] The report recognises and identifies much good work in youth service. We are worried that the services are declining not only because when expenditure has to be cut youth services have often been an easy target but also because there is sometimes a lack of suitable settings in which they can operate. The problems tend to be exacerbated when the services are absorbed into the leisure departments of local authorities where they can lose their identity. We recommend renewed reliance should be put on the youth services in providing drugs education taking into account the findings of OFSTED's report.

6.75    Perhaps the most important influence of all within the neighbourhood is the establishment of friendship networks but we cover that in the section on the individual.

## THE FAMILY

6.76    We reviewed the effects of family influence in chapter 3. Most families, most of the time, will act as bulwarks against drug misuse. They achieve this through the parents adopting an approach which includes listening and responding to their children, acting consistently, defining boundaries and supervising them well. This list of qualities is by no means exhaustive but covers some of the skills which are essential to good parenting and we are in no doubt that supporting parents through a range of interventions which will have benefits in influencing children's awareness and beliefs so as not to misuse drugs. That benefit is part of a wider one of producing socially responsible children. Conversely, harsh and erratic discipline, parental conflict, and lack of parental interest or time, will tend to work the other way.

6.77    No matter how good the parenting skills of these families they do need to be aware of, and know how to cope with, the existence of drugs. It is not just a matter of the parents being provided with information. They also need advice on how to approach the subject with their children. The Department of Health (whether directly or indirectly though the Health Education Authority) has undertaken publicity campaigns. They have over the years produced leaflets on drug and solvent misuse which have been pitched at parents. Their latest publication "A parents' guide to drugs and solvents" (1996) and the "Facts of drugs" issued by the Health Education Board for Scotland continues that pattern. The production of these sorts of publications we regard as a very necessary part of the information providing service and we were glad to see that the latest parents' guide included advice on how to approach their children on the subject.

6.78    What we have said in the last two paragraphs applies to most families. But it seems to us that there are situations where the awareness and beliefs of the family will not act to prevent drug misuse among children. Some families are more likely than others to have children who are vulnerable to the misuse of drugs; children who are looked after and those who have been abused are more likely to take drugs than their counterparts (and to progress to dependent or problematic misuse); and children of parents who are drug takers and children who have siblings who are drug takers are more likely than other children to take drugs. We believe therefore that these "family" situations should attract especial attention for drugs prevention and early intervention measures - they offer a promise of high rewards in reducing misuse. We recommend that the professionals who work in such situations, who will include social workers, educational welfare officers, health visitors, school nurses and general practitioners, should have some drugs training and that schools should be made aware of the possibility that children with problems may be part of families with drug related problems and should know where to seek advice, for example, from community drug teams.

## THE INDIVIDUAL

6.79   The level of awareness and beliefs of individuals will, of course, be influenced by the society and family in which they live but there is also an altogether more personal world in which they exist. They will have their own self-esteem and views on where they fit in with society, which will include their views on drugs.

6.80   It is doubtful that a young person's aspirations are much different from those of previous generations in terms of a wish for friends, housing, a job and security. But job and housing prospects are less good than they were a generation or so ago putting today's youngsters under different and increasing pressures.

6.81   The young person today is in a society where the acceptability of the use of drugs and the availability of them has changed markedly in recent years. The majority have still not yet tried drugs, although as many as 45% might have done, and around 15% may misuse regularly. But there is probably a general acceptance that illegal drugs, and especially cannabis, are "around". What separates the non-user, the person who has tried and the person who misuses regularly is unclear.

6.82   However as children get older it is probably friends who have the greatest influence over their awareness and beliefs. We think the concept of peer pressure is not a particularly useful one in trying to explain drug misuse among young people but that it is better to think in terms of youngsters seeking out and falling in with essentially like-minded friends. We considered the matter in some detail in chapter 3. Thus there will be groups of young people who have a tendency not to take drugs and groups which have a tendency to take them. The use of this characteristic in the cause of drug prevention should be considered further.

6.83   We have already seen in chapter 4 that there is a lack of clarity about what constitute peer interventions, programmes or education. But there is inherent attractiveness in drug prevention approaches which involve young people interacting with one another and it seems to be popular with those who take part. We would however wish to caution against regarding all peer approaches as a panacea. Because there is little evidence of their effectiveness we do not yet know whether they work in terms of reducing misuse although such evidence as there is points to some measure of success in terms of harm reduction. It is important that where peer approaches are adopted that clear objectives for them are established at the outset, that the whole process is carefully controlled and that the results are evaluated.

6.84   Throughout this chapter we have been considering the influences that bear on the individual and feel we must continue to emphasise that these are not compartmentalised but are part of a very broad range which are overlapping and interactive so that much of what has been said in earlier sections will also be relevant to this one.

*Chapter*

# 7 DRUG PREVENTION AND HOUSING

*Housing issues may bear on drug prevention and we see serious practical recommendations evolving from this conclusion. Indeed, the housing question seems to us in many ways to exemplify the fact that prevention must have an environmental dimension. Drug misuse among the homeless is a particularly worrying problem and we recommend action.*

## THE DILEMMA

7.1   Housing questions relating to drug (and alcohol) misuse set a considerable dilemma. On the one hand drug misusers and their families have housing needs like any other citizen and these needs must be met. Providing such people with satisfactory housing is often an integral part of rehabilitation and hence in everyone's interests. On the other hand drug misusers and drug dealers can be unwelcome and disruptive neighbours and communities will understandably be resistant to any policy which seems to dump such problems in their neighbourhood. Communities too have needs and rights.

7.2   Poor housing or lack of access to affordable housing is in many instances a contributory factor in drugs misuse and, at very least, will hinder drug prevention. There is a dearth of research in this area and in the relationship between drugs misuse and homelessness. We return to drugs misuse and homelessness in a later section.

## LOCAL SOLUTIONS ARE NEEDED

7.3   We believe that the general housing dilemma needs sensitive thinking through at local level and that the difficulties can only be resolved by local action and examination of clear and agreed local policies. What we offer in this chapter are some ideas to support that kind of local resolution rather than in any way seeking to propose a master plan for solution of a varied problem with many different kinds of local presentation. We recognise the fact that there are other problems, some of which will inevitably overlap with drug-related problems and especially those of mental health and alcohol.

7.4   While we see the effort having to be made at local level this can only be done in the national context. There is proportionately less social housing (that is, stock owned by local authorities and registered social landlords (the latter of which includes housing associations)) than there used to be and reductions in the state benefits which are available to young people have led to difficulties in them finding accommodation of their own. Under the Housing Act 1996 young homeless people are regarded as in priority need for accommodation if they are vulnerable in some way. Our understanding is that in practice it is very difficult for young homeless persons to qualify.

## "SOCIAL CONTRACT" AS BASIS FOR CONSTRUCTIVE LOCAL POLICIES

7.5    Fundamental to a constructive way of meeting the housing dilemma would perhaps be communities and the relevant agencies accepting as basis for dialogue the idea of a balanced and mutual "social contract". There is a public responsibility to meet the housing needs of drug misusers rather than reject them. That however must be balanced by the reasonable expectation that drug misusers will honour their side of the contract and not disrupt, disturb or threaten the neighbourhoods in which they are housed by anti-social behaviour brought on by misuse, littering with drug-misusing paraphernalia or dealing, whether or not the dealer is also a drug misuser.

7.6    For such a constructive approach to be acceptable and replace tension and confrontation, there must be appropriate support for drug misusers who have been housed in a locality. One part of the local authority (social services) is already under a statutory duty to plan for the needs of drug misusers under community care arrangements. There must be support also for communities and neighbours.

7.7    Another essential ingredient if constructive policies are to be acceptable and workable is that the expectation that drug misusers will respect agreed limits will so far as possible be enforced and antisocial drug-related behaviour (but not the drug taking itself) will not be tolerated. It will not always be easy to distinguish between anti-social behaviour which is drug-related and that which is not.

## MEETING THE HOUSING NEEDS OF DRUG MISUSERS

7.8    At this point it is again worth emphasising the diversity of the problems which are likely to be encountered. Many young drug misusers will have grown up on the estate or in the street in which they are now living and they may still be living in their parental home. Others may have been rehoused in this community after a period of homelessness, institutional treatment or a prison sentence. Some will be currently in treatment while others may not be seriously engaged in seeking help. And as ever we are talking about a spectrum of drugs and drug problems. And they need not be confined to urban settings but will exist in rural communities too.

7.9    We believe that individual housing allocations for drug misusers should be the responsibility of local authority housing departments or housing associations and that it would generally be invidious to involve tenants associations in these decisions although we understand that when in full possession of the facts some are known to have been very helpful. We strongly caution against policies which lead to concentration of drug users on any particular estate. We are unclear of the extent to which tenancies in the voluntary and private sectors may be able to play a part but the scope for them providing accommodation seems to us worth exploring and even stimulating. There may, for example, be a case for local and other authorities helping individuals into private tenancies by paying deposits which would in due course be returnable. We understand that in England at least 100 local authorities currently operate rent guarantee or cash deposit schemes.

7.10   When and if it becomes known by the local authority or housing association that a tenant is a drug misuser they will need to decide what action, if any, to take. We see two broad situations. The test, and the distinction between the two, is whether the misuser's behaviour impinges unreasonably on the community in which he or she lives.

7.11    First, where a drug misuser's activities do not interfere with the normal life of the community we do not believe that the local authority should feel obliged to act. In practice they are unlikely to be aware of the problem's existence. If this sort of drug misuse contravenes the tenancy agreement, as may sometimes be the case, a choice will have to be made on whether and how to enforce it. Rather than move immediately towards eviction we suggest, for reasons which we explain in paragraph 7.15, that an attempt should be made in the first instance to introduce the misuser to the local helping services (eg a community drug team or a local community drug project).

7.12    Second, where a drug misuser's behaviour does impinge on the community, for example, because it is anti-social, leads to dealing or results in used needles and syringes being irresponsibly discarded, we think several types of action might be taken. If dealing is occurring the police should be informed. If the nuisance is something less than that we suggest that the target should be the anti-social behaviour of the misuser. There might still be a need to involve the police but behaviour might also be altered through putting the misuser in touch with the local helping services (as described in the previous paragraph) for appropriate and continuing assistance. The local environment service may be able to assist in dealing with the nuisance of discarded needles and syringes. At the same time it might be appropriate for the local authority to lay down, perhaps in the form of a formal but positive contract, what behaviour is and is not acceptable. If after a period the misuser does not comply thought may have to be given to further sanctions.

7.13    In both these cases the ability of the housing authority to put misusers in touch with helping agencies points to a need for prior arrangements for co-operation to have been made between them at local level. Social services may sometimes also need to be contacted. Community care plans may offer a means of re-integrating misusers. Where children are members of a household where the parents are drug misusers we believe that their welfare is paramount but that the misuse of drugs by the parents should not automatically lead to the children being removed. In considering the welfare of the child it is sensible to involve both drug practitioner and child specialist to help decide what is the most appropriate course of action.

7.14    The types of sanction which are available, feasible and acceptable again need to be considered at local level. Eviction may be possible through the general processes of civil law but the Housing Act 1996 introduced new provisions which strengthened local authorities' powers (and those of housing associations and private landlords) to deal with anti-social behaviour of tenants and their visitors. These will enable local authorities to set up an introductory tenancy scheme for all new tenants. After a period of twelve months the tenancy would become secure unless the local authority had gained possession. The grounds for possession of an existing secure tenancy on the basis of nuisance or annoyance have also been widened to cover such behaviour in the locality of the tenant's home, the behaviour of visitors and the case where there has been a conviction for an arrestable offence in the locality.

7.15    There is a cost attached to the process of eviction. We understand that, in practice, it is cheaper to stabilise the behaviour of a tenant and have them in touch with local helping services and claiming any relevant state benefits than it is to evict them. We have heard how one organisation, Phoenix House, can provide services - sometimes called intensive housing management - to bring about these ends. There is therefore an economic case for considering other measures before eviction. The very fact that eviction is threatened may provide the opening to discuss and alter a tenant's behaviour. We recognise that the economic benefits may not accrue to the housing department but that we suggest is a weakness of the budgetary arrangements and should not be allowed to work against the overall benefit. These considerations lead us to believe that eviction should be an action of last resort.

7.16    There will, as we have already mentioned in paragraph 7.8, be individuals and families who have been treated for their drug misusing problems and need housing afterwards. We see great sense in ensuring that the progress that has been made in treatment or rehabilitation is not negated by inappropriate or delayed housing allocation. Detailed care plans for those moving on from treatment and rehabilitation regimes should include collaboration between drug workers, housing support workers, and others relevant to rehabilitation in the community. The questions of transfers and previous rent arrears should be addressed reasonably early on in a rehabilitation programme so that good, effective planning for housing can be seen as part of an overall package of care.

7.17    While what we have said so far is very much about drug misusers it would be naive to suppose that they are always a clearly discrete group. They may also have mental health, alcohol-related or other problems. These will necessarily have to be kept in mind and policy development should take into account the possibility of inter-related and overlapping problems.

7.18    We are well aware that many housing managers work under very great pressure and may regard our concerns for drug misusers as an unwelcome addition to their tasks. However we believe that in making plans for coping with drug misusers housing managers' work will become less reactive and the communities which they service better places to live.

## DRUGS AND HOUSING PROBLEMS

7.19    At times drug dealing has become a matter of great concern in some housing areas. The problem may relate to dealing behind closed doors, but with a constant to and from of customers, or taking the form of open dealing in corridors or precincts. Residents may feel that drug dealing has become a problem which contributes to an overall state of local environmental decline. It is not only the fact of dealing which is the concern but the fears which the activity generates.

7.20    We believe that communities deserve every possible support in tackling this kind of problem. Dealing in illicit drugs is a criminal act which should not be tolerated or condoned. The problem is likely to be met by police action and possibly also action on tenancies - see paragraph 7.14. Communities need and deserve the assurance of firm action.

7.21    These actions are likely to require different levels of intensity depending on the problems which are being tackled. For example, whereas some situations may require immediate and strict law enforcement to return a neighbourhood to some form of normality, in the longer term there is likely to be a need for different policies involving all the local services and the local community, including local young people.

7.22    In taking intensive action, consideration needs to be given to the probable effects of that action to ensure so far as possible that there are no unintended undesirable consequences. This is a point we also make in chapter 8.

7.23    We are aware that some communities have dealt with open drug dealing which has become a problem in their environment by hiring private security staff. That may be an understandable reaction by a community which rightly or wrongly feels under-supported, but we see dangers in this kind of solution. We are also aware that concierge arrangements have provided some benefits to some estates. They seem to be able to help reduce deterioration but the concierges have sometimes been susceptible to intimidation when they have lived on the estate.

## DRUG PROBLEMS IN THE NEIGHBOURHOOD: WHAT SHOULD COMMUNITIES EXPECT BY WAY OF INFORMATION, SUPPORT AND ACTION?

7.24    We suggest that local authority housing departments and housing associations should review their current policies on tenancies, drug misuse and drug dealing with a view to determining whether the concept of the two-way "social contract" is adequately operationalised. A policy in relation to drug problems should be stated and public, and conveyed to tenants' associations and other relevant bodies. A telephone number should be available for anyone wanting to consult on these issues and there should be ready access to advice and support.

7.25    Some communities have developed their own support systems for dealing specifically with anxieties about neighbourhood drug problems, volatile substance abuse and related housing questions, or such matters are dealt with through the tenants association. There is advantage in a community mobilising its own coping resources, but we are sure that some communities feel so burdened by multiple problems as to find it difficult to tackle these kinds of housing-related drug problems. We would however recommend that wherever possible local communities are empowered and supported so that they can share in finding solutions to the kinds of problems we are talking about here.

## DESIGNING OUT DRUGS

7.26    The concept of designing out crime both to reduce criminal activity and the fear of it is well-understood and is particularly relevant in the context of drugs misuse. Opportunities for dealing and administering drugs in public can be reduced, for example, by reducing the amount of space which does not have an obvious owner, ensuring that dark areas are lit, and making paths and access points to areas visible.

7.27    If necessary thought might be given to providing facilities for drug misusers to discard used needles and syringes so as to reduce risks to others.

7.28    We believe there is benefit to be gained in terms of making a locality less prone to drug related (and other) problems if premises are not allowed to stand empty for any appreciable length of time and repairs to be undertaken quickly. Children require space which has been specifically set aside for recreational purposes to be available to them.

7.29    In considering the facilities which should be available for young people we suggest that young people themselves should be consulted and their views taken into account. There is no point providing something which they will not use. The facilities need to be attractive to all including, for example, young people who may be truanting or who may be temporarily or permanently excluded from main stream schooling. In our view, such young people may be more vulnerable than many others and it is important that they remain in contact with some form of care and supervision. In their design and management, the facilities that are available to the young people should be viewed as offering opportunities for drug prevention and other related health education. The then Department for Education's School Circular 4/95 - Drug Prevention and Schools states particularly that "where a pupil has been excluded for a drug related offence there is clearly a particular continuing need to provide appropriate drug education and support".

7.30    Where community organisations or groups wish to play a part in providing facilities which will help drug prevention we understand that they can run into practical difficulties because the funders often require measurable outputs which in this field can be very difficult to find. We would urge funders not to be too prescriptive and inflexible in their demands. They should consider accepting proxy measures of output or perhaps help the community organisation or group identify acceptable measures.

## DRUG MISUSE AND HOMELESSNESS

7.31    The term "homeless" is used to describe people living in a wide range of circumstances, covering those who meet the statutory criteria for assistance from local housing authorities set out in Part VII of the 1996 Housing Act and those who fall outside it, a group frequently referred to as the single homeless. The single homeless population can include people in different levels of housing need ranging from the extreme of sleeping rough, through emergency night shelters, direct access hostels, squats, bed and breakfast accommodation, longer term hostels, to those staying with friends or relatives on a temporary basis.

7.32    There is no data available which shows the scale of the overall homeless population. In 1996 116,870 households were accepted by local housing authorities in England as statutorily homeless (on the basis that they were unintentionally homeless and in priority need). There are no national figures for the scale of the single homeless population. Researchers for the Joseph Rowntree Foundation have described the problem of producing such figures:

"There is no reliable national estimate of the scale of single homelessness in Britain in the 1990's. Estimates of homelessness and housing need are inextricably linked with definitions of these terms and constrained by the availability of data on persons who fall within given definitions" (Isobel Anderson, Access to housing for low income single people, 1994).

7.33   A limited amount of data is available on the number of rough sleepers in central London, where voluntary sector agencies working with rough sleepers undertake single night head counts twice a year. The most recent count in November 1996 found 357 people sleeping rough in central London.

7.34   The homeless population is heterogeneous. It includes people who are transiently homeless and those who have been homeless for many years; people in every age bracket; men and women; homeless single people and homeless families; British people and recent immigrants; healthy people and people with many different kinds of physical and mental disability.

7.35   The pathways into and out of homelessness are multiple. The size and characteristics of the homeless population will vary over time and across the country, and are likely to be influenced by such factors as economic cycles, unemployment, welfare provisions, housing provision, and the quality of mental care provision.

7.36   The health care needs of the homeless population are many and diverse, while the provision of good quality care is intrinsically difficult. Many homeless people are geographically mobile and may not be registered with general practitioners.

7.37   Within this needful population with its multiple problems, drug misuse is today prevalent as one further problem within the wider mix. It may sometimes constitute the individual's primary and most handicapping disorder, be central to an understanding of why that individual is homeless, and a strong factor in perpetuating that person's state of homelessness. Dealing with the drug dependence may then be the priority need. Other homeless people will however be misusing drugs while also experiencing one or more of a wide range of psychiatric comorbidities including alcohol dependence. Drug problems may in this population co-exist with major physical health problems such as HIV infection and tuberculosis.

7.38   Prevalence estimates for alcohol and drug misuse (and psychiatric disorder) among homeless people are available from the OPCS Psychiatric Morbidity Survey.[1] Dr Michael Farrell has collated publication data which are reproduced in Tables 1 and 2 (below). Explicit operational criteria are given in the original text for the approach used in the diagnosis of both alcohol and drug dependence (see also paragraph 9.38). The comparisons which are made in the following paragraphs between the homeless and the general population can only be indicative because correction for class and age has not been attempted.

7.39   Some of the major inferences which can be drawn from the analysis of the OPCS data for drug misuse among homeless populations in the previous 12 months (Table 1) are as follows:-

   • In overall terms cannabis is the most frequent drug being used (25% aggregate), but significant misuse of other drugs is also found at a level considerably beyond that occurring in the general population.

   • The level of misuse varies greatly between sub-categories of the homeless. The major concern must attach to those categories of people who are sleeping rough or using night shelters. While both of these groups show a 13% prevalence for opiate use, what needs also to be underlined is that in comparison with the general population there is in this sector a greatly increased prevalence for every category of drug.

**Table 1.  Reported drug use "ever" by homeless people during year prior to interview**

Source: Farrell et al (1997).[2] Figures give percentage prevalence within categories
"-" indicates a prevalence too small to estimate

| Drugs | Cannabis | Stimulant | Hallucinogen or Ecstasy | Hypnotic | Opiates | Solvents | Any Drug |
|---|---|---|---|---|---|---|---|
| **General Population** (n = 9741) | 5 | 1 | 1 | 1 | - | - | 5 |
| **Homeless** (n = 1061) | | | | | | | |
| Using hostels | 23 | 8 | 7 | - | 4 | 1 | 25 |
| Using private sector leased accommodation | 15 | 3 | 2 | 1 | 1 | - | 16 |
| Using night shelters | 40 | 20 | 18 | 20 | 13 | 15 | 46 |
| Sleeping rough, but using day centres | 31 | 15 | 13 | 14 | 13 | 3 | 37 |
| Aggregate | 25 | 10 | 9 | 6 | 6 | 3 | 28 |

7.40   Turning to Table 2 and the data on prevalence of dependence we make the following points:-

- Within the operational terms which these investigators employed, alcohol dependence is a considerably more prevalent problem than drug dependence.

- Prevalence for drug dependence varies between categories of homelessness and it is those using night shelters or sleeping rough who record the highest rates. What is to be the cut-off level is somewhat arbitrary, but the 8% prevalence of drug dependence among those sleeping rough and the 11% prevalence in the night shelter group must be cause for concern.

**Table 2.  Diagnosed rates of alcohol and drug dependence among homeless people.**

Source: Farrell et al (1997).[2] Figures give percentage prevalence within categories.
"-" indicates a prevalence too small to estimate

| | Alcohol dependence | Drug dependence on any drug excluding cannabis |
|---|---|---|
| **General population** | 5 | - |
| **Homeless** | | |
| Using hostels | 16 | 3 |
| Using private sector leased accommodation | 4 | 1 |
| Using night shelters | 31 | 11 |
| Sleeping rough, but using day centres | 36 | 8 |

7.41   We have found these OPCS data helpful in the factual basis they provide for estimating the prevalence of drug misuse and drug dependence among different sectors of the homeless population. As already emphasised this is a population with multiple needs, and it is only within that context that one can understand or hope to deal with the levels of drug misuse and dependence which are shown to be part of the picture. Society has a responsibility to try as best possible to help the individual drug user who is homeless in terms of care for that person. We also believe that there are issues here which potentially bear on prevention. First, homelessness may constitute a lifestyle which not only attracts established drug users, but it is also a situation which may for several reasons enhance the risk for initiation of drug use and escalation toward dependence. A young person who becomes homeless is likely to enter an unsupported environment where many people are using many different types of drugs and where drugs will probably be freely available: it is difficult to envisage a situation more encouraging of drug misuse. Any measures which deal more adequately with the root causes of homelessness or which get people out of this state sooner rather than later, are in our view likely to contribute significantly to prevention of drug misuse.

7.42    Along with the emphasis which we place on the need to address the basic problem of homelessness, we also believe that appropriate help needs meanwhile to be targeted at the drug misusing homeless population. We are aware of the inherent difficulties in helping people who will often be out of touch with primary care services, and who may find it difficult to respond to specialist help until housing and other social needs are met. Homeless drug users with multiple problems are going to require an integrated, multisectoral response. We recommend, however, that where a significant problem of homelessness exists within an area, DATs should ensure that responses are developed to meet the needs of homeless drug users. A strong element of outreach is likely to be part of the formula, while co-morbidity problems in this population will often imply the need for support from mental health services. Meeting housing needs will often constitute a priority. Where one intervention is dependent upon another (eg a housing place on medical treatment) services must avoid the situation where an individual benefits from neither because he or she is not immediately eligible for the first intervention. Otherwise the risk is that he or she will never receive the requisite care. Specifically GPs should be willing to fully register patients even if they are homeless.

7.43    Although we believe that there are practical responses to drug problems among the homeless which can and should immediately be got in place or strengthened without further delay, we also believe that this is an issue which would benefit from the insights gained from intersectoral pilot projects and sharing of the experience which would derive.

7.44    There is, we understand, a legislative provision which can inhibit the ability of services to provide accommodation and support to some drug misusers. Section 8 of the Misuse of Drugs Act 1971 makes it an offence for a person concerned in the management of premises to knowingly permit smoking of cannabis on those premises but not the use of most other controlled drugs. For some drug misusers abstinence from cannabis use is, in the short term at least, an unrealistic aim and to them the anomaly of other drug use being permissible on the premises is hard to explain. In providing misusers with treatment, rehabilitation or other forms of intervention which stop short of prohibiting cannabis use on the premises these services break the law; or if they enforce the prohibition they have to evict the misuser exposing him to the harms which the treatment is intended to prevent. For services it is an unsatisfactory position which should be reviewed.

## CONCLUSIONS

7.45   As will be apparent from the foregoing we see a great deal of scope for housing-related decisions and actions to be used for drug misuse prevention. The question remains of how the ideas should be put into practice.

7.46   Traditionally housing managers have tended to regard their role very much as confined to the mechanics of allocation and management without much regard for the problems of individuals which might impact on the wider community. We think this approach should and could be broadened through training. Training is essential if our recommendations are going to be successfully put into effect. Housing managers need, for example, to be aware of the problems to which drug misusers can give rise and where to obtain advice and help for drug misusing tenants. There should, as we said in paragraph 7.13, be formal links between helping agencies and housing authorities which might, in practice, amount to little more than an established telephone contact number. The link between drug misuse and crime is such that in operating a policy for drug misusers housing managers may find other problems which they have to address diminishing.

7.47   The role of housing managers should be part of the housing policy for drugs misusers – see paragraph 7.24. A person in the housing department needs to be responsible for that policy. The policy should include liaison as necessary with social services, health services, education services, and the local police.

7.48   We regard it as an omission if any DAT does not have on it the local director of housing. There is a need for housing to be taken into account at the strategic level when dealing with drug misuse locally and the right place for this is the Drug Action Team.

7.49   We also believe that there is a danger of housing departments up and down the country going through the same hoops as one another without building on experience from elsewhere. We are not aware of a mechanism for developing and sharing good practice and believe that one should be found.

7.50   Drugs misuse and homelessness represents a special problem which requires particular attention and we believe that at a local level DATs should engineer the development of responses to meet the needs of homeless drug users. This will require co-operation between a number of services. However, part of the problem, it seems to us, arises at national level from the way housing benefit regulations operate for young people and we believe that they should be reviewed by the Government.

*Chapter*

# 8 DRUG MARKETS

*The environmental issue on which this chapter focuses is the existence within some communities of open, concentrated drug markets which may both facilitate dissemination of drugs and become a public nuisance. Probably only a small percentage of drugs are sold in this way and there can be a downside as well as an upside to attempting to close down such dealing. But on balance we believe that it is in the public interest to take planned action against such markets.*

## INTRODUCTION

8.1     In this chapter we consider the effect of drug markets on the environment. It is the open street drug markets which have such an impact on a locality and it is with these that this chapter is mostly concerned. Where they exist a blind eye should not be turned. The effect on the environment is not simply a function of the supply transaction but comprises everything which goes with it. For example, markets will attract drug misusers to the area, which may lead to increased fear of crime for residents, the possibility of violence between dealers, and discarded needles and syringes.

8.2     While it is these markets which have the most effect on a neighbourhood, paradoxically they probably do not account for a very large proportion of the drug dealing which takes place. It seems to us that, for the most part, drug transactions in the United Kingdom go unnoticed by the community at large, taking place in pubs, clubs and behind closed doors (for example, from private homes).

8.3     In its earlier report on "Police, Drug Misusers and the Community"[1] the Advisory Council considered in detail the interactions between misusers and enforcement and prosecution agencies, drug services and the community, and with the extent to which there is scope for reducing the supply and demand for drugs and the harm they cause to individuals and society. It is not our intention in this chapter to try and cover all the same issues again but we feel this report would be incomplete without some reference to drugs markets.

8.4     Before moving on, however, there is one theme which we would wish to highlight from the 1994 report and that is the need to site drugs prevention in the wider context of community safety. As we said then, there is a need for local partnerships to be established with all the relevant local agencies involved and a common purpose formulated among them. Communities themselves also need to be part of the process. It is in this setting, and not the police acting in isolation, that the rest of this chapter should be read.

## MARKETS

8.5     A drugs market's characteristics are, like any other market, formed by

- the type of good which is being sold

- who is buying, and

- who is selling.

And, as with any other market, it will constantly adjust to changes in circumstances – for example, change in what people want, what the goods cost to supply, and effects of policy changes.

## TYPES OF DRUG

8.6   Markets for drugs will be influenced by the different types of drugs and the levels of use. For example, frequent and regular purchases of a drug will lead to a different sort of market from one where purchases are infrequent. And the market where a large number of purchasers gather for one event (even if the users are individually infrequent purchasers) is going to be different again.

## TYPES OF USER

8.7   Dependent users will tend to seek assured sources of supply and assurance of the quality of the drug being bought. There are advantages to both the user and the dealer in maintaining that relationship. Regular business and lower prices are likely to be the outcome when compared with more open deals, perhaps in the street.

8.8   Occasional users may be deterred from use if search costs are high. The "price" paid for any drug includes not just the money which changes hands but also the time taken to find a supplier, the risk of being ripped off, the risk of poor quality drugs and the risk of being caught by the police.

## TYPES OF SUPPLIER

8.9   The supply line runs from the producers, sometimes through importers, wholesalers and retailers. Drug markets are complicated by the fact that many frequent users are also dealers, but not all dealers are users and in the main people engage in supplying drugs to make profits. Dealers who are users are more likely to be involved in supplying dependence forming drugs than a drug such as ecstasy, for example. The profits available depend on the level of demand from users and the risks involved (both from law enforcement bodies and competitors) in the trade. The numbers willing to engage in the trade may be affected by the profits which can be made from other legitimate and illegitimate activities.

8.10   Selling networks are often complex and users are most likely to find their way into them, for the first time at least, through friends or someone known to them in the local community. Telephone networks, with an apparent increase in mobile telephones, and delivery services may develop as market conditions change. Many people are supplied by members of their own family.

8.11   There is also little doubt that some doctors through liberal prescribing or insufficient care in prescribing help supply the illicit market as therapeutic drugs are diverted to it. The Department of Health's review of the guidelines on clinical management for drug misuse and dependence should provide some scope for addressing these problems. There are also occasional diversions from wholesale sources.

8.12    Solvents which may be misused are, of course, available through regular retail outlets and around the home. Sometimes when sniffable substances have been diverted or stolen from industrial premises, they may be sold specifically for misuse.

*THE ROLE OF PRICES*

8.13    Most market transactions are governed by the maxim "if the price is right". The ability of drug users to purchase and how much they can purchase of a particular drug will depend on

- the price of the drug

- the price of substitutes

- the price of complements (i.e. associated paraphernalia)

- availability of income

- search or other costs

8.14    While it has tended to be thought that frequent or dependent users would be insensitive to price changes evidence is beginning to emerge from the United States and Holland that such changes can lead to behavioural change.[2,3] Even where the price change is small it may nonetheless have an effect on consumption.

8.15    Marketing techniques are as evident in the drugs market as any other. For example, one drug will be sold in a quantity and a purity so as to compete with another and dealers will sometimes encourage people into debt so as to ensnare them. Unscrupulous money lenders can become involved in the process too.

## DRUG MARKETS, PROBLEMS AND THE ENVIRONMENT

8.16    Open street markets have an effect on the environment which is obvious. They tend to be confined to deprived areas in large urban conurbations and are often used by drug users as the markets of "last resort" if regular sources fail. The sites are liable to be associated with disruption and violence from trade disputes, intensive local drug use may lead to discarded drug using equipment, legitimate traders can be affected and an area go into serious decline, and they lead to a fear of crime in local residents.

8.17    While the environmental impact of other dealing, for example at pubs, clubs, sporting venues, or through dealers' houses may not be so great they can also lead to noise nuisance and other disturbance and indirect effects by, for example, drawing attention to the pervasiveness of drugs in the community and fear of crime brought on by consumption and dealing.

## POLICY INTERVENTIONS DIRECTED AT MARKETS

8.18    Any intervention directed at a market should, in assessing the overall outcome, take account of the fact that markets respond to change quickly and sometimes unexpectedly. The intervention will lead to benefits and harms which should as far as possible be foreseen and always evaluated. Complete elimination of an established market is probably an unrealistic aim. Interventions against newly emerging drugs would be expected to be more effective than those against established markets.

8.19    Intervening at the point of production or some other point of major transaction unfortunately now seems to have little, if any, effect on the drugs market. That is not to say that we think it is useless intervening at these points – such actions are necessary in order to stop the market mushrooming.

8.20    While they may not be responsible for the majority of drugs transactions we believe that enforcement action against open markets is necessary either to reduce the chances of an area going into decline or to help re-vitalise an area. Not to take action against blatant dealing, whether in these sites or elsewhere, must have a symbolic importance which should not be disregarded. It suggests a "don't care" attitude which can only affect the climate of beliefs adversely.

8.21    Open markets will tend to be disrupted – that is, the buyer and seller kept separate – by enforcement action whether this is through surveillance, stop and search, use of close circuit television (CCTV) etc. And the more open the market the more it will be affected. The market is likely to respond by sellers and buyers adopting less open transactions, moving transactions to a different place locally, or moving the market site.

8.22    It seems to us that this form of enforcement will probably help to deter inexperienced users from buying drugs in these markets although it may add to the excitement for some. There is also a prospect of a market becoming regarded as a particularly risky place for both buyers and sellers which undermines its reputation – just how real that prospect is, is unclear.

8.23    In taking this action an open market may become more closed. For the local community that in itself is likely to be a desirable consequence.

8.24    Another possible consequence is that an open market may be displaced through enforcement action and some people would argue that the use of resources to produce that result is not worthwhile and might even have the result of spreading misuse.

8.25    Our view however is that the benefits are likely to outweigh the disadvantages. Experience from the United States suggests that when displacement of a drugs market occurs the effect may not be total and that some dealing stops. In additional the local community is likely to be glad to see a drugs market displaced from its neighbourhood (although a neighbourhood which receives the residual market will not be). Dealers will probably regard a new site as second best. Casual buyers may have greater difficulty in making contact with sellers.

8.26    In considering taking action against dealers police forces should bear in mind that there are different sorts of dealers. While there can be little sympathy for regular dealers primarily motivated by financial gain there will be some smaller scale sellers, who are engaged in low-level dealing while they are unable or unwilling to secure legitimate employment and who are also misusers, for whom it will be appropriate to try and secure help from treatment agencies.

8.27    As has often been remarked the contact which drug misusers have with the criminal justice system provides a prime opportunity for helping misusers which should not be missed. Arrest referral schemes offer an example of how that contact can be used. The

1994 ACMD report "Police, Drug Misusers and the Community"[1] (paragraphs 4.10 and 4.11) suggested that there was a need for drug services and the police to develop a common purpose and shared agenda if community strategies were going to be successfully implemented. We see an important role for DATs, which were established after the 1994 report, in helping to establish the necessary partnerships (see also paragraph 8.4).

8.28    There appear to be some conditions which help sustain an open market. For example, ease of access, a level of street activity to help mask illicit activity, and good using sites (for example, lavatories in fast food restaurants).

8.29    These examples are by no means exhaustive and it may well be possible to identify other characteristics which help to keep a particular market in being. Once identified it may be possible to influence these characteristics so as to make life difficult for the market to operate. Developing and implementing these policies is likely to require involvement of the local community, local authority, the police, local business interests and others. In deciding what can be done care will need to be taken to ensure that there are no unacceptable consequences – see paragraph 8.18.

8.30    The street scene which can develop around an open market in dependent drugs can unwittingly be exacerbated by

• planning decisions which lead to the surrounding area having high levels of temporary accommodation such as hostels, and bed and breakfast hotels

• managers of these establishments ensuring that residents spend only a small amount of time in them

• accommodation in the area being allocated to problem drug users.

8.31    The undesirability of perpetuating a street culture through practices of this sort is obvious. Young people are particularly at risk of being exploited by those selling drugs.

8.32    The location of health service facilities and dispensing chemists can impact on the development of the street scene. For example, needle exchanges can attract large numbers of drug users to one place. A more dispersed network of provision for example through pharmacies might reduce that clustering effect but might also increase the incidence of equipment sharing. The particular circumstances of the area will be paramount and any changes would need careful planning and phasing.

8.33    The Home Office report "Tackling Local Drug Markets",[4] which was published in February 1997, and on which this section has drawn, provided some detailed suggestions for tackling drug markets through treatment services, enforcement, and situational prevention.

8.34    We think it is also worth mentioning in this chapter dealing in semi-public places like pubs, clubs, fast food restaurants etc which are places where drug deals are also struck. The report referred to in the previous paragraph suggested some ways in which situational prevention methods could be used to impede dealing. In relation to pubs we are aware that the licensed trade has, with assistance from the police, taken steps to reduce dealing on their premises. These have included use of CCTV, the installation of special lighting and smoke detectors in lavatories, improved visual supervision and restricting access to out of the way areas. In some cases where pubs have had very serious problems they have been totally re-designed and refurbished. These efforts have used existing licensed victuallers associations and pubwatch schemes where they have been in place. Broad approaches in partnership, of the sort which these pub schemes exemplify, seem to us to be the right way to tackle drug dealing in semi-public places.

*Chapter*

# 9 DRUGS AND SOCIAL DEPRIVATION

*Building on the review of environmental factors given in chapter 3, we focus here on the importance of social deprivation. Deprivation, although far from being the sole cause of drug misuse, is on the balance of evidence significantly and causally related to problematic drug misuse. From that conclusion we derive recommendations both for local action and national policy.*

## DRUGS AND DEPRIVATION: AN EVIDENCE-BASED APPROACH

9.1     The purpose of this chapter is to explore the relationships between drug use and deprivation and the practical bearing of any such connections on strategies for prevention. We have already, in chapter 3, had a preliminary look at the significance of deprivation when it forms part of an individual's macro-environment. Here we consider the issue in more detail.

9.2     Many observers of the current British scene would probably contend that the social conditions associated with poverty evidently and significantly facilitate initial drug misuse, encourage a move into problematic use, and exacerbate risks of harmful outcome. Others are, however, likely to advise caution and will point out the limitations in the evidence and the difficulties in drawing firm conclusions, and they will remind us that the rich as well as the poor can develop drug problems. The approach which we take to this question in the present chapter will be critical, and we believe that it is necessary and timely to address the question. We pay attention both to the research base and to views which derive from the experience of agency workers.

9.3     The way this chapter will be structured is as follows. We will start by defining what is meant by social deprivation and will identify some of the several different aspects of drug misuse with which deprivation might be expected to have a connection. Some pertinent data illustrating the way in which deprivation relates to health and crime are then given by way of background, and the relationship between cigarette smoking and socio-economic grouping is also discussed. American experience on the relationship between deprivation and drug use is briefly considered. The UK evidence is then examined in relation to evolutions in the drug use and poverty connections which have occurred over time, and the recent or current picture regarding different facets of these connections is considered. We sum up our views on how this complex evidence is best to be interpreted and then in a final section consider the implications of these conclusions for prevention policies.

## THE MEANING OF THE TERM "DEPRIVATION"

9.4     The experience of deprivation may have within it a number of constituents such as, for instance, poverty, inadequate housing, educational disadvantage, and lack of job opportunities. Unemployment and low or relatively low income are often key factors.[1] There are several widely used indices which summate specified elements into overall deprivation scores.[2]

9.5    Whatever the objective criteria which are employed to measure deprivation it is important to realise that what we are talking about here is a condition which at the same time will often exist as a potent, corrosive, subjective and personal experience.[3] The mix of feelings are likely to include worthlessness and a sense of failure, powerless and the feeling of not being in control, alienation and apathy and loss of any role as stakeholder, the sense of lacking any hope of a personal way out or up and of there being no better future in sight for one's children. Deprivation is a psychological burden.

9.6    Measures of deprivation can be used to describe an individual's position or, alternatively, to describe the state of a defined geographical area, by averaging the deprivation characteristics of its population.

9.7    There is debate as to whether absolute or relative deprivation is the more relevant index for social and public health purposes.[4] Absolute deprivation is measured by the score on any chosen index and indicates the level of deprivation experienced by individual or community in direct terms. Relative deprivation describes the person's or community's deprivation level in relation to background population averages. There is evidence to show that it is sometimes relative rather than absolute deprivation which is associated with adverse health consequences: people feel bad about themselves when they feel disadvantaged in comparison to others. Research on drug use has to date generally focused on absolute rather than relative deprivation and in this particular arena the question is open as to which type of deprivation is more relevant.

9.8    There are statistics which demonstrate that the level of deprivation in present-day Britain, with the likely knock-on effect for related problems in health inequalities, should be cause for acute concern. For instance, in Britain between 1982 and 1996, there was a rise from 10% to 19% in those whose income was at a level below half the national mean. A recent report from the UN Development Program[5] has shown that the poorest fifth of the British population have less spending power than equivalent strata in other major Western countries: within terms of this measure the poor in Britain are also poorer and worse off than the poor in the United States, or Hong Kong. The report charts the fact that poverty levels in Britain had been decreasing up to the early 1980s, but since then we are the only major Western nation to have experienced a significant increase in poverty. Relative deprivation is susceptible to economic cycles and can be influenced by fiscal and welfare policies. Concern over the problems set by deprivation and how they are best to be ameliorated is of course by no means new. There is a long tradition in Britain, dating back to Charles Booth's pioneering work in the last century, of studying poverty and its consequences.[6,7,8]

9.9    Lower socio-economic status is sometimes used as a marker for deprivation, although the two concepts are not identical. Within terms of the Registrar General's 5-part classification Social Class V comprises those who are working in unskilled manual occupations, and Social Class I those who are in professional, executive or managerial employment.

9.10    Deprivation is often very evidently a problem in areas of inner city decay, but it can be haphazard as well as concentrated. It exists as a rural as well as an urban problem.

## SPECIFYING THE "DRUGS" PART OF ANY CONNECTION

9.11    If deprivation is one part of the deprivation and drugs connection which requires definition before developing our substantive discussion, it is necessary also to scrutinise how the "drugs" element in the equation may be envisaged. We would suggest that if deprivation is related to drug misuse it is likely to be in a subtle and multiple way, rather than in any monolithic sense. For instance:-

   • Deprivation has at times and in different localities been associated with problematic use of particular drugs (for instance, heroin or crack cocaine). Such associations can change quickly over time and should never be interpreted as implying that use of a particular drug is exclusively related to poverty. And much problematic use is poly-drug use.

   • Rather than deprivation being strongly related only to the simple fact of use "ever", it may relate more subtly to age of first use, progression to dependence, intravenous use and risky use, health and social complications of use, and to criminal involvement.

   • We would expect the connection to be strongest for the extremes of problem drug use, and weakest for what might be termed casual, recreational or intermittent use.

   • We would expect deprivation adversely to influence the drug user's access to care and treatment.

   • The chances for either spontaneous or post-treatment recovery will probably be influenced by those aspects of deprivation which decrease access to positive alternatives to drug misuse, which make access to meaningful employment unlikely and which generally hamper the individual's integration or re-integration within society.

   • A deprived area might suffer from greater and more visible public nuisance from drug taking in comparison to an area with more resources.

   • A potentially vulnerable community may be purposely selected as a potential market by drug dealers.

   • A poor area with high levels of unemployment can provide an environment where drug dealing becomes established as part of the alternative economy.

   • Deprived areas may at community level find it more difficult to deal with drug problems than more advantaged areas.

   • Among networks of marginalised drug users who are living in circumstances of intense deprivation and often sharing crowded and sub-standard accommodation, TB and HIV infection may be transmitted and become prevalent.[9]

9.12    It should be understood that what we are seeking to do here is put forward a set of conjectures to illustrate the contention that the drug element in the possible connection that we are considering, needs dissection. We are not presuming that there is at present evidence available which can differentiate the question in all these ways.

9.13   In this preliminary discussion of the nature of the questions with which we will be dealing, there is one important note of caution which should be entered. Statistical correlation is not the same thing as cause. If deprivation is shown to be related to any aspect of drug misuse it will still be necessary to probe the nature and direction of causality rather than jump to conclusions.

9.14   If there is a statistical finding of any kind between deprivation and drug misuse, an important question relates to the significance of the relationship. The conventional approach is to describe a relationship in terms of the likelihood of its having happened by chance. Thus a relationship significant at $p<.05$ (probability less than .05) is one which has a 5% likelihood of chance occurrence and thus a 95% likelihood of being due to other than chance. A $p<.05$ relationship is often described as "statistically significant" - it is significant to a degree on which most people would happily place a bet. Similarly, a finding at $p<.01$ (one in a hundred likelihood of chance relationship) is described as "highly significant", and one at $p<.001$ (one in a thousand) as "very highly significant". We hope that the non-statistical reader will not find the use of this notation too burdensome, but to strengthen the scientific credibility of the presentation we will provide when reviewing research material probability estimates when appropriate.

## DEPRIVATION AND PROBLEMS: THE LARGER BACKGROUND

9.15   There is evidence in relation to a wide range of health and social problems to show that deprivation can be associated with mortality, morbidity and impaired access to health care.[10,11,12] Deprivation is in addition associated with certain types of offending. Some of this research deals directly with measures of deprivation, while other analyses have examined health differentials across the socio-economic spectrum. A common and underlying mechanism whatever the problem, may be the damage which deprivation can cause to ties in the community.[13]

9.16   For the purposes of this chapter it would be inappropriate to go into this kind of material at great length. We believe, however, that this evidence is relevant to our present concerns insofar as it supports the general contention that the quality of people's environment can widely affect their health and behaviour. Here are some illustrations:-

• A child coming from a family belonging to the least advantaged end of the socio-economic spectrum, in comparison to a more advantaged child is twice as likely to die before age 15.[14]

• For the 15-29 year age group and both for men and women, suicide rates are about twice as high in deprived as compared with affluent areas.[15]

• Research has generally identified higher rates of mental illness, including depressive illness, among socially deprived groups.[16]

• Unskilled men in the UK now have an overall age-adjusted mortality rate three times that of professional men. In the early 1970s the differential was two-fold.[4]

• The British Crime Survey has consistently shown that people who live in the poorest areas are most likely to be the victims of crime.

9.17   A review[17] on health inequalities in the early years of life, suggests that for many problems a phasic relationship with parental socio-economic status may exist. In early childhood impoverished home circumstances will bear negatively on the infant's health; during school years many types of disadvantage may be buffered by school experience (although success or failure at school is itself related to relative family advantage); in later adolescence and the post-school period there is a re-emergence of class-related disadvantage.

9.18   We would suggest therefore that the basic proposition that the individual's social situation can have a significant relationship with their health and social adjustment is well supported. And we would argue that with deprivation so widely relating to the individual's health and behaviour, it would be surprising if drug misuse were found to be immune to this influence. Health, research repeatedly tells us, is a property of the individual, but it is a property which is in significant degree conferred or impaired by the individual's environment.

## CIGARETTE SMOKING

9.19   Before turning to our specific focus on drug misuse, let us for a moment sketch out the background a little further and look at trends in cigarette smoking over a recent thirty year period.[11,18] We believe that two conclusions which are relevant to our present concerns can be drawn from Figure 1.

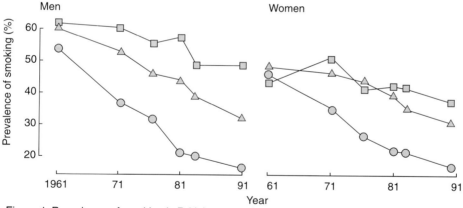

Figure 1. Prevalence of smoking in British men and women during 1961-91 by socio-economic group. ○, group I; □, group III △, group V.

• Class differences in prevalence of smoking have varied greatly over recent years. This suggests that to talk of similar interactions between drug misuse and social factors as if these were relationships fixed for all time, is likely to be similarly misleading. What on the contrary is needed is an understanding of how such relationships are likely to be operating at any particular time and in changing fields.

• At the beginning of the 1990s, cigarette smoking had in this country become a strongly class-related drug behaviour. The data show that the less privileged have thus far found it significantly more difficult to give up smoking than have the more privileged sectors. Cigarettes in Britain are moving toward becoming a poverty drug.[19]

We do not wish to over-interpret the smoking data nor argue simplistically that because cigarettes show a socio-economic relationship, illicit drug use should be expected to behave in exactly the same way. We would on the contrary suggest that different drugs and different modes of drug use are likely to show very different types and intensities of relationship with socio-economic status, but with the smoking data demonstrating that in some circumstances this kind of influence can be powerful. We see our "different drugs may behave differently" argument as strengthened by the finding that alcohol consumption in Britain is greater among the richer than among the poorer segments of society.

## DRUG MISUSE, DEPRIVATION, AND THE EXPERIENCE OF THE USA

9.20    The American epidemiological experience with drug misuse has some important historical differences as compared with Britain. We believe, however, that aspects of what happened in the US parallel what has occurred here, except that in the USA the connection with deprivation came to be established earlier. The American experience suggests that what has more recently happened in our own country is not unique, and might even have been expected.

9.21    Prior to the 1960s, America had a long and fluctuating history of problems with opioids and cocaine, and patterns of misuse varied both geographically and over time. To summarise the experience of those decades in one short sentence, it is probably fair to conclude that up to some time soon after the end of the Second World War there was no evidence in the US for a strong and consistent relationship between deprivation and major types of drug misuse.[20,21,22]

9.22    The nature of what happened with heroin use in America during the 1960s can be illustrated by reference to a study by Isidor Chein and his colleagues.[23] They sampled a number of multi-ethnic communities in New York City and explored the relationship between aspects of social deprivation and the likelihood of an area being affected by epidemic heroin misuse. They focused on the time period 1949-1955. Employing measures which are of relevance to our present British concerns, they found that the geographical distribution of heroin was strongly related to ecological measures of poverty, unemployment, overcrowding and family breakdown. They "interpreted the correlation not in terms of the direct impact of poverty on the youth, but in those of the community atmosphere. The youngsters react to the values and practices which they experience and not simply to the material deprivations from which they suffer".

9.23    Chein's findings were much in line with other research conducted around that time. Thus Ball and Chambers,[24] in reviewing the overall epidemiology of drug misuse in the US, stated that "The areas of high rates of drug abuse tend to be deteriorating neighbourhoods and slum ghettos." In the 1980s when crack cocaine made an entry on the US scene, the use of this drug again showed strong clustering in areas of urban poverty.[25]

9.24    A recent ecological study of cocaine and opiate overdose deaths in New York City over the years 1990-1992 showed a highly significant correlation between overdose mortality and the poverty status of communities, so much so that the authors suggest that poverty accounted for 69% of the variance in overdose mortality rates.[26]

## THE RELATIONSHIP BETWEEN SOCIAL CLASS, DEPRIVATION AND DRUG MISUSE IN THE UK: THE HISTORICAL CONTEXT

9.25 Before turning to the problems of more recent decades, it may be interesting briefly to consider the historical depth of the issues with which we are today dealing, and enter a note on the nineteenth century experience. Alcohol was undoubtedly in this country the major substance problem for that century and there is vivid contemporary testimony as to the appalling social consequences of slum drinking which were embedded in social deprivation of an extent and intensity which is today fortunately long since gone.[27] The more privileged sectors of society at the same time also drank heavily. What we may perhaps tend to overlook is that opium use was in that century also widespread.[28] There was considerable evidence for socio-economic patterning of opium taking in terms, for instance, of urban opium use in the mill towns and a high prevalence of rural use in the fever-prone Fenlands. But it is also well substantiated that opium was not restricted to the poor or deprived: it was a habit widely accepted among all classes with notable literary figures such as Coleridge and De Quincey famed for their opium taking.[29] Drug taking, the historical records suggests, always has been a behaviour with socio-economic connections, but never a behaviour susceptible to any one simple social explanation.

9.26 When in the 1960s Britain experienced a significant increase in heroin misuse, largely concentrated in London, there was no evidence that this epidemic was influenced by socio-economic grouping. In a monograph which reported on a representative sample of heroin misusers who in 1969 were attending London DDUs, Stimson found that the socio-economic distribution for the parents of his subjects did not differ from that of the general population and these subjects had high levels of employment.[30] The same type of conclusion was reached by Blumberg when he reviewed research on the characteristics of heroin users coming to treatment nationally over the previous 10 years.[31] These data were restricted to clinic attenders, but it is likely they gave a fair representation also of the wider heroin-using population.

9.27 In the early 1980s many parts of this country experienced a steep increase in heroin misuse. In the context of that epidemic the ecology of UK drug misuse for the first time began to show a strong patterning by social environment. This occurred at a different pace in different parts of the country, but in some areas with great rapidity. The change was more in relation to heroin and heavy poly-drug use than casual use of cannabis.

9.28 The evidence is persuasive that major drug problems during the 1980s became increasingly associated with social disadvantage.[32,33] Research to support this contention came from Glasgow,[34] the north of England,[35] the Wirral,[36] Nottingham,[37] Liverpool,[38] and South London.[39]

9.29 Rather than reviewing these reports in detail we will give here some of the key findings from the Wirral study as illustrative of the kinds of evidence which emerged over this period. Howard Parker and his colleagues[36] conducted their research in the Wirral area of Merseyside, between July 1984 and June 1985. For research purposes this geographical area was well-chosen, with the Wirral peninsular constituting a patchwork of contiguous neighbourhoods representing a wide spectrum of income levels. A total of 1305 opioid users were identified by the research team as known to agencies, with a prevalence rate of 18.2 per 1000 among the 16–24 years age group. What became apparent was a great variation in prevalence rates across different townships, ranging in the 16–24 age group from a low of zero to a high of 162 per 1000. The variation in geographical prevalence was highly correlated with each of seven indicators of the background deprivation level within a given area. These indicators related to the following measures and in each instance we bracket the correlation (a concept which is explained at the end of this paragraph) with geographical rates for youth opiate agency referrals: local rates of unemployment (0.72), council tenancies (0.67), overcrowding (0.62), larger families (0.49), unskilled employment (0.39), single parent families (0.69), and lack of access to a car (0.58). All these correlations reached a level of statistical significance. (A correlation co-efficient is a measure of how closely two variables move together or, as it were, go hand in hand. A co-efficient of 1.0 indicates that those variables move absolutely together while one of zero means that they are totally unrelated.)

9.30    The echoes between these findings for Merseyside and Chein's earlier research in New York City are obvious. Britain seems in the 1980s to have been in an unhappy sense recapitulating the American experience, and discovering that when heroin is widely available and geographical clustering of deprivation exists, the two factors are likely to make a connection

## DRUG USE AND DEPRIVATION IN THE UK: THE RECENT EVIDENCE

9.31    The paragraphs which follow will look at recent evidence on the relationship between deprivation and drug misuse and dependence in the UK. Research on this topic is still at a relatively early stage of development, but in preparing this chapter we have been able to locate a number of interesting and relevant reports. We believe that from these separate studies a coherent and persuasive picture begins to emerge. We will consider in sequence a report which relates volatile substance abuse (VSA) deaths to ecological measures of deprivation; a study which explores the relationship across London between ecological measures of deprivation and rates of enrolment for treatment of drug problems; a report from Glasgow on the relationship between emergency admissions for drug misuse and area measures of deprivation; a national survey relating deprivation to drug dependence at individual level; a national survey which reports on the relationship between drug use and features of the individual's residential area.

## DEATHS FROM VOLATILE SUBSTANCE ABUSE (VSA) AND DEPRIVATION CHARACTERISTICS OF AREAS FROM WHICH SUCH DEATHS ARE REPORTED

9.32    Although VSA is not covered by the Misuse of Drugs Act, ACMD has taken the position that VSA is an integral part of the national drug problem and has published a report which deals specifically with this topic.[40] There is continuing concern about the level of VSA deaths which after a dip has again risen slightly.[41] In any consideration of the link between deprivation and drug misuse insights which can be gained from study of the relationship between deprivation and VSA will be valuable.

9.33   Within this context a recent report by Esmail and colleagues deserves note.[42] These authors took as basis for their study the 775 deaths due to VSA which occurred in England, Scotland and Wales between the years 1985 and 1991. A ward-level analysis was conducted which determined variations for VSA in age standardised mortality ratios (ASMR) for VSA-related deaths. This index gives the ratio between observed levels of VSA deaths in an area and the average expected level, with correction for age. ASMR was then related to an ecological measure of deprivation within each ward (the Townsend deprivation index with higher scores relating to lower owner housing occupation, higher unemployment, overcrowding, and less access to a car).

9.34   Two findings emerged from this study which are relevant to our present concerns.

• Areas where any VSA death had occurred over the stated period scored an average of 2.8 on the Townsend index, while the average score for areas which had not had a death was 0.2: the difference between these two averages is very highly significant ($p < .0001$).

• A statistical technique known as multiple regression was used to determine how much of the variance (variation) in ASMR at country level can be accounted for by variation in deprivation. Forty five per cent of variance in VSA deaths (ASMR) was in these terms accounted for by variation in deprivation.

The first finding quoted above points to a statistical relationship between deprivation and VSA deaths, while the second goes an important step further and tells us about the size of the relationship. But a further and perhaps equally important insight to be derived from this finding is that although deprivation accounts for 45% of variation in VSA deaths, an outstanding 55% must be accounted for by other and unexplained influences.

9.35   The authors of this report point out that they are employing area measures of deprivation and are not seeking to measure individual deprivation experience.


## DEPRIVATION AND LEVEL OF TREATED DRUG MISUSE IN LONDON

9.36   A document from the Thames Regional Drug Misuse Databases[43] analysed data collected between April 1991 and March 1994 on problem drug users seen by services in the Greater London Area. The presentation rates per 100,000 population aged between 15 and 44 were first calculated for Family Health Service Areas. For these same areas measures of deprivation were available in terms of Under-Privileged Area or UPA scores. Figure 2 shows report rates against UPA Index with a line of best fit drawn in. The correlation between the two measures was 0.75 ($p < .001$). The authors were cautious in emphasising that the research is based on residence at time of reporting rather than its being indicative of the subject's area of origin. Leaving for a moment the causality question aside, this study provides evidence to support the contention that areas of higher deprivation are likely to experience high levels of the kinds of drug misuse which put people in need of help.

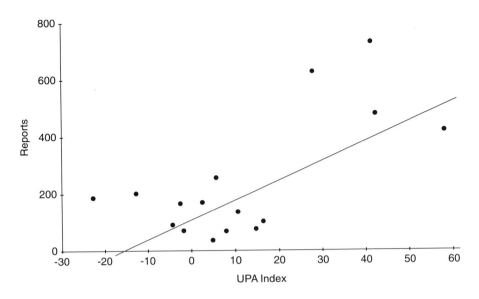

Figure 2. Relation between area rates of agency reported drug problems and area deprivation (UPA) scores, Greater London.

## DRUG MISUSE EMERGENCY ADMISSIONS AND DEPRIVATION IN GLASGOW

9.37    Dr Laurence Gruer and his colleagues[44] have kindly made available an analysis of the area of residence of persons admitted to hospital for drug-related emergencies in Greater Glasgow during the five years 1st April 1991 to 31 March 1996. Drug-related admissions were defined as those given an ICD9 diagnostic code on discharge for drug dependence, non-dependent drug abuse or drug psychosis. Each patient's postcode sector of residence was then classified according to the Carstairs Deprivation Index.[45] This index assigns to each postcode sector a deprivation score from 1 (most affluent) to 7 (least affluent) based on the following four variables as recorded in the 1991 census; namely

*overcrowding* - persons in private households living at a density of greater than 1 person per room as a proportion of all persons in private households;

*male unemployment* - proportion of economically active males who are seeking work;

*low social class* - proportion of all persons in private households with head of household in social class 4 or 5; and

*no car* - proportion of all persons in private households with no car.

During the period there were 3,715 admissions. Figure 3 shows that the standardised admission rates rose sharply with increasing deprivation. The admission rate from the most deprived areas of Greater Glasgow exceeded that of the least deprived by a factor of 30. Male rates exceeded female rates by 2.2:1. Rates peaked at 25-29 years of age. If the admission rate for the most affluent areas applied to all parts of the city, the number of admissions would be reduced by 92%. The authors observe that the relationship between deprivation and drug misuse-related admission is far stronger than any other health-related variable they have studied. They also found a very strong correlation across postcode sectors between rates for drug related and alcohol related admissions (correlation coefficient 0.94 or p<.001).

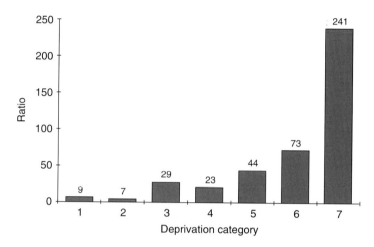

Figure 3. Drug-related emergency hospital admissions in Greater Glasgow, 1 April 1991 to 31 March 1996. Age and sex standardised ratios by Carstairs deprivation category (All Greater Glasgow = 100).

## DEPRIVATION SCORES AND THE RISK OF DEPENDENCE: EVIDENCE FROM THE OPCS PSYCHIATRIC MORBIDITY SURVEY

9.38    The Parker study which we discuss earlier dealt specifically with the relationship between rates of known opioid use within local areas and the deprivation characteristics of those areas. A recent analysis[46] of data from the 1995 OPCS national 10,000 person sample survey on psychiatric morbidity, took a different approach. The analysis was restricted to subjects aged 15-35 years. For every individual data were available which allowed categorisation of that person's degree of dependence (0-4) on illicit drugs, with all such drugs considered together: the items employed in this scale dealt with intensity of use, sensed need, inability to cut down, tolerance, and withdrawal symptoms. A 0-4 point rating of deprivation was constructed for each individual with items relating to unemployment, living in rented accommodation, not having use of a car, and manual work status. The statistical technique (regression analysis) used by the authors eliminated the possible confounding effect of sex and age (for example, young people probably living in rented accommodation, young people more probably being dependent on drugs and hence if uncorrected a possibly artefactual correlation between living in rented accommodation and being drug dependent). That the likelihood of incurring a 1-4 score on the dependence scale as opposed to a zero score increased stepwise and significantly with increase in personal deprivation score, is shown in Figure 4. A person with a 4-point (extreme) deprivation score was almost 10 times more likely to have a positive score on drug dependence than an individual who had a zero deprivation score. Here as with other studies we quote, the results are likely to be influenced by sampling, response rate and choice of instruments, and scoring technique but the evidence for a statistical link between drug dependence and deprivation is seemingly further strengthened.

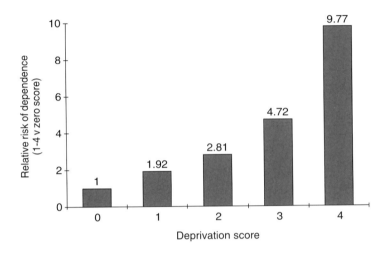

Figure 4. Likelihood of scoring positively on a drug dependence scale by deprivation score: odds ratios.

9.39    It should be emphasised that what Farrell and his colleagues were dealing with was the relationship between on the one hand individual-level ratings of deprivation (as compared with Esmail's, Taylor's and Parker's geographical measure of deprivation), and on the other hand measures of the individual's dependence on any illicit drug (as contrasted with Esmail's use of death rates and Jones's and Parker's approach in terms of whether or not an individual had come to the attention of an agency by reason of their opioid misuse). Furthermore, the Farrell and Esmail teams made use of national data while Jones and Parker were reporting regional studies. Despite these varied research approaches, the essential confluence in the findings from these four studies is strong.

## SOCIO-ECONOMIC POSITION AND DRUG MISUSE: ANALYSIS DERIVING FROM THE 1996 BRITISH CRIME SURVEY

9.40    The Home Office report 'Drug Misuse Declared in 1996'[47] analyses information on drug misuse deriving from the 1996 British Crime Survey (BCS) which interviewed a representative sample of 16,500 people living in England and Wales. Some of the output from this survey has already been discussed in chapter 2 of this report. We will focus here on what this survey shows about the relationship between drug misuse and socio-economic position.

9.41    The Home Office researchers use as the descriptor of drug misuse report by subjects regarding "use" of any kind of illicit drug, separately by "last 12 months" and "ever". This approach does not seek to differentiate between types of drugs, higher or lower quantity or frequency of use, or between dependent and non-dependent use. A six part ACORN rating classification (A Classification of Residential Areas), described features of the subjects' area of residence.

9.42    We quote below the key relevant findings from the Home Office report:-

"ACORN has six basic categories, one of which - Rising - has significantly higher rates of drug misuse than the other five, irrespective of age group. Rising areas are urban ones populated by professional people who tend to have active and varied leisure lives. Those living in Rising areas are more at risk of drug misuse even than those in impoverished areas with a high proportion of council housing (Striving). The sole - limited - exception to this generalisation is that a particular sub-category within the Striving classification, covering areas of high unemployment, has rates of drug misuse in line with those for the Rising category as a whole, but less than those of one particular sub-category within the Rising classification which has the highest level of all (better-off executive areas in inner-city settings)."

9.43    We interpret these findings as suggesting that drug misuse per se[47] probably shows a different relationship with deprivation than VSA related deaths,[42] problematic use which has reached clinical significance[36,43] or dependence.[46] The subjects who admitted to drug misuse in the BCS survey included in the 16-29 year age group a significant proportion of cannabis users, including 57% who used cannabis alone. We therefore see the Home Office analysis as usefully contributing to the total jigsaw, but not as weakening the conclusion that in present-day Britain, not all but some aspects of problematic drug misuse are related to deprivation. BCS again usefully reminds us that drug misuse has multiple causes and deprivation is likely, even when important, to be interacting with other factors to bring about the behaviour.

## HOW IS THE STATISTICAL RELATIONSHIP BETWEEN DRUG MISUSE AND DEPRIVATION BEST TO BE INTERPRETED?

9.44    In the paragraphs above we have examined a quantity of evidence. Let us now try briefly to identify the conclusions which can be drawn from this material. In this section we will focus strictly on the question of whether the sum of evidence can be read as pointing to socially significant connections between drug misuse and deprivation, while the relevance of any such conclusions for prevention strategies will be dealt with in the final section.

9.45    At a factual level we first conclude that research points strongly to a statistical association between social deprivation and drug use when that use is of a kind and intensity which leads to significant health and social problems. That type of drug taking is sadly today in sum a common occurrence in Britain (see chapter 2), with adverse implications for the individual and family and expensive consequences for the health care, welfare and criminal justice system. We are far from suggesting that all types and levels of drug use are at all times and in all circumstances deprivation-related. What we do however feel confident in asserting is that deprivation relates statistically to types and intensities of drug use which are problematic.

9.46    To establish that a statistical association can legitimately be interpreted as indicative of underlying causal linkage, is always difficult. Within the traditions of epidemiology it is accepted that the stronger the observed relationships and the more often the connection has been observed in different circumstances and at different times, the greater is the likelihood of causation being at work. We believe that these criteria are reasonably well met in relation to our present concerns, but the research base here is not as yet so well developed as, say, that in relation to the persistent and consistent findings which support the conclusion that the statistical relationship between cigarette smoking and lung cancer can, beyond reasonable doubt, be interpreted as evidence that smoking causes cancer. We would like to see the relevant research in the drugs area in due course further replicated and strengthened.

9.47    Epidemiologists in general are also more willing to interpret association as evidence of cause if feasible causative mechanisms can be proposed. We believe that several such mechanisms can be envisaged as credible links between deprivation and problematic drug use.

• Deprivation weakens family and social bonding and cohesiveness and there are strong arguments from social psychology to support the conclusion that the individual growing up or living in such circumstances will be prone to ignore the expectations of a society with which they see themselves as having no or weak bonds.

• Deprivation gives rise to personal distress and psychological discomfort of a kind which can result in depressive illness as well as lesser and more amorphous types of mood disturbance.[16] In such circumstances mind-acting drugs (including illicit drugs) can be used as self-medication to relieve distress or as substitute source of excitement and good feelings.

• Research has shown that in communities where unemployment is high and many young people are without a job-related role or structure, being a drug taker or being a dealer confers the status of being someone.[48] Hustling for drugs becomes a meaningful occupation.

• As already suggested above (paragraph 9.11), drugs can become established in a deprived environment as a significant part of the alternative economy. There may be no other such easy way of earning a living and specially so for youth who are poorly educated and lack job skills.

• A deprived area may not have the resources effectively to respond to an incipient drug problem in the way that a more privileged area might find possible. In such circumstances an initially low prevalence drug problem will easily spread and become endemic.

9.48    While noting the strength of the arguments for causal connections we would also point out that these explanations are unlikely ever to constitute the whole story. For instance, the housing market and resettlement policies may concentrate people who are prone to drug use on one estate. Furthermore, rather than the direction of causation always being in terms of deprivation causing drug misuse, drug misuse may itself lead the individual into unemployment or poor housing, or cut that person off from their community. Paradoxically, extreme poverty may actually reduce access to drugs except among those willing to take up crime.

9.49    Having stated our belief that there is a statistical relationship between deprivation and drug use (paragraph 9.45) and having then gone on to examine the difficult questions around potential causal implications, what conclusions can now reasonably be drawn? Are the observed associations more probably "just statistical" in a dismissive sense, or do they have real-world meaning? In our view a balanced conclusion should be couched in the following terms. Not all the observed association is likely to be the result of direct cause and effect, and the complexities should be admitted. Deprivation is only ever likely to be one risk factor within a multiple system of causes. But with all the complexities noted, the immensely wide background literature on the connection between deprivation and health; the historical experience with drugs and alcohol; smoking research; the American experience with drugs; and then finally and most importantly and directly, the strength of the developing British drugs research base together with a set of credible explanatory theories, make it legitimate to reach a strong rather than weak conclusion. We thus assert without any of the familiar hedging with "on the one hand but on the other", that on strong balance of probability deprivation is today in Britain likely often to make a significant causal contribution to the cause, complications and intractability of damaging kinds of drug misuse.

## DEPRIVATION AND DRUG MISUSE: THE POLICY IMPLICATIONS OF THE RELATIONSHIP

9.50    Let us first address a question which may perhaps best be posed as "Can anything be done until everything is done?" If a significant causal relationship between deprivation and drug misuse is accepted as established, does that imply that we have to wait for the root and branch elimination of deprivation before making any progress at all on this front? Or is it possible to use insights deriving from this connection toward immediate, practical, step-wise locally-based strategies aimed at amelioration of drug misuse, while larger and longer term efforts to deal with deprivation continue in the background? It is this latter and ameliorative view of the way forward which we favour, coupled with a belief that to ignore the relevance of deprivation offers no way forward at all.

9.51    Within that perspective we believe that Drug Action Teams (DATs) should, where there is presumptive cause for concern, assess and respond to significant relationships between drug misuse and deprivation which may exist within their own localities. Local surveys should be conducted either through agency identifications or sample interviewing, with drug problem prevalence related to personal or community indicators.

9.52    That kind of evidence should be used for accurate targeting of environmental prevention strategies of the many different kinds identified in other chapters of this report. We are thus calling for strong new initiatives at local level drawn up within an awareness of the importance of the deprivation connection. Resource allocation formulas should include a measure of deprivation. We are not suggesting that prevention resources within a locality should be targeted exclusively at areas of deprivation. We are however concerned that unless salience is given to the special needs of deprived areas, the needs of these areas will not be adequately met. For instance, where schools are under strain it may be particularly difficult for them to mount effective drug education or involve parents in drug education. Community projects, community mobilisation, housing projects, youth work, and community policing may all require special attention in these kinds of environments. It is our argument that these geographical needs should be assessed, and the needed multi-agency and multi-sectional interventions planned and delivered, and we see DATs as crucial to the achievement of such targeting. We believe that every DAT should consider these aspects of the local problem and include suitable responses within their overall action plans.

9.53    Special attention should be given to developing more accurate perceptions of the health education needs of deprived people, together with more sensitive insights into the real-world possibilities for uptake of health messages within contexts of poverty and blocked opportunity. A prerequisite might be research which established the specific health preoccupation of the poor and of poor families, in relation to illicit drugs, alcohol, smoking and wider issues.

9.54    We also believe that when areas are identified where drug misuse and deprivation have made a strong connection, such evidence must be seen as relevant to the planning and targeting of local drug treatment services as provided by both statutory and non-statutory agencies. New impetus may be needed to overcome any problems with access to treatment, either by establishing satellite clinics or by putting emphasis on outreach. Court diversion programmes may be of special relevance. Where high levels of deprivation exist, treatment services will need to develop strategies which make effective links with rehabilitation in terms of rehousing, job training and employment. Purchasers of health care should ensure that these expectations are met. What we are recommending here is fully in accord with more general policies on inequalities in health and with wider health service concern with targeting areas of social need.[49] The tools are available for such targeting. We recommend that evidence should be given over time by DATs of tangible progress on this front.

9.55    We deal with housing as a specific issue in chapter 7 of this report and make recommendations. Within the context of the policy recommendations which stem from the present chapter, we would urge that the policy implications for housing authorities should be noted. Where concentrations of poor housing contribute to and perpetuate social deprivation, it will be strongly supportive of drug prevention if such housing problems can be targeted and ameliorated.

9.56    We wish now finally to return to the implications for national policies at the strategic level which may derive from the conclusion that deprivation has at present a significant causal link with problematic drug misuse. Income levels and reduction in poverty, employment levels, housing provision, the quality of education and skills training, health care and correction of inequalities in health, support for rewarding leisure facilities, an adequate welfare safety-net, are of course salient policy issues in their own right, but the connection between deprivation and drug problems provides a forceful reminder that all these background issues are salient to public health as well as standing in their own right. It is not within our competence or the remit of ACMD to suggest what policies should be pursued at the macro-level to ameliorate deprivation.

9.57    However the Government's welfare-to-work programme may have particular relevance in this context although it will need to find imaginative ways of adapting to the specific needs of drug users and of communities suffering from the effects of deprivation, unemployment and drug misuse. A focused intervention at a national level is needed to identify best practice in employment generation and re-training for drug misusers and promoting their locally targeted implementation. Adequate funding should be earmarked for a drug misusers' welfare-to-work initiative.

9.58 Even with deprivation eliminated we would not expect to see drug misuse disappear. Steering well clear of the Utopian and staying within our remit we do however feel it proper to conclude that when macro-level social and economic policies significantly fail and social deprivation, structural unemployment and poverty becomes rife, one of the prices which will have to be paid is the added cost and tragedy of deprivation-related drug misuse. The recent establishment by the Government of the Social Exclusion Unit at the Cabinet Office to co-ordinate the policies and programmes across Departments to combat social exclusion is accordingly to be welcomed.

9.59 It is appropriate at this juncture again to enter a reminder that deprivation is far from being the total explanation of drug misuse - we cannot stress this point too often or too hard. Yet the analysis of the links between deprivation and drug misuse developed in this chapter forces the conclusion that deprivation sets questions of major relevance to prevention of drug misuse at both the local and strategic levels. This connection has too often in the past been neglected when formulating the policy mix. We want now and in the future to see deprivation given its full and proper place in all considerations of drug prevention policy, held in that policy consciousness, and not let slip from sight.

*Chapter*

# 10 THE RESOURCES AVAILABLE TO SUPPORT COMMUNITY ACTION ON PREVENTION

*Rather than propose substantial new funding we give here a brief directory of existing funding sources and other types of support which are potentially available to agencies wishing to strengthen or initiate community action on drug prevention.*

## INTRODUCTION

10.1　Inspired by the Government's drugs strategies for England, Wales, Scotland and Northern Ireland there is now a great deal of activity, particularly at local level, aimed at preventing drugs misuse.

10.2　This activity needs to be nurtured and sustained. As evidence begins to emerge of the practices which are effective in drug prevention the activity should increasingly focus on these practices.

10.3　The intention of this chapter is to be practical by highlighting some (it would be impossible to cover all) of the resources which might be tapped for assistance. And here we mean resources in the widest possible sense - people, information, money and advice.

## VOLUNTEERS

10.4　There are vast numbers of people in the United Kingdom who do voluntary work. We understand that in 1991 it was estimated that over 20 million people did some voluntary work and that over 10 million people did so on a regular basis. Some of that work will have been in the cause of drug prevention but we suspect that this vast reservoir of willing workers has not yet been used as well as it might have been for that cause.

10.5　Most volunteers, probably over 90%, get started by being motivated by an issue which, for whatever reason, strikes a chord with them. Only a small proportion are interested in voluntary work for its own sake. It is thus difficult to establish completely coherent systems for the recruitment of volunteers.

10.6　We are aware that the Government produced a paper "Make a Difference" in 1995 drawing together "action plans" for the promotion and development of volunteering by Government Departments. That demonstrates the very diverse activities in which volunteers can become involved. For drugs prevention related work which is often very localised and not centrally directed we think that the provider or initiator of that work should as a matter of course consider if and how voluntary effort could be harnessed. Drug Action Teams, Drug Prevention Teams, and other agencies should keep in mind the scope for the use of volunteers.

10.7   It is not possible here to suggest how this should be done because the circumstances of drug prevention work or initiatives will vary enormously. However we think there are a few matters which should be borne in mind.

10.8   The questions should be asked, why volunteers would help and what would they bring? If the reason is a simple desire to save money then experience apparently shows that the arrangement is unlikely to succeed. Volunteers should be engaged for their willingness and enthusiasm. They may need some training but care needs to be taken to prevent them being used (usually on economic grounds) as substitutes for professionals where professionals are needed.

10.9   There may be other organisations locally who engage volunteers from whom advice and assistance may be available on the basis of their experience and there are Councils for voluntary service around the United Kingdom who can be consulted. They can be contacted through the National Association of Councils for Voluntary Service in England; the Scottish Council for Voluntary Organisations; the Wales Council for Voluntary Action; and the Northern Ireland Council for Voluntary Action. The National Centre for Volunteering promotes, develops and supports volunteering in England. Community Service Volunteers promotes and encourages volunteering within the local community. The addresses and telephone numbers of all these organisations are in paragraph 10.24.

## MONEY

10.10   Limitless funds are not available for drugs prevention work any more than they are for anything else. Our interest here is not so much with established funding arrangements as where additional funding might be available to help local drug prevention work.

10.11   The Single Regeneration Budget which is administered by the ten Government Offices of the Regions (GORs), the addresses of which are in Appendix C, is capable of providing large sums of money on the basis of bids. These bids are usually expected to comprise comprehensive proposals for regenerating an area which include strong partnerships and community involvement. Drug Action Teams have been recommended to get in touch with their GORs to seek guidance on potential funding opportunities but, if the Single Regeneration Budget continues in being, we see scope for a rather more fundamental approach. While we understand the intention is that GORs should not be prescriptive in laying down the contents of bids we believe there is a case for requiring bidders to consider whether drug prevention should form a part of their bids - it need not necessarily do so but should only be rejected after consideration.

10.12   The twelve Home Office Drug Prevention Teams, which are spread throughout England, are also able to provide some funds for community orientated drug prevention work. Money which is provided under this scheme is not intended to act as an established form of funding but to get things started. Further information can be obtained from the relevant local offices, the addresses of which are in Appendix D.

10.13   Grants for Education Support and Training (GEST) from the Department for Education and Employment can be bid for by local education authorities under two heads for activities relating to drugs. One is for teacher training and drug prevention and education programmes. The other is for the youth service, a major objective of which is to support youth and community workers in the delivery of drug education and prevention.

10.14  The National Lottery Charities Board (NLCB) has in the past funded some projects which have involved drugs prevention. Each funding round has a theme - for example, "new opportunities and choices" and "voluntary sector development" - which seems usually to offer the prospect of covering an aspect of drug related work. Enquiries can be made of the regional NLCB offices (a list of which is at Appendix E) for information about the prospects of a project being eligible for funding. The NLCB is likely to consider whether a proposal fits with the local Drug Action Team's priorities. Potential applicants would therefore be well-advised to discuss their proposals with their local Drug Action Team first.

10.15  In November 1996 the Department of Health announced a mental health services challenge fund for England for 1997-98 for £10m for which health authorities, social services and other local services could bid. The bids were to be assessed against their ability to enable services to target people with severe or enduring health problems including those with associated problems of mental illness and substance misuse. At the same time the Department announced £100 million for the development of primary care and community services in England which was intended in part for the further development of shared care services for drug misusers - health authorities were expected to discuss their proposals with their local Drug Action Teams.

10.16  The European Commission action programme to combat drug abuse is another possible source of funding. At the moment there is about £4.3 million available each year throughout the Community. The programme is administered by the Public Health and Safety at Work Directorate DGV/F of Directorate General V (Employment, Industrial Relations and Social Affairs) in Brussels. There are two bidding rounds in each year. SCODA has a European liaison office who are in close contact with the Commission and who can advise on funding matters.

10.17  The Central Drugs Co-ordination Unit has administered for the years 1996-97 and 1997-98 challenge funds of £2 million for which Drug Action Teams in England could bid. Its purpose is to get local partnerships off the ground through a combination of public sector support and commitment from the private and voluntary sectors. Its long term future is uncertain.

10.18  There are also many Trusts and foundations who may be willing to provide pump priming funds for drug prevention projects. Additionally, companies may be willing to sponsor projects. These are too numerous to mention. Some operate at a local level while others take applications from all over the country. The Directory of Social Change annually publishes two documents giving valuable advice. The Guide to Major Trusts gives details of the top 300 grant making trusts in the UK. A Guide to Company Giving gives details of 1400 companies who give money to charitable causes. The Directory of Social Change (24 Stephenson Way, London NW1 2DP (tel: 0171 209 5151)) also publishes information on smaller and local charities.

10.19  Local authorities also sometimes contribute to community organisations and activities supporting drug prevention initiatives. The local Council should be contacted in the first instance. Alternatively, the local Drug Action Team may be able to offer advice.

## ADVICE/ASSISTANCE

10.20    Given the level of activity which is current in the field of drug prevention it is no surprise that there is a large array of sources which can be tapped for advice and assistance.

10.21    In England, the Health Education Authority has run a small grants scheme which is a result of their work in stimulating commercial and private sources of funding. SCODA also has a fundraising and sponsorship advisory service which advises drug services and others on support for drug prevention activities.

10.22    Drug Action Teams (DATs) in England and Scotland, and Drug and Alcohol Action Teams (DAATs) in Wales are constituted to lead and co-ordinate local efforts to tackle drug misuse. They are therefore natural places to call on. In England Drugs Reference Groups (DRGs) have been set up to advise DATs, and in Wales Local Action Teams have been set up to advise DAATs, and provide a local forum to exchange information, involve local communities, and will also provide a natural source of assistance.

10.23    The Home Office's Drugs Prevention Teams (the addresses of which are in Appendix D) will do the same and already have developed close relationships with their local DATs and DRGs.

10.24    There is also a range of organisations which can provide advice and information, a selection which we include below with a very brief description of what they do.

Adfam National
Waterbridge House
32-36 Loman Street
London SE1 0EE
Tel 0171 928 8900

Provides training and support for people, projects and groups with families of drug users, including parents themselves and members of family support groups.

Alcohol Concern
Waterbridge House
32-36 Loman Street
London SE1 0EE
Tel 0171 928 7377
Fax 0171 928 3343

Works to reduce the cost and incidence of alcohol misuse and improve the provision of services for people with drinking problems.

Community Service Volunteers
237 Pentonville Road
London N1 9NJ
Tel 0171 278 6601
Promotes and encourages volunteering within the local community.

Crime Concern
Signal Point
Station Road
Swindon SN1 1FE
Tel 01793 514596
Fax 01793 514654

Crime Concern is a national, not-for-profit, crime prevention organisation. It can help with consultancies, surveys and training. It runs a drug education programme.

The Drug Education Forum at
the National Children's Bureau
8 Wakley Street
London EC1V 7QE
Tel 0171 843 6111

Provides information on drug education in schools and promotes good practice in drug education.

Health Education Authority
Hamilton House
Mabledon Place
London WC1H 9TX
Tel 0171 383 3833
Web http://www.trashed.co.uk

The HEA is responsible for the Government's publicity campaign on drugs. It publishes research reports and a small number of leaflets. It has also run a small grants scheme on behalf of a major company. It will be publishing a directory of prevention activities in England produced for them by SCODA.

Health Education Board
for Scotland
Woodburn House
Canaan Lane
Edinburgh EH10 4SG
Tel 0131 447 8044
Web http://www.hebs.scot.nhs.uk

HEBS is responsible for the Government's publicity campaign on drugs in Scotland.

Health Promotion Wales
Ffynnon Las
Ty Glas Avenue
Llanishen
Cardiff CF4 5DZ
Tel 01222 752222
Fax 01222 756000

Promotes the health of the people of Wales.

Institute for the Study of Drug Dependence
Waterbridge House
32-36 Loman Street
London SE1 0EE
Tel 0171 928 1211
Fax 0171 928 2599
Web http://www.isdd.co.uk

ISDD has a comprehensive library of drug misuse literature and is a focal point for information in the United Kingdom. It has many publications available on drugs misuse.

The Local Government Drugs Forum
Tel 0171 227 2813
26 Chapter Street
London SW1P 4ND
Fax 0171 222 0878

The LGDF speaks on behalf of local authorities in England, Scotland and Wales. It seeks to promote best practice and help local authorities in partnership with others to tackle problem drug use in their community.

National Association for the Care and Resettlement of Offenders
169 Clapham Road
London SW9 0PU
Tel 0171 582 6500

As its name suggests NACRO's focus is on caring for and re-settling past offenders. Many of these will have substance abuse related problems. It is also concerned to prevent crime and runs many local crime prevention projects.

National Association of Councils for
Voluntary Service in England
3rd Floor
Arundel Court
177 Arundel Street
Sheffield S1 2NU
Tel 0114 278 6636

Will provide advice on the use of volunteers in England.

National Centre for Volunteering
Carriage Row
183 Eversholt Street
London NW1 1BU
Tel 0171 388 9888

Promotes, develops and supports volunteering in England.

National Drugs Prevention Alliance
PO Box 137
London N10 3JJ

The Alliance is a network of concerned citizens and prevention professionals whose aim is to promote drug free healthy lifestyles.

National Youth Agency (NYA)
17-23 Albion Street
Leicester LE1 6GD
Tel 01162 471200
Fax 01162 471043

The NYA is a source of information across the whole range of health education topics and publishes a wide range of material for informal educators.

Northern Ireland Council for
Voluntary Action
127 Ormeau Road
Belfast BT7 1SH
Tel 01232 321224

Will provide advice on the use of volunteers in Northern Ireland.

Northern Ireland Health
Promotion Agency
18 Ormeau Avenue
Belfast BT2 8HS
Tel 01232 311611

Promotes the health of everyone in Northern Ireland.

Release
388 Old Street
London EC1V 9CT
Tel 0171 729 9904
Fax 0171 729 2599

Release offers advice, particularly on drugs and legal issues.

Research Group on Clinical
Dependency
Graham House
1 Albert Square
Belfast BT1 3EQ
Tel 01232 240900
Fax 01232 331498

The Group publish information on services available in Northern Ireland, including prevention.

Scottish Council for Voluntary
Organisations
18-19 Claremont Crescent
Edinburgh EH7 4QD
Tel 0131 556 3882

Will provide advice on the use of volunteers in Scotland.

The Scottish Drugs Forum
5 Oswald Street
Glasgow G1 5QR
Tel 0141 221 1175

The forum co-ordinates in Scotland services for people with drug problems. It also publishes a range of information about drug services.

Standing Conference on Drug Abuse
Waterbridge House
32-36 Loman Street
London SE1 0EE
Tel 0171 928 9500
Fax 0171 928 3343

SCODA is the umbrella organisation for drugs services and others who are concerned about the effects of drug use on individuals and communities. It has specialist advice services on education, prevention, and fundings as well as information about drug services.

TACADE
(The Advisory Council on Alcohol
and Drug Education)
1 Hulme Place
The Crescent
Salford
Manchester M5 4QA
Tel 0161 745 8925
Fax 0161 745 8923

TACADE produces a wide variety of drug and health education material and material on other aspects of personal and social education.

The Wales Council for Voluntary
Action
Llysfor
Crescent Road
Caephilly
Mid Glamorgan CF83 1XL
Tel 01222 869224

Will provide advice on the use of volunteers in Wales.

Welsh Drug and Alcohol Unit
4th Floor
St Davids House
Wood Street
Cardiff CF1 1EY
Tel 01222 667766
Fax 01222 665940

The WDAU, which is managed by SCODA, provides information, advice and professional development services in Wales on all aspects of prevention, education, treatment and rehabilitation.

10.25   Other sources of advice and information which could be helpful in the cause of environmental drug prevention include the local press, schools, the police, the probation service, and health promotion and health education units.

10.26   The Central Drugs Co-ordination Unit has published and issued a useful practical digest for DATs which distils some of the ideas, good practices and recurring themes which their plans have brought out. The Central Drugs Prevention Unit has produced a number of papers on prevention projects and have summarised good practice points for the first eight papers in a digest - all these papers are available free from the Unit (Tel 0171 217 8631).

10.27   These suggestions and ideas of available resources are not exhaustive but we hope they will prove useful to some readers. Much has been, and is being done, and it would be a mistake not to build on that existing experience.

*Chapter*

# 11 THE RELEVANCE OF THIS REPORT TO THE INDIVIDUAL

*This tailpiece to our report re-emphasises what we see as its most fundamental message. There is a very broad need to construct and keep in repair a social, psychological and physical environmental surround which supports the individual's capacity to stay away from drug misuse and its harms, and which help them to pull out sooner rather than later from damaging drug misuse should it occur.*

11.1   In this concluding chapter, our aim is to make the link between the issues which we have highlighted in the report and the needs and position of the individual. In chapter 1, we pointed to the fact that it is the individual who is the ultimate agent who does or does not make the personal decision to misuse drugs. The question which arose from that fact was how could stronger awareness of the environmental dimension be used so as to put in place policies which render it less likely that the individual will be harmed by drugs.

11.2   We should perhaps start from the present position which tells us that the current environment is probably to some extent protective. Thus by the time a person is between 16 and 19 there is, looking at the country as a whole, more than a 50% possibility that he or she will not have taken illicit drugs, even experimentally. And 80% of that age group will not be taking illicit drugs regularly. As they become older many individuals grow out of misusing as they take on responsibilities, for example, of family and career. The figures may not remain constant and it would be negligent to be complacent about them. Nonetheless they are not a reason for despair.

11.3   There are many things which we still do not know about drug misuse, some of which we have alluded to in the report. For example, we do not have a good understanding of whether the phenomenon is a seamless and interactive whole or whether in reality it is a collection of distinct and discrete behaviours with different causes and consequences. And it is impossible for generalisations, in which a report of this sort must to a large extent deal, to take account all the differences which exist between individuals in terms of age, attitudes, values, social background etc.

11.4   However, what we attempt to do in this short concluding chapter is to say what the individual should expect from the environment around him or her to help protect them from the harms of drug misuse.

11.5   The family and the school must be the places where the young individual gains initial support which keeps them away from the harms of drugs. The effectiveness of altering behaviour through school education for the moment remains uncertain, but our view is that education which enhances the individual's capacity to make informed choices about drugs is a necessary part of the young person's formative years. The child would be educated about drugs during personal social health education classes. If he or she became caught up with drugs at school they should find that the school operated to a consistent and known policy, which would include liaison with parents, and that exclusion was likely only as an act of last resort. They may also be provided with drugs education by the youth services. If they are absent from school special effort should still be made to reach them.

11.6   The home environment should also, but not always will, provide support against the misuse of drugs. Parents and carers need to be aware of the issues involved and to have ready access to material which will assist them - this might come through local sources initiated by central Government (e.g. by the Health Education Authority in England and Wales), through Drug Action Teams or other local groups. The child should find himself or herself in a caring and supportive environment which helps prevent initiation into drug misuse.

11.7   And at this early stage, the young person should be aware that alcohol and tobacco and volatile substance abuse are part of the context of the misuse of drugs.

11.8   Outside the family peer influences have a significant impact on the individual. If he or she falls in with friends who do not then, or in the future, take drugs, the more likely it is that they will not take drugs themselves. The opposite is also true.

11.9   Once the individual has started misusing he or she may give up, may carry on occasionally or may carry on regularly. They may become problematic misusers. There should be a prevailing environment which helps them all reduce the harms of drug misuse - and which continues to discourage the non-user. In the case of the non-problematic misuser (whether occasional or regular) they need to be aware of the problems, health, social and criminal, to which their misuse could give rise. They might expect to receive this through centrally co-ordinated effort, through Drug Action Teams or other local drugs projects. They should not have to search out for this information, but it should be put to them through effective targeting - in chapter 6 we give some examples of where and how. They should find themselves engaged in the process of drug prevention in their normal social settings, at work, and through the local, if not national, media.

11.10  In the case of the problematic user there are benefits for both him or her and the community if their surrounding environment gives them the support which they require to deal with their problems. If they live in a deprived area there is a greater likelihood of them being a problematic user than if they lived elsewhere. The problematic misuser here therefore should expect to see special effort directed towards environmental drug prevention. They should find access to treatment easy and sympathetic housing policies in place. He or she should also find that there are effective links between treatment services, re-habilitation services, housing services, and training and employment services. They and their community should also find that the nuisance of drug dealing is dealt with firmly and that anti-social behaviour is not tolerated whether drug related or not. He or she should see the built environment being altered in such a way as to inhibit dealing and misuse. Even as negative features in the environment may generally encourage the initiation and perpetuation of problematic drug misuse, so will positive environmental interventions help to reduce the incidence of problematic use and help the user to find an earlier pathway out of their misuse.

11.11   In a more general way if they live in a deprived area they would be aware of efforts to reduce social deprivation and unemployment.

11.12   In some areas environmentally-directed activity of this sort should already be apparent but it crosses a wide range of activity and requires impetus. We regard Drug Action Teams as being especially well-placed to provide that impetus for the good of the individual and the community as a whole. Such activity whatever its immediate and detailed content can also be seen as broadly targeted at overcoming entropy, despair and the writing off of people or communities because of their drug problem.

11.13   Drug misuse will remain a feature of United Kingdom life for the future. It is a problem with linked personal and social origins. In matching terms the concept of prevention favoured by this report is therefore one of partnership between individual and society. The individual, whether younger or older, and whatever their circumstances, has personal responsibility for many aspects of their own good health, including avoidance of drug misuse and other types of substance misuse. They also bear individual responsibility for good citizenship and contribution toward their society. The additional and entirely complementary contention made by this report is that besides individual responsibility there is a societal responsibility to construct and keep in repair a social, psychological and physical environmental surround which supports the individual's capacity to stay away from drug misuse and the harms of drug misuse and helps them pull out of damaging drug misuse. The task is difficult but it must be addressed.

# APPENDIX A

**WORKING GROUP ON PREVENTION**

**Members including co-opted members**

Professor G Edwards, Institute of Psychiatry, Addiction Research Unit, London

Mrs J Barlow, Aberlour Child Care Trust, Stirling

Ms J Christian, Druglink, North Staffs

Dr W Clee, General Practitioner, near Cardiff

Mrs C Godfrey, Centre for Economics, University of York

Mr T Herbert, Independent consultant and counsellor for drug and alcohol problems, Nottingham

Mr R Howard, SCODA, London

Mr R Ives, Independent consultant on young people and drugs, London

Ms R Joyce, SCODA, London

Mr J Kay, Healthwise, Liverpool

Dr N McKeganey, Centre for Drug Misuse Research, Glasgow University

Mr P Martin, APA Community Drug and Alcohol Initiatives, London

Professor G Pearson, Goldsmiths College, London

Mr A Ramsay, Health Education Department, Glasgow City Council

Mr I Robinson, Hammersmith Drug Action Team, London

Mr P Walker, The Abbey School, Faversham

Ms M Ward, Black Drugs Initiative, Nottingham

Inspector P Wotton, Metropolitan Police, London

*Secretary:* Mr R Rhodes
*Assistant Secretary:* Mrs D Greene (to July 1997)
              Miss J Wright
*Assisted by:* Mrs J Leppert

*Officials:*

| *Home Office* | *Department of Environment, Transport and the Regions* |
| --- | --- |
| Ms L Rogerson | Mrs H Barton |
| Dr M Ramsay | Mr D Nixon |
| Mr C Lloyd | |
| *Department of Health* | *Scottish Office* |
| Dr A Thorley | Mrs M Cuthbert |

*Department for Education
and Employment*

Mr J Ford

*Northern Ireland Office*

Dr W B Smith

*Central Drugs Co-ordination
Unit*

Mr S Rimmer

Mr J Fitzpatrick

*Welsh Office*

Ms M McCabe

*OFSTED*

Dr M Gee

# APPENDIX B

## ACKNOWLEDGEMENTS

**The working group is grateful to the following who gave presentations:**

Mrs Sue Coleman
Ms Lynne Chapman
Ms Glenys Hester
Mr Rob Gilham
Ms Marlene Kneller
Mr Denis Hamilton, Wolverhampton drug prevention initiatives

Professor Peter Reuter, University of Maryland

Ms Sarah Gregory, Priority Estates Project

Mr Mick Chick, Government Office for the Eastern Region

Professor Susanne Macgregor, Middlesex University

Mr Paul Henderson, Community Development Foundation

PC Les Bullamore, Metropolitan Police

Mr Danny Levine, North West London Housing Association

Mr Roger Howard, Standing Conference on Drug Abuse

Professor David Farrington, Cambridge University

Mr Tony Herbert, Independent consultant and counsellor for drug and alcohol problems

Ms Dee McLean, Health Education Authority

Mr Stephen Rimmer, Central Drugs Co-ordination Unit

Mr Dennis Muirhead, Institute for the Study of Drug Dependence

Mr Harry Shapiro, Institute for the Study of Drug Dependence

Ms Andrea Kelmanson, National Centre for Volunteering

Professor Ivor Gaber, Goldsmiths College

Ms Clare Tickell, Phoenix House

Mr Hugh Boatswain, Housing Community Unit, London Borough of Hackney


In addition we are grateful to the following who made valuable contributions to the content of chapters 2, 3, 4, 5
and 9 of the report:

Dr John Ball

Elaine Buist

Dr M Donmall

Dr Ernest Drucker

Karen Duke

Dr Aneez Esmail

Dr Michael Farrell

Dr D Goldberg

Dr Laurence Gruer

Dr R Hammersley

Sally Haw

Dr J Heptonstall

Dr M Jones

Mr Charles Lloyd

Professor Susanne Macgregor

Doctor Neil McKeganey

Professor Michael Marmot

Eileen O'Gorman

Professor Geoffrey Pearson

Dr Malcolm Ramsay

Ms Lorraine Rogerson

Mr Colin Taylor

Mr John Whitton

# APPENDIX C

**GOVERNMENT OFFICES FOR THE REGIONS - ADDRESSES OF REGIONAL DIRECTORS**

Government Office for Eastern Region
Building A
Westbrook Centre
Milton Road
Cambridge  CB4 1YG

Tel: 01223 461939
Fax: 01223 461941

Government Office for the East Midlands
The Belgrave Centre
Stanley Place
Talbot Street
Nottingham  NG1 5GG

Tel: 0115 971 9971
Fax: 0115 971 2404

Government Office for London
Riverwalk House
157-161 Millbank
London  SW1P 4RR

Tel: 0171 217 3456
Fax: 0171 217 3450

Government Office for Merseyside
Cunard Building
Pier Head
Liverpool  L3 1QB

Tel: 0151 224 6301
Fax: 0151 224 6470

Government Office for the North East
Stanegate House
2 Groat Market
Newcastle Upon Tyne  NE1 1YN

Tel: 0191 201 3300
Fax: 0191 202 3768

Government Office for the North West
Sunley Tower
Piccadilly Plaza
Manchester  M1 4BE

Tel: 0161 952 4000
Fax: 0161 952 4099

Government Office for the South East
Bridge House
1 Walnut Tree Close
Guildford
Surrey  GU1 4GA

Tel: 01483 882255
Fax: 01483 882259

Government Office for the South West        Tel: 0117 900 1700
The Pithay                                  Fax: 0117 900 1900
Bristol BS1 2PB


Government Office for the West Midlands     Tel: 0121 212 5050
77 Paradise Circus                          Fax: 0121 212 1010
Queensway
Birmingham B1 2DT


Government Office for Yorkshire and         Tel: 0113 280 0600
 the Humber                                 Fax: 0113 283 6394
PO Box 213
City House
New Station Street
Leeds LS1 4US

# APPENDIX D

**HOME OFFICE DRUGS PREVENTION INITIATIVE**

| | | |
|---|---|---|
| **Central Drugs Prevention Unit** | Home Office<br>Room 354<br>Horseferry House<br>Dean Ryle Street<br>London  SW1P 2AW | Tel: 0171 217 8631<br>Fax: 0171 217 8230 |

**Local Teams**

| | | |
|---|---|---|
| Avon and Somerset | Prudential Buildings<br>2nd Floor<br>Wine Street<br>Bristol  BS1 2BQ | Tel: 0117 922 7997<br>Fax: 0117 925 0949 |
| Birmingham, Dudley,<br>Sandwell, Walsall and<br>Wolverhampton | Daviot House<br>3rd Floor<br>Lombard Street West<br>West Bromwich  B70 8EG | Tel: 0121 553 5553<br>Fax: 0121 553 1339 |
| Bolton, Manchester,<br>Rochdale, Salford<br>and Stockport | MSF Building<br>3 Acton Square<br>Ground Floor<br>The Crescent<br>Salford  M5 4NY | Tel: 0161 736 9540<br>Fax: 0161 736 9750 |
| East Midlands<br>(Nottingham, Leicester<br>and Derby and<br>surrounding areas in<br>the East Midlands) | Albion House<br>3rd Floor<br>Canal Street<br>Nottingham  NG1 7EG | Tel: 0115 924 0648<br>Fax: 0115 924 0649 |
| Essex | French's Gate<br>1st Floor<br>20 Springfield Road<br>Chelmsford  CM2 6FA | Tel: 01245 353124<br>Fax: 01245 353134 |
| Merseyside | Silkhouse Court<br>Suite B<br>Ground Floor<br>Tithebarn Street<br>Liverpool  L2 2LZ | Tel: 0151 236 4434<br>Fax: 0151 258 1387 |

| | | |
|---|---|---|
| North East London (Newham, Tower Hamlets, Camden, Islington, Hackney and Harringey) | Units 8/9 Angel Gate City Road London EC1V 2PT | Tel: 0171 837 7477 Fax: 0171 837 7455 |
| North West London (Westminster, Kensington and Chelsea, Hammersmith and Fulham, Brent and Ealing) | 1st Floor 4-6 York Street London W1A 1FA | Tel: 0171 224 7229 Fax: 0171 224 7237 |
| Northumbria | Lombard House Ground Floor 4 Lombard Street Newcastle Upon Tyne NE1 3AE | Tel: 0191 233 1972 Fax: 0191 233 1973 |
| South London (Wandsworth, Lambeth, Southwark, Lewisham and Greenwich) | County House 1st Floor 190 Great Dover Street London SE1 4YB | Tel: 0171 378 1488 Fax: 0171 403 4867 |
| Sussex | Castle Square House 4th Floor 9 Castle Square Brighton BN1 1DZ | Tel: 01273 722221 Fax: 01273 748813 |
| West Yorkshire | 3rd Floor Metrochange House Hall Ings Bradford BD1 5SG | Tel: 01274 741274 Fax: 01274 732846 |

# APPENDIX E

## NATIONAL LOTTERY CHARITIES BOARD

**Corporate Head Office**

Enquiries: 0171 747 5299
Reception: 0171 747 5300
Textphone: 0171 747 5347
Fax: 0171 747 5214

St Vincent House
30 Orange Street
London WC2H 7HH

Press Officer: 0171 747 5200
Internet homepage: ww.nlcb.org.uk

Main grant programme application
forms and guides: 0345 919191

**Wales Office**

Director for Wales
Ladywell House
Newtown
Powys SY16 1JB

Tel: 01686 621644
Textphone: 01686 610205
Fax: 01686 621534

**Northern Ireland Office**

Director for Northern Ireland
2nd Floor
Hildon House
30-34 Hill Street
Belfast BT1 2LB

Tel: 01232 551455
Textphone: 01232 551431
Fax: 01232 551444

**Scotland Office**

Director for Scotland
Norloch House
36 Kings Stables Road
Edinburgh EH1 2EJ

Tel: 0131 221 7100
Textphone: 0131 221 7122
Fax: 0131 221 7120

**England Office**

Director for England
Readson House
96-98 Regent Road
Leicester LE1 7DZ

Tel: 0116 258 7000
Textphone: 0116 255 5162
Fax: 0116 255 7398

## ENGLAND REGIONAL OFFICES

### London

3rd Floor
Whittington House
19-30 Alfred Place
London WC1E 7EZ

Tel: 0171 291 8500
Textphone: 0171 291 8526
Fax: 0171 291 8503

### South East

3rd Floor
Dominion House
Woodbridge Road
Guildford
Surrey GU1 4BN

Tel: 01483 462900
Textphone: 01483 568764
Fax: 01483 569893

### South West

Pembroke House
Southernhay Gardens
Southernhay East
Exeter EX1 1UL

Tel: 01392 849700
Textphone: 01392 490633
Fax: 01392 491134

### Eastern

Great Eastern House
Tension Road
Cambridge CB1 2TT

Tel: 01223 449000
Textphone: 01233 352041
Fax: 01223 312628

### East Midlands

3rd Floor
33 Park Row
Nottingham NG1 6NL

Tel: 0115 934 9300
Textphone: 0115 946 4436
Fax: 0115 948 4435

### West Midlands

4th Floor
Edmund House
12-22 Newhall Street
Birmingham B3 3NL

Tel: 0121 200 3500
Textphone: 0121 212 3523
Fax: 0121 212 3081

### Yorkshire and Humberside

3rd Floor
Carlton Tower
34 St Pauls Street
Leeds LS1 2AT

Tel: 0113 224 5300
Textphone: 0113 245 4104
Fax: 0113 214 0363

## North West (including Merseyside)

Dallam Court
Dallam Lane
Warrington WA2 7LU

Tel: 01925 626800
Textphone: 01925 231241
Fax: 01925 234041

## North East

Ground Floor
Bede House
All Saints Business Centre
Broad Chare
Newcastle Upon Tyne NE1 2NL

Tel: 0191 255 1100
Textphone: 0191 233 2099
Fax: 0191 233 1997

# APPENDIX F

## REFERENCES

### CHAPTER 1

1. Advisory Council on the Misuse of Drugs (1984) Prevention, London, HMSO.
2. Advisory Council on the Misuse of Drugs (1993) Drug Education in Schools: the need for new impetus, London, HMSO.
3. Advisory Coucil on the Misuse of Drugs (1995) Volatile Subtance Abuse, London, HMSO.
4. Advisory Council on the Misuse of Drugs (1994) Drug Misusers and the Criminal Justice System, Part II: Police Drug Misusers and the Community, London, HMSO.
5. Advisory Council on the Misuse of Drugs (1988) AIDS and Drug Misuse, Part I, London, HMSO.
6. Advisory Council on the Misuse of Drugs (1989) AIDS and Drug Misuse, Part II, London, HMSO.
7. Advisory Council on the Misuse of Drugs (1993) AIDS and Drug Misuse, Update, London, HMSO.

### CHAPTER 2

1. Goddard, E (1987) The Feasibility of a National Survey of Drugs Use. New Methodology Series, Social Science Division, Office of Population Censuses and Surveys, No. NM 15.
2. Home Office (1997) Statistics of Drug Addicts Notified to the Home Office, United Kingdom, 1996. Home Office Statistical Bulletin 22/97.
3. Home Office (1996) Statistics of Drugs Seizures and Offenders Dealt With, United Kingdom, 1995. Home Office Statistical Bulletin 25/96.
4. Home Office (1971) Misuse of Drugs Act, London: HMSO.
5. Department of Health Statistical Bulletin (1997) Drug Misuse Statistics - for the six months ending 31 March 1996: England. Government Statistical Service.
6. Ramsay M and Spiller J (1997) Drug Misuse declared in 1996: latest results from the British Crime Survey Home Office Research Study 172 London: Home Office.
7. Anderson S and Frischer M (1997) Drug Misuse in Scotland: Findings from the 1993 and 1996 Scottish Crime Surveys. Scottish Office Central Research Unit: Edinburgh.
8. Northern Ireland Office (1996) Experience of Drugs in Northern Ireland: Preliminary Research Findings from the 1994/1995 Northern Ireland Crime Survey Statistics and Research Branch, Northern Ireland Office. Research Findings 1/96.
9. Meltzer H, Gill B, Petticrew M and Hinds K (1995) Prevalence of Psychiatric Morbidity among Adults living in Private Households. OPCS Surveys of Psychiatric Morbidity in Great Britain, Report 1.
10. Leitner M, Shapland J and Wiles P (1993) Drug Usage and Drug Prevention: the views and habits of the general public. London: HMSO.
11. Sutton M and Maynard A (1993) Are Drug Policies Based on 'Fake' Statistics? Addiction;88:455-458.
12. Welsh Office (1995)Welsh Drug Misuse Database Report: Report 8.
13. Frischer M, Leyland A, Cormack R, Goldberg D, Bloor M, Green S, Taylor A, Covell R, McKeganey N and Platt S (1993) Estimating the Population Prevalence of Injection Drug Use and Infection with Human Immunodeficiency Virus among Injection Drug Users in Glasgow, Scotland. American Journal of Epidemiology;138:170-181.
14. Squires N, Beeching N, Schlecht B and Ruben S (1995) An Estimate of the Prevalence of Drug Misuse in Liverpool and a Spatial Analysis of Known Addiction. Journal of Public Health Medicine;171:103-109.
15. Hay G and McKeganey N (1996) Estimating the Prevalence of Drug Misuse in Dundee: An Application of Capture-recapture Methods. Journal of Epidemiology and Community Health; 50: 469-472.
16. Bloor M, Wood F and Palmer S (1997) Estimating the Prevalence of Injecting Drug Use and Serious Drug Use in Wales. Cardiff: Social Research Unit.
17. McGourty H and Hotchkiss J (1994) Drug Misuse and Services for Drug Users in Chester. Observatory Report Series No. 18. Liverpool Public Health Observatory.
18. Ramsay M and Percy A (1996) Drug Misuse Declared: results of the 1994 British Crime Survey. Home Office Research Study 151. London: Home Office.

19. Robins L and McEnvoy L (1990) Conduct Problems as Predictors of Substance Abuse, in L Robins and M Rutter (eds) Straight and Devious Pathways from Childhood to Adulthood, pp. 182-204 Cambridge: Cambridge University Press.

20. Balding J (1996) Young People in 1995. University of Exeter: Schools Health Education Unit.

21. Adelekan M, Gowers S and Singh D (1994) Substance Use Among Secondary School Pupils in Blackburn Borough. Drugs: Education, Prevention and Policy;1:111-120.

22. Barnard M, Forsyth A and McKeganey N (1996) Levels of Drug Use Among a Sample of Scottish Schoolchildren. Drugs: Education, Prevention and Policy ;3:81-89.

23. McKeganey N, Forsyth A, Barnard M and Hay G (1996) Designer Drinks and Drunkenness Amongst a Sample of Scottish Schoolchildren. British Medical Journal;313:1397-1398.

24. Parker H, Measham F and Aldridge J (1995) Drugs Futures: Changing Patterns of Drug Use Amongst English Youth. London: ISDD.

25. Advisory Council on the Misuse of Drugs (1995) Volatile Substance Abuse. London:HMSO.

26. Health Promotion Agency for Northern Ireland (1995) The Health Behaviour of School Children in Northern Ireland: A report on the 1994 survey. Belfast.

27. Miller P and Plant M (1996) Drinking, smoking, and illicit drug use among 15 and 16 year olds in the United Kingdom. British Medical Journal;313:394-7.

28. Smith C and Nutbeam D (1992) Adolescent Drug Use in Wales. British Journal of Addiction;87:227-233.

29. Forsyth A (1996) Places and patterns of drug use in the Scottish dance scene. Addiction;91:511-522

30. The University of Manchester Drug Misuse Research Unit. Personal communication from M Donmall.

31. Oppenheimer E, Tobutt C, Taylor C and Andrew T (1995) Death and survival in a cohort of heroin addicts from London clinics: a 22-year follow-up study. Addiction;89:1299-1308.

32. Frischer M, Goldberg D, Rahman M and Berney L (1996) Mortality and Survival amongst a cohort of drug injectors in Glasgow 1982-1994. Addiction;92:419-427.

33. Eskild A, Magnus P, Samuelson S, Sohlberg C and Kittleson P (1995) Differences in mortality rates and causes of death between HIV-positive and HIV-negative intravenous drug users. International Journal of Epidemiology; 22:315-320.

34. Roberts I, Barker M and Li L (1997) Analysis of trends in deaths from accidental poisoning in teenagers 1985 to 1995 British Medical Journal;315:289.

35. Henry, J. Personal Communication

36. Home Office (1993) Statistics of Drug Addicts Notified to the Home Office, United Kingdom, 1992. Home Office Statistical Bulletin 15/93.

37. Arrundale J and Cole S (1997) Drug-related Deaths in Scotland in 1996. Edinburgh:GRO(S).

38. General Register Office, Northern Ireland. Personal communication from the Statistics Section.

39. Unlinked Anonymous HIV Surveys Steering Group (1995) Unlinked Anonymous HIV Prevalence Monitoring Programmes in England and Wales. London: Department of Health, PHLS with the Institute of Child Health, London.

40. Davies A, Dominy N, Peters A, Bath G, Burns S and Richardson A (1995) HIV in Injecting Drug-users in Edinburgh - Prevalence and Correlates. Journal of Acquired Immune Deficiency Syndrome and Human Retrovirology; 8:399-405.

41. Haw S, Higgins K, Bell D, Johnston B and Richardson A (1996) Evidence of Continuing Risk of HIV Transmission among Injecting Drug Users from Dundee. Scottish Medical Journal;41:3-4.

42. Johnson A, Wadsworth J, Wellings K, Bradshaw S and Field J (1992) Sexual Lifestyles and HIV Risk. Nature;330:410-412.

43. Giesecke J, Noone A, Nicoll A, Johnson A, Hawkins A, Wadsworth J, Wellings K and Field J (1994) An Estimate of the Prevalence of Human Immunodeficieny Virus Infection in England and Wales by Using a Direct Method. Journal of the Royal Statistical Society A;157:89-103.

44. Hickman H, Bardsley M, de Angelis D, Ward H, Carrier J (1997) A sexual health ready reckoner. The Health of Londoners Project, East London and The City Health Authority. London.

45. Day N (1996) The Incidence and prevalence of other severe HIV disease in England and Wales for 1995 to 1999: projections using data to the end of 1994. Communicable Disease Report; 6:7.

46. CDSC. AIDS and HIV-1 Infection in the United Kingdom: Monthly Report. Communicable Disease Report Vol 7, No 4, 24th January 1997.

47. Wodak A and Crofts N (1996) Once more unto the breach: controlling hepatitis C in injecting drug users. Addiction;91:181-184.

48. Brind A, Serfaty A, Lawrie A, Watson J, Johnson S, Gilvarry E and Bassendine M (1996) Hepatitis-C virus (HCV) infection in a drug dependency centre in North-East England. Hepatology;23:102.

49. Smyth R, Keenan E, Dorman A, and O'Connor J (1995) Hepatitis-C infection among injecting drug-users attending the national drug-treatment center. Irish Journal Of Medical Science;164:267-268.
50. Scottish Health Service, Personal communication from the Information and Statistics Division
51. Gossop M, Griffiths P, Powis B, Williamson S and Strang J (1996) Frequency of non-fatal heroin overdose recruited in non-clinical settings. British Medical Journal;313:402.
52. Taylor A, Frischer M and Goldberg D (1996) Non-fatal overdose is related to poly drug use in Glasgow. British Medical Journal;313:1400-1401.
53. Darke S, Ross J and Hall W (1996) Overdose among heroin users in Sydney, Australia: I. Prevalence and correlates of non-fatal overdose. Addiction; 91:405-411.
54. Barnard M (1993) Needle sharing in context: patterns of sharing among men and women injectors and HIV risks. Addiction; 88:805-812.
55. Donoghoe M (1992) Sex, HIV and the injecting drug user British Journal of Addiction;87:405-416.
56. McKeganey N and Barnard M (1996) Sex Work on the Streets: Prostitutes and their Clients: Open University Press.

**CHAPTER 3**

1. R Power, S Jones, G Kearns and J Ward (1995) Drug User Lifestyles and Peer Education, Druglink, 10, 14-16.
2. National Institute Of Justice (1991) Drug Use Forecasting: Drugs and and Crime. 1990 Annual Report. Washington DC: US Department of Justice.
3. A Golub and B D Johnson (1994) A Recent Decline in Cocaine Use among Youthful Arrestees in Manhattan, 1987 through 1993, American Journal of Public Health, 84, 1250-1254.
4. E Dunlap and B D Johnson (1992) The Setting for the Crack Era: Macro Forces, Micro Consequences 1960-92, Journal of Psychoactive Drugs, 24, 307-322.
5. A Golub and B D Johnson (1997) Crack's Decline: Some Surprises Across US Cities, Washington DC: National Institute of Justice, US Department of Justice
6. N E Zinberg (1984) Drug, Set, and Setting: The Basis for Controlled Intoxicant Use. New Haven: Yale University Press.
7. M B Lyons, R Toomey, J Meyer et al (1997) How do genes influence marijuana use? The Role of subjective effect, Addiction, 92, 409-417.
8. H S Becker (1963) Becoming a Marijuana User, Outsiders: Studies in the Sociology of Deviance, 41-58, New York, Free Press.
9. G Pearson (1992) The Role of Culture in the Drug Question, in M Lader, G Edwards and D C Drummond eds., The Nature of Alcohol and Drug Related Problems. Society for the Study of Addiction Monograph No. 2, 109-132, Oxford: Oxford University Press.
10. E Preble and J J Casey (1969) Taking Care of Business: The Heroin User's Life on the Street, International Journal of the Addictions, 4, 1-24.
11. M Gilman and G Pearson (1991) Lifestyles and Law Enforcement, in D K Whynes and P T Bean eds., Policing and Prescribing, 85-124, London: Macmillan.
12. G Pearson (1987) The New Heroin Users. Oxford: Blackwell.
13. M H Moore (1977) Buy and Bust: The Effective Regulation of an Illicit Market in Heroin. Lexington, Mass: Lexington Books.
14. M A R Kleiman (1992) Against Excess: Drug Policy for Results. New York: Basic Books.
15. G Pearson (1992) Drugs and Criminal Justice: A Harm Reduction Perspective, in R A O'Hare, R Newcombe, A Matthews, E C Buning and E Drucker eds., The Reduction of Drug-Related Harm, 15-29, London: Routledge.
16. J G Bachman, L D Johnston and P M O'Malley (1990) Explaining the Recent Decline in Cocaine Use Among Adults: Further Evidence That Perceived Risks and Disapproval Lead to Reduce Drug Use, Journal of Health and Social Behavior, 31, 173-184.
17. S Peele (1985) The Meaning of Addiction: Compulsive Experience and Its Interpretation. Lexington: Lexington, Mass: Lexington Books.
18. S R Goldberg and I P Stollerman eds (1986) Behavioural Analysis of Drug Dependence, New York, Academic Press.
19. D Waldorf, C Reinerman and S Murphy (1991) Cocaine Changes: The Experience of Using and Quitting. Philadelphia: Temple University Press.
20. H J Shaffer and S B Jones (1989) Quitting Cocaine: The Struggle Against Impulse. Lexington, Mass: Lexington Books.

21. Biernacki P (1986) Pathways from Heroin Addiction: Recovery without Treatment. Philadelphia: Temple University Press.
22. D Waldorf (1983) Natural Recovery from Opiate Addiction: Some Social-Psychological Processes of Untreated Recovery, Journal of Drug Issues, 13, 237-280.
23. L N Robins (1973) The Vietnam Drug User Returns. Washington, DC: US Government Printing Office.
24. J Long and D Scherl (1984) Developmental Antecedents of Compulsive Drug Use: A Report on the Literature, Journal of Psychoactive Drugs, 16, 169-182.
25. D B Kandel ed (1978) Longitudinal Research on Drug Use: Empirical Findings and Methodological Issues. New York: Wiley.
26. J D Hawkins, R F Catalano and J Y Miller (1992) Risk and Protective Factors for Alcohol and Other Drug Problems in Adolescence and Early Adulthood: Implications for Substance Abuse Prevention, Psychological Bulletin, 112, 64-105.
27. J M Chaiken and M R Chaiken (1990) Drugs and Predatory Crime, in M Tonry and J Q Wilson eds., Drugs and Crime. Crime and Justice: A Review of Research. 13, 203-239, Chicago: University of Chicago Press.
28. G D Walters (1994) Drugs and Crime in Lifestyle Perspective. London: Sage.
29. J Fagan and J G Weis (1991) Drug Use and Delinquency among Inner City Youth. New York: Springer-Verlag.
30. T Williams and W Kornblum (1985) Growing Up Poor. Lexington, Mass: Lexington Books.
31. L E Wells and J H Rankin (1991) Families and Delinquency: A Meta-Analysis of the Impact of Broken Homes, Social Problems, 38, 71-93.
32. D P Farrington (1994) Human Development and Criminal Careers, in M Maguire, R Morgan and R Reiner eds., The Oxford Handbook of Criminology, 511-584, Oxford: Clarendon Press.
33. L Robins (1992) Detecting Individual Factors in Substance Abuse Problems, in M Lader, G Edwards and D C Drummond eds., The Nature of Alcohol and Drug Related Problems. Society for the Study of Addiction Monograph No 2, 133-150, Oxford: Oxford University Press.
34. D Cahalan and R Room (1972) Problem Drinking among American Men Aged 21-59, American Journal of Public Health, 62, 1473-1482.
35. D B Kandel (1980) Drug and Drinking Behaviour among Youth, Annual Review of Sociology, 6, 235-285.
36. H Parker, K Bakx and R Newcombe (1988) Living With Heroin: The Impact of a Drugs 'Epidemic' on an English Community. Milton Keynes: Open University Press.
37. G Pearson, M Gilman and S McIver (1985) Young People and Heroin: An Examination of Heroin Use in the North of England. London: Health Education Council.
38. L Steinberg, A Fletcher and N Darling (1994) Parental Monitoring and Peer Influences on Adolescent Substance Use, Pediatrics, 93, 1060-1064.
39. N McKeganey and M Barnard (1992) AIDS, Drugs and Sexual Risk. Buckingham: Open University Press.
40. E R Oetting and F Beauvais (1988) Common Elements in Youth Drug Abuse: Peer Clusters and Other Psychosocial Factors, in S. Peele ed., Visions of Addiction: Major Contemporary Perspectives on Addiction and Alcoholism, pp 141-161, Lexington, Mass: Lexington Books.
41. M Barnard and N McKeganey (1994) Drug Misuse and Young People: A Selective Review of the Literature. Glasgow: Centre for Drug Misuse Research, University of Glasgow.
42. D S Elliott, D Huizinga and S S Ageton (1985) Explaining Delinquency and Drug Use. London: Sage.
43. D S Elliott, D Huizinga and S Menard (1989) Multiple Problem Youth: Delinquency, Substance Use and Mental Health Problems. New York: Springer-Verlag.
44. G R Patterson and T J Dishion (1985) Contributions of Families and Peers to Delinquency, Criminology, 23, 63-79.
45. P Townsend, N Davidson and M Whitehead (1988) Inequalities in Health. London: Penguin.
46. P Mayhew, N A Maung and C Mirrlees-Black(1993) The 1992 British Crime Survey. Home Office Research Study no. 132. London: HMSO.
47. R Kaestner (1991) The Effect of Illicit Drug Use on the Wages of Young Adults, Journal of Labour Economics, 9, 381-412.
48. C E Faupel (1988) Heroin Use, Crime and Employment Status, Journal of Drug Issues, 18, 467-479.
49. C R Shaw and H McKay (1942) Juvenile Delinquency and Urban Areas. Chicago: University of Chicago Press.
50. R E L Faris and H W Dunham (1939) Mental Disorders in Urban Areas. Chicago: University of Chicago Press.
51. B Dai (1937) Opium Addiction in Chicago. Chicago: University of Chicago Press.
52. I Chein, D Gerard, R Lee and E Rosenfield (1964) The Road to H: Narcotics, Delinquency and Social Policy. London: Tavistock.

53. P H Hughes (1977) Behind the Wall of Respect: Community Experiments in Heroin Addiction Control. Chicago: University of Chicago Press.
54. P Bourgois (1989) Crack in Spanish Harlem: Culture and Economy in the Inner City, Anthropology Today, 5, 6-11.
55. J Fagan and K L Chin (1991) Social Processes of Initiation into Crack, Journal of Drug Issues, 21, 313-43.
56. S Haw (1985) Drug Problems in Greater Glasgow. London: Standing Conference on Drug Abuse.
57. J Giggs, P Bean, D K Whynes and C Wilkinson (1989) Class A Drug Users: Prevalence Characteristics in Greater Nottingham, British Journal of Addiction, 84, 1473-80.
58. A Burr (1987) Chasing the Dragon: Heroin Misuse, Delinquency and Crime in the Context of South London Culture, British Journal of Criminology, 27, 333-357.
59. H S Mirza, G Pearson and S Phillips (1990) Drugs, Services and People in Lewisham. London: Lewisham Safer Cities Committee and Goldsmiths College.
60. G Pearson and M Gilman (1994) Local and Regional Variations in Drug Misuse: The British Heroin Epidemic of the 1980s, in J Strang and M Gossop eds., Heroin Addiction and Drug Policy: The British System, 102-120, Oxford: Oxford University Press.
61. A E Bottoms and P Wiles (1986) Housing Tenure and Residential Community Crime Careers in Britain, in A J Reiss Jr and M Tonry eds., Communities and Crime. Crime and Justice: A Review of Research, 8, 101-162, Chicago: University of Chicago Press.
62. H W Feldman (1968) Ideological Supports to becoming And Remaining a Heroin Addict, Journal of Health and Social Behaviour, 9, 131-139.
63. I B Ricardo (1994) Life Choices of African-American Youth Living in Public Housing: Perspectives on Drug Trafficking, Pediatrics, 93, 1055-1059.
64. P Reuter, R MacCoun and P Murphy (1990) Money from Crime: A Study of the Economics of Drug Dealing in Washington, DC. Santa Monica, CA: RAND Corporation.
65. B D Johnson, P J Goldstein, E Preble, J Schmeidler, D S Lipton, B Spunt and T Miller (1985) Taking Care of Business: The Economics of Crime by Heroin Abusers. Lexington, Mass: Lexington Books.
66. N Dorn, K Murji and N South (1992) Traffickers: Drug Markets and Law Enforcement. London: Routledge.
67. N Dorn, O Baker and T Seddon (1994) Paying for Heroin: Estimating the Financial Cost of Acquisitive Crime Committed by Dependent Heroin Users in England and Wales. London: Institute for the Study of Drug Dependence.
68. T Williams (1989) The Cocaine Kids. New York: Addison-Wesley.
69. M Rosenbaum (1981) Women on Heroin. New Jersey: Rutgers University Press.
70. A Taylor (1993) Women Drug Users: An Ethnography of a Female Injecting Community. Oxford: Clarendon Press.
71. D F Peck and M A Plant (1986) Unemployment and Illegal Drug Use: Concordant Evidence from a Prospective Study and National Trends, British Medical Journal, 293, 929-932.
72. G Pearson (1987) Social Deprivation, Unemployment and Patterns of Heroin Use, in N Dorn and N South eds., A Land Fit for Heroin? Drug Policies, Prevention and Practice. London: Macmillan.
73. G Pearson (1991) Drug Control Policies in Britain, in M Tonry ed., Crime and Justice: A Review of Research, 14, 167-227, Chicago: University of Chicago Press.
74. S Weir (1985) Qat in Yemen: Consumption and Social Change. London: British Museum.
75. L J Francis and K Mullen (1993) Religiosity and Attitudes Towards Drug Use among 13-15 Year Olds in England, Addiction, 88, 665-672.
76. W W Wiebel (1988) Combining Ethnographic and Epidemiological Methods in Targeted AIDS Interventions: The Chicago Model, in R J Battjes and R W Pickens eds., Needle-Sharing among Intravenous Drug Abusers: National and International Perspectives, NIDA Research Monograph 80, 137-150, Rockville, MA: National Institute on Drug Abuse.
77. G Pearson, H S Mirza and S Phillips (1993) Cocaine in Context: Findings from a South London Inner-City Drug Survey, in P Bean ed., Cocaine and Crack: Supply and Use, 99-129, London: Macmillan.
78. M Leitner, J Shapland and P Wiles (1993) Drug Usage and Drugs Prevention: The Views and Habits of the General Public. London: HMSO.
79. H Parker, F Measham and J Aldridge (1995) Drug Futures: Changing Patterns of Drug Use Amongst English Youth, ISDD Research Monograph Seven. London: Institute for the Study of Drug Dependence.
80. J Mott and C Mirrlees-Black (1995) Self-Reported Drug Misuse in England and Wales: Findings from the 1992 British Crime Survey, Research and Planning Unit Paper no. 89. London: Home Office.
81. G Pearson and K Patel (1998) Drugs, Deprivation and Ethnicity: Outreach Among Asian Drug Users in a Northern English City, Journal of Drug Issues, March 1988, in press.

82. J Graham and B Bowling (1995) Young People and Crime. Home Office Research Study, no. 145. London: Home Office.

83. M Ramsay and A Percy (1996) Drug Misuse Declared: Results of the 1994 British Crime Survey. Home Office Research Study, no. 151. London: Home Office.

84. M Ramsay and J Spiller (1997) Drug Misuse Declared in 1996: Latest Results from the British Crime Survey. Home Office Research Study 172. London: Home Office

85. J Awiah, S Butt and N Dorn (1992) Race, Gender and Drug Services. ISDD Research Monograph Six. London: Institute for the Study of Drug Dependence.

86. M R D Johnson and M Carroll (1995) Dealing With Diversity: Good Practice in Drug Prevention Work with Racially and Culturally Diverse Communities. London: Central Drugs Prevention Unit, Home Office.

87. H Shapiro (1988) Waiting for the Man: The Story of Drugs and Popular Music.    London: Quartet.

88. D Courtwright, H Joseph and D Des Jarlais (1989) Addicts Who Survived: An Oral History of Narcotic Use in America, 1923-1965. Knoxville: University of Tennessee Press.

89. G Pearson (1983) Hooligan: A History of Respectable Fears. London: Macmillan.

90. M Gilman (1988) Comics as a Strategy in Reducing Drug-Related Harm, in N Dorn, L Lucas and N South eds., Drug Questions: An Annual Research Register, 4, 125-132, London: Institute for the Study of Drug Dependence.

91. H Blagg, G Pearson, A Sampson, D Smith and P Stubbs (1988) Inter-Agency Cooperation: Rhetoric and Reality, in T. Hope and M. Shaw eds., Communities and Crime Reduction, 204-220, London: HMSO.

92. G Pearson, H Blagg, D Smith, A Sampson and P Stubbs (1992) Crime, Community and Conflict: 'The Multi-Agency Approach', in D Downes ed., Unravelling Criminal Justice: Eleven British Studies, 46-72, London: Macmillan.

93. J Foster and T Hope (1993) Housing, Community and Crime: The Impact of the Priority Estates Project. Home Office Research Study no. 131. London: HMSO.

94. J Fagan (1990) 'Intoxication and Aggression', in M. Tonry and J.Q. Wilson eds., Drugs and Crime. Crime and Justice: A Review of Research, 13, 241-320, Chicago: University of Chicago Press.

95. B D Johnson, T Williams, K A Dei and H Sanabria (1990) Drug Abuse In the Inner City: Impact on Hard-Drug Users and the Community, in M Tonry and J Q Wilson eds., Drugs and Crime. Crime and Justice: A Review of Research. 13, 9-67, Chicago: University of Chicago Press.

96. E Currie (1993) Reckoning: Drugs, the Cities, and the American Future. New York: Hill and Wang.

## CHAPTER 4

1. Bangert-Drowns R L (1988) The effects of school-based substance abuse education - a meta-analysis. Journal of Drug Education, 18, 243-264.

2. Schaps E, DiBartolo R, Moskowitz J, et al (1981) A review of 127 drug abuse prevention program evaluations, Journal of Drug Issues, 11, 17-43.

3. Advisory Council on the Misuse of Drugs (1993) Drug Education in Schools: the need for new impetus, London, HMSO.

4. Moskowitz J M, (1985) Evaluating the effects of parent groups on the correlates of adolescents' substance abuse, Journal of Psychoactive Drugs, 17, 173-178.

5. Klitzner M, Bamberger E and Gruenewald P (1990) The assessment of parent-led prevention programs: a national descriptive study, Journal of Drug Education, 20, 111-125.

6. DeMarsh J and Kumpfer K L (1986) Family oriented interventions for the prevention of chemical dependency in children and adolescents, Childhood and Chemical Abuse: prevention and intervention edited by S Ezekaye, K Kumpfer and W Bukoski, New York, Haworth Press.

7. McDonald L, Bradish D C, Billingham S, et al (1991) Families and schools together: an innovative substance abuse prevention program, Social Work Education, 13, 118-128.

8. Tobler N S (1986) Meta-analysis of 143 adolescent drug prevention program: quantiative outcome results of program participants compared to a control or comparison group, The Journal of Drug Issues, 16, 537-567.

9. Tobler, NS (1992) Drug prevention programs can work: research findings, Journal of Addictive Diseases, 11, 1-28.

10. Shiner M and Newburn T (1996) Young People, Drugs and Peer Education: an evaluation of the Youth Awareness Programme (YAP), Drugs Prevention Initiative Paper 13, London, Home Office.

11. Leitner M, Shapland J and Wiles P (1993) Drug Usage and Drugs Prevention: the views and habits of the general public, London, Home Office Drugs Prevention Initiative.

12. Davis G and Dawson N (1995) Using diversion to communicate drugs prevention messages to young people: an examination of six projects, Drugs Prevention Initiative Paper 12, London, Home Office.

13. Dorn N and Murji K (1992) Drug Prevention: a review of the English language literature, ISDD, London, Research Monograph Five.

14. Osterloh J (1990) Drug testing in the workplace, Occupational Medicine, 5, 617-632.

15. Dorn N and South N (1994) The power behind practice: drug control and harm minimisation in inter-agency and criminal law contexts, Heroin Addiction and Drugs Policy: the British System, edited by J Strang and M Donmall, Oxford University Press, Oxford, 292- 300.

16. Advisory Council on the Misuse of Drugs (1984) Prevention, London, HMSO.

17. Stimson G V, Aldritt L, Dolan K, Donaghue N C and Lart R (1988) Injecting Equipment Exchanges Schemes:final report, London, Goldsmiths College.

18. Rhodes T J, Hartnoll R L and Johnson A M (1991) Out of the Agency and on to the Streets: a review of HIV outreach health education in Europe and the United States, London, ISDD Research Monograph 2.

19. Maudsley Alcohol Pilot Project (1975) Designing a comprehensive community response to problems of alcohol abuse. Report to the Department of Health and Social Security, London.

20. Strang J and Clement S (1994) The introduction of Community Drug Teams across the UK, Heroin Addiction and Drug Policy: the British System (edited by J Strang and M Donmall), Oxford, Oxford University Press, 207-221.

21. Friedman S R, Neaigus A, Des Jarlais D C et al (1992) Social intervention against AIDS among injecting drug users, British Journal of Addiction 87, 393-405.

22. Turnbull P J, Stimson G V and Stillwell G (1994) Drug Use in Prison, AVERT.

23. Advisory Council on the Misuse of Drugs (1996) Drug Misuse and the Prison System - an integrated approach, London, HMSO.

24. Rock P (1988) Crime reduction initiatives on problem estates, Communities and Crime Reduction, edited by T Hope and M Shaw, London, HMSO.

25. Skogan W and Lurigio A J (1992) The correlates of community antidrug activism, Crime and Delinquency, 38, 510-521.

26. Skogan W G (1990) Disorder and Decline, New York, New York Free Press .

27. Lurigio A J and Davis R C (1992) Taking the War on Drugs to the Streets: the perceptual impact of four neighbourhood drug programs, Crime and Delinquency, 38, 522-538.

28. Blackman T (1995) Urban Policy in Practice, London, Routledge.

29. Kress J S and Elias M J (1993) Substance abuse prevention in special education populations: review and recommendations, The Journal of Special Education, 27, 35-51.

30. Van Hasselt V B , Hersen M, Null, J, et al (1993) Drug abuse prevention for high risk African American children and their families: a review and model program, Addictive Behaviours, 18, 213-234.

31. Hawkins J D, Catalano R F and Associates (1992) Communities that Care: Action for Drug Abuse Prevention, San Francisco, Jossey-Bass.

32. Duke K, MacGregor S and Smith L (1996) Activating Local Networks: a comparison of two community development approaches to drug prevention. Drugs Prevention Initiative Paper 1, London, Home Office.

33. Henderson P (1996) Drugs Prevention and Community Development: principles of good practice. Drugs Prevention Initiative Paper 7, London, Home Office.

34. Compass Partnership (1993) Drugs Prevention Initiative: an Evaluation. Final Report, Compass Partnership, London.

35. Crow I (1991) Community based drug misuse prevention: a report on the work of NACRO's Drug Misuse Prevention Unit 1988-1990, University of Sheffield

36. Kumpfer K L and Hopkins R (1993) Prevention: Current research and trends, Recent Advances in Addictive Disorders, Psychiatric Clinics of North America, 16, March 11- 20.

37. Russell N, Booth M and Merrony B (1987) Report of the Evaluation of the CADAP Project, Canberra, Alcohol and Drug Foundation Australia.

38. Hawkins J D, Catalano R F and Miller J Y (1992) Risk and protective factors for alcohol and other drug problems in adolescence and early adulthood: implications for substance abuse prevention, Psychological Bulletin, 112, 64-105.

39. Newcomb M D and Felix-Ortiz M (1992) Multiple protective and risk factors for drug use and abuse: cross-sectional and prospective findings, Journal of Personality and Social Psychology, 63, 280-296.

40. Farquhar J W, Wood P D, Breitrose H, et al (1977) Community education for cardiovascular health, Lancet 1 (8023), 1192-1195.

41. Johnson C A and Solis J (1983) Comprehensive Community Programs for Drug Abuse Prevention: implications of the community heart disease prevention programs for future research, National Institute on Drug Abuse Monograph Series, 47, 76-114. Washington DC, US Dept of Health and Human Services.

42. Kumpfer K L (1991) Children and adolescents and drug and alcohol abuse and addiction: review of prevention strategies, Comprehensive Handbook of Drug and Alcohol Addiction edited by N S Miller, Marcel Dekker.

43. Pentz M A, Dwyer J H, Mackinnon D P, et al (1989) A multi-community trial for primary prevention of adolescent drug abuse, Journal of the American Medical Association, 261, 3259-3266.

44. Pentz M A (1993) Comparative effects of community-based drug abuse prevention Addictive Behaviour across the life span: prevention, treatment and policy issues, edited by J S Baer, G A Masters and D J McMahon, London, Sage.

45. Johnson C A, Pentz M A, Weber M D, et al (1990) Relative effectiveness of comprehensive community programming for drug abuse prevention with high-risk and low-risk adolescents, Journal of Consulting and Clinical Psychology, 58, 447-456.

46. Botvin, GJ, and Botvin, E M (1992) School-based and community-based prevention approaches, Substance Abuse: a comprehensive textbook second edition edited by J H Lowinson, P Rruiz, R B Millman and J G Langrod. Williams and Wilkins, 910-927.

47. Botvin G J, Baker E, Dusenbury L, et al (1995) Preventing adolescent drug abuse through a multimodal cognitive-behavioural approach: results of a three year study, Journal of Consulting and Clinical Psychology, 58, 437-446.

48. Wing K T (1993) Lessons from experience: the role of research in improving substance abuse prevention, Journal of Community Psychology, 21, 246-255.

## CHAPTER 5

1. Turner D (1994) The Voluntary Sector. In eds J Strang and M Gossop Heroin Addiction and Drug Policy: the British System. Oxford, Oxford University Press.

2. Leech K (1972) The Role of the Voluntary agencies. The British Journal of Addiction to alcohol and other drugs, 67, 131-6.

3. MacGregor S, Ettore B, Coomber R, Croiser A, Lodge H (1991) Drug Services in England and the impact of the Central Funding Initiative. ISDD Research Monograph Series No 2. London, Institute for the Study of Drug Dependence.

4. Advisory Council on the Misuse of Drugs (1982) Treatment and Rehabilitation. London, HMSO.

5. Strang J (1989) A model service: tuning the generalist onto drugs. In S McGregor editor Drugs and British Society. London, Routledge.

6. Strang J, Donmall M, Webster A, Abbey J and Tantam D (1991) A bridge not far enough: community drug teams and doctors in the North Western Region 1982-86. ISDD Research Monograph No 3. London, Institute for the Study of Drug Dependence.

7. Duke K and MacGregor S (1997) Tackling Drugs Locally, the implementation of Drug Action Teams in England. London. The Stationery Office.

## CHAPTER 6

1. Ramsay M and Spiller J (1997) Drug misuse declared: results of the 1996 British Crime Survey, London, Home Office

2. Yamaguchi K and Kandel D (1984) Patterns of Drug Use from Adolescence to Young Adulthood: Sequences of Progression American Journal of Public Health 74 668-672

3. Balding J (1995) Young People in 1994, Social Health Education Report, University of Exeter

4. Barnard M, Forsyth A, McKeganey N (1996) Levels of Drug Use Amongst a Sample of Scottish Schoolchildren, Drugs: Education, Prevention and Policy, 3:81-89

5. Roker D and Coleman J, (1997) Education and Advice About Illegal Drugs: what do young people want? Drugs, Education, Prevention and Policy, 4, 53-64

6. London Drug Policy Forum (1996) Dance till dawn safely - a code of practice on health and safety at dance venues, London, LDPF

7. The Scottish Office (1994) Drugs in Scotland: meeting the challenge: report of the Ministerial Drugs Task Force, London, HMSO

8. Advisory Council on the Misuse of Drugs (1993) Drug Education in Schools: the need for new impetus, London, HMSO

9. Office for Standards in Education (OFSTED) (1997) Drug Education in Schools: a report from the Office of Her Majesty's Chief Inspector of Schools, London, The Stationery Office

10. Office for Standards in Education (OFSTED) (1997) The contribution of Youth Services to Drug Education: a report from the Office of Her Majesty's Inspector of Schools, London, The Stationery Office

## CHAPTER 7

1. Gill B, Meltzer H, Heinz K, Petticrew M (1996) Psychiatric Morbidity among homeless people. OPCS survey of psychiatric morbidity in GB. Report 7. London. HMSO
2. Farrell M, Jenkins R, Bebbington P, et al C (1997) Substance misuse and psychiatric comorbidity. An overview of the National Psychiatric Morbidity Survey. Draft report

## CHAPTER 8

1. Advisory Council on the Misuse of Drugs (1994) Drug Misusers and the Criminal Justice System Part II: Police, Drug Misusers and the Community, London, HMSO.
2. M Grapendaal (1992) Cutting Their Coat According to Their Cloth: Economic Behaviour of Amsterdam Opiate Users, International Journal of the Addictions, 27, 487-501.
3. M Grossman, F J Chaloupka, and C C Brown (1996) The demand for cocaine by young adults: a rational addiction approach. National Bureau of Economic Research Working Paper 5713, NBER: Cambridge, MA.
4. M Edmunds, M Hough, and N Urquia, (1997) Tackling Local Drug Markets, Crime Detection and Prevention Series, 80. London, Home Office

## CHAPTER 9

1. Wilkinson R G (1996) Unhealthy Societies: The Afflictions of Inequality. London, Routledge.
2. Morris R and Carstairs V (1991) Which deprivation? A comparison of selected 21. O'Donnell J (1969) Narcotic Addicts in Kentucky. Chevy Chase, Maryland, Department of Health, Education and Welfare.
3. Jahoda M (1982) Employment and Unemployment: A Social-Psychological Analysis. Cambridge, Cambridge University Press.
4. Wilkinson R G (1997) Socio-economic determinants of health. Health inequalities: relative or absolute material standards? BMJ 314, 591-595.
5. United Nations Development Program (1997) Human Development Report. Oxford, Oxford University Press.
6. Townsend P (1979) Poverty in the United Kingdom. Harmondsworth, Penguin.
7. Townsend P and Davidson N (1982) Inequalities in Health: The Black Report. Harmondsworth, Penguin.
8. Whitehead M (1987) The Health Divide. London, Health Education Council.
9. Drucker E, Alcabes P, Bosworth W and Sckell B (1994) Childhood tuberculosis in the Bronx. Lancet 343, 1482-1485.
10. Hakim C (1987) The social consequences of high employment. Journal of Social Policy II.
11. Marmot M (1997) Inequality, deprivation and alcohol use. Addiction 92 (Supplement†1), 513-520.
12. Marmot M G, Davey Smith G, Stansfeld S, Patel C, North F, Head J White I et al (1991) Inequalities in health twenty years on: the Whitehall II study of British Civil Servants. Lancet 337, 1387-1393.
13. Wallace R and Wallace D (1997) Community marginalisation and the diffusion of disease and disorder in the United States. B M J 314, 1341-1345.
14. Woodroffe C, Glicksman M, Barker M and Power C (1993) Children, teenagers and health: the key data. Buckingham, Open University Press.
15. McLoone P (1996) Suicide and deprivation in Scotland. BMJ 312, 543-544.
16. Brown G W and Harris T (1978) Social Origins of Depression. London, Tavistock Press.
17. West P (1977) Health inequalities in the early years: is there equalisation in youth? Social Science and Medicine 44, 833-858.
18. Townsend J, Roderick P and Cooper J (1994) Cigarette smoking by socio-economic group, sex, and age: effects of price, income and health publicity. BMJ 309, 923-927.
19. Marsh A and McKay S (1994) Poor smokers. London. Policy Studies Unit.
20. Terry C E and Pellens M (1928). The Opium Problem. Montclair NJ., Patterson Smith.
21. O'Donnell J (1969) Narcotic Addicts in Kentucky. Chevy Chase, Maryland, Department of Health, Education and Welfare.
22. Musto D F (1973) The American Disease. Origins of Narcotic Control. New Haven, Yale University Press.
23. Chein I, Gerard D L, Lee R S and Rosenfeld E (1964) Narcotics, Delinquency and Social Policy: the road to H. London, Tavistock.
24. Ball J C and Chambers C D eds (1970) The epidemiology of opiate misuse in the United States. Springfield Ill., Charles C Thomas.
25. Bourgois P (1989) Crack in Spanish Harlem: culture and economy in the inner city. Anthropology Today 5, 6-11.

26. Marzuk P M, Tardiff K, Leon A C, Hirsch C S, Stajic M, Porters L et al (1997) Poverty and fatal accidental drug overdose of cocaine and opiates in New York City: an ecological study. American Journal of Drug and Alcohol Abuse 23, 221-228.
27. Booth W (1890) In Darkest England and the Way Out. London, International Headquarters of the Salvation Army.
28. Berridge V and Edwards G (1981) Opium and the People. Opium Use in Nineteenth Century English Society. London, Allen Lane.
29. Hayter A (1968) Opium and the Romantic Imagination. London, Faber and Faber.
30. Stimson G V (1973) Heroin and Behaviour. Shannon, Irish University Press.
31. Blumberg H H (1981) Characteristics of people coming to treatment. Chapter 5, pps.77-116 in Edwards G and Busch C. eds. Drug Problems in Britain. A review of Ten Years. London, Academic Press.
32. Pearson G (1987) Social deprivation, unemployment and patterns of heroin use, in Dorn N and South N. eds. A Land Fit for Heroin? Drug policies, prevention and practice. London, MacMillan.
33. Pearson G and Gilman M (1994) Local and regional variations in drug misuse: the British heroin epidemic of the 1980s. Chapter 8, pps. 102-120 in Strang J and Gossop M eds. Heroin Addiction and Drug Policy. The British System. Oxford, OUP.
34. Haw S (1985) Drug problems in Greater Glasgow. London, HMSO.
35. Pearson G, Gilman M and McIver S (1985) Heroin use in the North of England. Health Education Journal 45, 186-189.
36. Parker H, Newcombe R and Bakx K (1987) The new heroin users: prevalence and characteristics in Wirral, Merseyside. British Journal of Addiction 82, 147-157.
37. Giggs J, Bean P, Waynes D and Wilkinson C (1989) Class A drug users: prevalence and characteristics in Greater Nottingham. British Journal of Addiction 84, 1473-1480.
38. Fazey C, Brown P and Batey P (1990) A socio-demographic analysis of patients attending a drug dependency clinic. Liverpool, Centre for Urban Studies.
39. Mirza H S, Pearson G and Phillips S (1991) Drugs, people and services in Lewisham: final report of the Drug Information Project. London, Goldsmiths College (University of London).
40. Advisory Council on the Misuse of Drugs (1995) Volatile Substance Abuse, London, HMSO.
41. Taylor J C, Norman C L, Bland J M, Ramsey J D , Anderson H R (1997) Trends in Deaths Associated with Abuse of Volatile Substances 1971-1995. Report No.10. London, St George's Hospital Medical School.
42. Esmail A, Warburton B, Bland M, Anderson H R, Ramsey J (1997) Regional variations in deaths from volatile solvent abuse in Great Britain. Addiction 92, in press.
43. Jones M, Bolton K, Edmond I, Hanstock R, Horrigan I, Olearnik H and Sondhi A (1995) Problem drug use reported by services in Greater London. London, Thames Regional Drug Misuse Databases.
44. Gruer L, Murray S, Boyd A, et al (1997) Extreme variations in the distribution of serious drug misuse-related morbidity in Greater Glasgow. Personal Communication.
45. Carstairs V, Morris R (1991) Deprivation and health in Scotland. Aberdeen, Aberdeen University Press.
46. Farrell M, Jarvis M, Taylor C, Lewis G, Bebbington P, Brugha T, Gill B, Jenkins R and Meltzer H (1997) Nicotine, alcohol and other drug dependence and the association with deprivation. [Publication awaited]
47. Ramsay M and Spiller J (1997) Drug misuse declared in 1996: latest results from the British Crime Survey. London, Home Office.
48. Preble E and Casey J J (1969) Taking care of business - the heroin user's life on the street. International Journal of the Addictions 4, 1-24.
49. Talbot R J (1991) Underprivileged areas and health care planning: implications of use of the Jarman indicators of urban deprivation. B M J 302, 383-386.

# INDEX